Refugee and Mixed Migration Flows

Also by Bimal Ghosh

The Global Economic Crisis and the Future of Migration: Issues and Prospects. What Will Migration Look Like in 2045? Palgrave Macmillan, England/New York (2012), (2015, Revised)

The Global Economic Crisis and Migration: Where Do we go from Here? IOM/The Hague Process on Refugees and Migration. Geneva/The Hague (2010)

Human Rights and Migration: The Missing Link. University of Utrecht/The Hague Process on Refugees and Migration, Utrecht/The Hague (2008)

Myths, Rhetoric and Realities: Migrants' Remittances and Development. IOM/The Hague Process on Refugees and Migration. Geneva/The Hague (2006)

Elusive Protection, Uncertain Lands: Migrants' Access to Human Rights, IOM, Geneva (2003)

Managing Migration: Time for a New International Regime? Oxford University Press, England (2000)

Return Migration: Journey of Hope or Despair? United Nations/IOM, Geneva (2000)

Huddled Masses and Uncertain Shores: Insights into Irregular Migration, IOM/Kluwer Law International/Martinus Nijhoff Publishers, Geneva/The Hague (1988)

Gains from Global Linkages: Trade in Services and Movement of Persons, Macmillan Press, St. Martins Press, England/New York (1987)

Bimal Ghosh

Refugee and Mixed Migration Flows

Managing a Looming Humanitarian and Economic Crisis

Bimal Ghosh
Graduate Institute of International
 and Development Studies
Geneva, Switzerland

ISBN 978-3-319-75273-0   ISBN 978-3-319-75274-7 (eBook)
https://doi.org/10.1007/978-3-319-75274-7

Library of Congress Control Number: 2018933046

© The Editor(s) (if applicable) and The Author(s) 2018
This work is subject to copyright. All rights are solely and exclusively licensed by the Publisher, whether the whole or part of the material is concerned, specifically the rights of translation, reprinting, reuse of illustrations, recitation, broadcasting, reproduction on microfilms or in any other physical way, and transmission or information storage and retrieval, electronic adaptation, computer software, or by similar or dissimilar methodology now known or hereafter developed.
The use of general descriptive names, registered names, trademarks, service marks, etc. in this publication does not imply, even in the absence of a specific statement, that such names are exempt from the relevant protective laws and regulations and therefore free for general use.
The publisher, the authors and the editors are safe to assume that the advice and information in this book are believed to be true and accurate at the date of publication. Neither the publisher nor the authors or the editors give a warranty, express or implied, with respect to the material contained herein or for any errors or omissions that may have been made. The publisher remains neutral with regard to jurisdictional claims in published maps and institutional affiliations.

Cover credit: © Petrov Vladimir/Alamy Stock Photo

Printed on acid-free paper

This Palgrave Macmillan imprint is published by the registered company Springer International Publishing AG part of Springer Nature
The registered company address is: Gewerbestrasse 11, 6330 Cham, Switzerland

To all who deserve humanitarian protection and need empathy and support to regain their hopes and start their life again

Preface

When late in 2015 I started writing this book, several parts of the world were gripped by a looming crisis in refugee and mixed migration flows. In Europe, member states of the European Union were feeling overwhelmed by an inflow of more than one million refugees and migrants, with ominous signals of many more yet to come. As the EU states were agonising over how to cope with the situation, several other regions of the world were facing massive internal displacements, alongside huge, and often unwanted, outflows of a mixture of refugees, persons deserving humanitarian protection, and irregular migrants. As noted in the Introduction of the book, these were triggered by geopolitical and religious tensions, violent conflicts, persecution and extreme insecurity and, in many cases, abject poverty or a varying combination of them.

Massive human displacements, whether internal or external, are surely not new. But, as will be discussed in the book, several of these flows have been throwing new challenges or making the existing ones more difficult to manage with the available migration policies and tools. For the discussion in the book, I have selected four major instances of these flows—two of them in Europe and one each in Central America and

Asia. I have done this in a global context as cross-border migration has become an integral part of the global human society.

Clearly, each of these flows has its distinctive features and presents specific issues, and therefore needs to be addressed separately as I have tried to do in different chapters of the book. But they also reveal many issues common to all of them, and these are addressed in the concluding chapter.

An overarching, common problem that bedevils the present migration system lies in the inadequacy of attention given to its root causes—the mismatch between high emigration pressure in the origin countries, accentuated by powerful demand-pull in receiving countries, on the one hand and, on the other, dwindling opportunities for legal entry in destination countries that are often fearful of losing control of their borders.

The challenge involved in achieving orderly, safe and less unpredictable flows lies in bringing these two powerful, opposing forces closer into a state of dynamic harmony. Issues of effective internal management of migration, including protection of migrants' rights, avoidance of discrimination and migrant integration, are closely interwoven with that challenge; they defy isolation. History also shows that although each type of migratory, including refugee, flow has its distinctive characteristics, they are also interlinked. Malfunctioning of any one channel is likely to have a negative spillover effect on the functioning of all or some of the other channels as well. Hence, the need for a coherent and comprehensive approach to management of migration and refugee flows.

As argued in the concluding section of the book, this calls for a new form of global partnership, based on a common understanding and collective self-confidence and determination of nations. It is promising that in 2016 the United Nations finally decided to step in and agreed to develop two global compacts dealing, respectively, with migration and refugees. It is sad that under the new administration the USA (subsequently followed by Hungary) has decided to dissociate itself from the initiative. Even so, it remains a golden, long-awaited opportunity, and every effort must be made to make sure that the new initiative moves in the right direction.

Geneva, Switzerland   Bimal Ghosh
March 2018

Contents

1 Introduction 1

Part I The European Refugee and Mixed Migration Crisis in a Global Context

2 The Backdrop of the Crisis in Europe 9

3 The European Union's Response 19

4 The European Union's Agonies 37

5 The Way Forward 59

6 Asylum-Seeking and Externalisation of the Screening Process: Why so Controversial? 79

7 Refugees and Asylum-Seekers: Eroding Rights, Less-Friendly Welcome 89

| 8 | Economic Effects of Migration/Refugee Inflows in Europe | 121 |

Part II Challenges Across Regions

9	Conflicts in Eastern Europe: Exodus from Ukraine and Russia	155
10	Central America: The Unresolved Migration Conundrum	167
11	South-East Asia: The Sad Plight of the Rohingya	189

Part III How to Manage the Crisis and Avoid Its Recrudescence

| 12 | A Synoptic Overview of Policy Issues and Prescriptions | 219 |

Glossary	235
Bibliography	237
Index	245

Abbreviations

AFD	Alternative for Germany
ASEAN	Association of South-East Asian Nations
BBC	British Broadcasting Corporation
EEA	European Economic Area
EU/EC	European Union/European Commission
GDP	Gross Domestic Product
IDP	Internally Displaced Person
IFC	International Finance Corporation
ILO	International Labour Organisation
IMF	International Monetary Fund
IMO	International Maritime Organization
ISIS	Islamic State of Syria, Iraq and Levant Organization
KIND	Kids In Need of Defense
MENA	Middle East and North Africa
MSF	Médecins Sans Frontières
NATO	North Atlantic Treaty Organization
NGO	Non-Governmental Organisation
OAU	Organisation of African Unity
OECD	Organisation for Economic Cooperation and Development
PEGIDA	Patriotic Europeans Against the Islamization of the West

Abbreviations

PWC   Pew Research Center
UN   United Nations
UNHCR   United Nations High Commission for Refugees
UNICEF United Nations Children Fund
WFP   World Food Programme

List of Figures

Fig. 1.1	Deaths on the fatal journey worldwide, January–September 2014 (*Source* IOM)	4
Fig. 1.2	Global migrant deaths, 2015–2016 (*Source* IOM)	4
Fig. 2.1	Migration flows in the Mediterranean region and beyond. **a**. Overview of migration flows to Europe (*Source* UNHCR). **b**. Total inflows in countries of first arrival in 2015 (*Source* IOM)	18
Fig. 3.1	Sea arrivals in Greece and onward movements (*Source* UNHCR)	25
Fig. 5.1	Growing unhappiness with the EU's handling of refugee flows (*Source* Pew Research Center)	71
Fig. 5.2	Declining positive views of the EU (*Source* Pew Research Center)	77
Fig. 7.1	Growing concern over the links between refugee flows and terrorism (*Source* Pew Research Center)	93
Fig. 7.2	Does diversity make your country a better place to live? (*Source* Pew Research Center)	94
Fig. 7.3	Germany: Attacks on asylum-seekers' shelters, January–March 2015 (*Source* German Federal Criminal Police/FT)	101

Fig. 7.4	**a.** Refugee population worldwide. **b.** Share of annual resettlement of refugees in the USA and all other countries	110
Fig. 8.1	Ageing in Europe (*Source* UN Population Division/Pew Research Center, 2015)	131
Fig. 8.2	Asylum-seekers' access to labour markets: minimum waiting periods in selected OECD countries (*Source* OECD)	132
Fig. 9.1	Ukraine internally displaced people as a result of the conflict (*Source* UNHCR)	157
Fig. 10.1	Apprehensions of unaccompanied child migrants at the US south-west border by country of origin, FY 2008–FY 2016 (*Source* William A. Kandel, Congressional Research Service May 2016. US Department of Homeland Security, US Border Patrol; and Customs and Border Protection)	171
Fig. 10.2	Homicide rate in Northern Triangle countries (per 100,000 people) (*Source* Insight crime, David Gagne, January 2016)	175
Fig. 10.3	Central Americans seeking asylum in neighbouring countries (*Source* UNHCR)	181
Fig. 11.1	Refugees and migrants abandoned at sea (*Source* UNHCR)	190
Fig. 11.2	The plight of the Rohingya: South and South-East Asia (prior to 2016) in thousand (*Source* IOM/FT)	191

1

Introduction

Gathering Violence, Widespread Persecution and Record Human Displacements: The Challenge of a Looming Crisis

The world of migration and refugees has been witnessing two contrasting scenarios: slow and wavering increase in new inflows of migrants through regular channels in the aftermath of the 2008/2009 economic crisis juxtaposed with the highest recorded level of uprooted people in the post-World War II era. These human displacements were being caused by waves of violent conflicts and persecution, combined with a worsening geopolitical and security situation and, in many cases, abject poverty. Much of these displacements have taken place in the last few years, especially since 2012 when their total number was hovering around 45.2 million. In 2013, an estimated total of 51.2 million individuals were found forcibly displaced worldwide. Some 16.7 million were refugees (including 5.0 million Palestinian refugees), 33.3 million were displaced within their own countries (IDPs), then the highest number on record, and close to 1.2 million were asylum-seekers. In the following year (2014), there were 59.5 million uprooted people, including 38.2 million internally displaced persons, 19.5 million refugees (including 5.1 million Palestinian refugees) and nearly 1.8 million asylum-seekers. This was 8.3 million persons more than the year before—yet again, the highest annual increase ever in a single year.

© The Author(s) 2018
B. Ghosh, *Refugee and Mixed Migration Flows*,
https://doi.org/10.1007/978-3-319-75274-7_1

The trend continued in 2015. The total number of uprooted people rose to 65.6 million (comprising 22.5 million refugees, 40.3 million IDPs and 2.8 million asylum-seekers). Figures most recently released by UNHCR show that there was no diminution of the level of human displacement in 2016; instead, the total number rose slightly more to 65.5 million.[1]

The UNHCR estimated that in 2015, some 12.4 million persons (excluding *returns*) were newly displaced from their home. The enormity and poignancy of the problem become clearer when it is reckoned this implies that in 2015 on average 24 persons were forced to abandon their home and hearth every minute.[2]

We were thus living in a world in which one in every 107 persons had been forcibly uprooted. If all these displaced people were in one country, it would already have been the twenty-first most populous country in the world, with a population larger than that of the UK or Italy.

* * *

Roughly speaking, there has been a 55% increase over the number of refugees under UNHCR mandate in just four years since the end of 2011. In 2015, developing regions were hosting 13.9 million—or 86%—of the world's refugees under UNHCR's mandate. This was then the highest number in more than two decades. The trend was also reflected in the number of new asylum applications, especially in Europe. Figures collected by UNHCR showed that more than 2 million asylum applications were lodged in 2015 in 38 European countries,[3] almost three times the number (709,800) registered in 2014. According to the European Union's Statistical Office, the number of *first time* asylum-seekers in 2014 in its member states was 562,000; it jumped to 1.26 million in 2015 and remained nearly as high in 2016 at 1.2 million. As a region, the Middle East has seen the sharpest increase in human displacements which more than doubled between 2005 and 2016, from about 25 million to around 54 million. Some of these

---

[1] The world's total displacement figures for 2017, released by the UNHCR after this script went to press, reached 68.5 million, an increase of five consecutive years.

[2] There was a slight deceleration in the increase of new (*excluding returns*) in 2016, totaling 10.3 million and the number of newly displaced persons every minute was 20, compared with 24 in 2015.

[3] This, however, includes considerable instances of double accounting and is therefore somewhat exaggerated.

persons were economically motivated, but the majority of them, especially after 2011, were victims of forced displacement, according to an analysis by Pew Research Center of the United Nations data.

As the script was going to press, and the conflicts and violence, especially in the Middle East, continued unabated, there was hardly any sign of a break in these relentless waves of human displacements.

Deaths on the Fatal Journeys

Worse still, many of those seeking escape abroad in desperation are not making it at all. The episodes of deaths of migrants on their way to the elusive destination are not entirely new. According to Amnesty International, as many as 23,000 migrants have lost their lives in trying to reach the EU across the Mediterranean in the past 15 years. The International Organization for Migration (IOM) recently raised the number as high as 46,000 since 2000 and 60,000 over the past 20 years. More worryingly, the number of such risky journeys has been increasing in recent years.

In 2014, worldwide, some 4077 migrants[4] lost their lives at sea or in remote deserts or mountains, making it the deadliest year on record and doubling the number of deaths in 2013. More than 540 migrants faced death in the Bay of Bengal, and at least, 307 migrants paid the same ultimate price in trying to cross the land border between Mexico and the USA (Figs. 1.1 and 1.2).

Since then, the situation turned still deadlier, with the number of migrants who died or disappeared worldwide rising to 5740 in 2015 and 7872 in 2016, making a 30% increase over the number in 2015, and representing an average of over 21 deaths a day, according to the figures released by IOM in January 2017.

The rising global trend in fatalities among migrants on their way to their destinations was particularly marked in the Mediterranean, where nearly 4600 of them perished in 2015. The UNHCR estimates that in two years,

---

[4]The UNHCR puts the number a little higher at 4272.

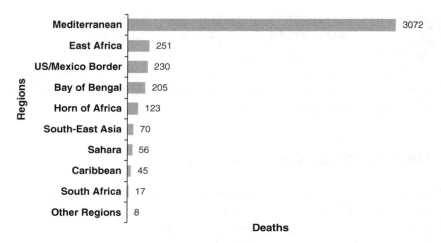

Fig. 1.1 Deaths on the fatal journey worldwide, January–September 2014 (*Source* IOM)

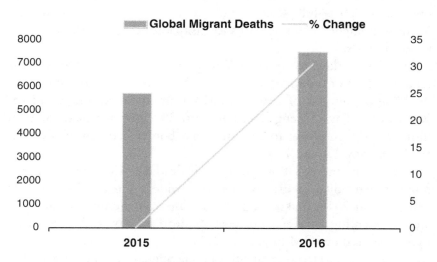

Fig. 1.2 Global migrant deaths, 2015–2016 (*Source* IOM)

2014–2015 over 10,000 migrants lost their life on the fatal journey; and with at least 5079 deaths or disappearances in 2016, these became the deadliest three years on record. And the trend, even if slightly subdued, seemed to continue, with the number reaching 1770, as of 10 June 2017.

The massive and cruel deaths in the small islands of Greece were starkly symbolic of the poignancy of the situation in some areas, with its painfully sobering effect. In October 2015, citing the local mayor, *Al Jazeera* reported that the Greek island of Lesbos had run out of room to bury the growing number of deaths at sea. Since autumn 2015, the accumulation of drowned bodies has become part of a wider migration crisis in Greece. The town morgue at Mytilene was full and so was a section of a Christian burial site which the church, in response to the emergency, had set aside for Islamic internment. As *The Economist* observed, in 1923 the region's affairs were settled by a vast separation between Christians and Muslims. In 2016, such separation no longer seems possible, either of the living or of the dead.[5]

According to Médecins Sans Frontières (MSF), every month 5000 Eritreans were leaving the country to escape oppression, but as they try to cross the desert and the Mediterranean to reach Europe, a good many of them perish on the way. Half of those interviewed by MSF reported that they had seen their fellow travellers dying on the way.

The available figures of deaths certainly understate the real numbers, as many migrants perish during the lengthy and harsh Sahara crossing, in the deep jungles or on hostile hilltops elsewhere. In June 2015, for example, the remains of 30 migrants were found in Dirked, Niger, who most probably were trying to reach Libya on their way to Europe.[6] Exactly one year later in June 2016, the dead bodies of 34 migrants—20 children, nine women and five men—were discovered in the desert of Niger. They, too, were trying to reach Libya on their way to Europe, which they never made. Mass graves of trafficked migrants were suddenly discovered on the Thai/Malaysian borders (further discussed in later Chapter 11).[7] A recent *BBC* investigation found that over 1250 unnamed

---
[5] *The Economist*, 21 April 2016.
[6] *IOM News*, 14 July 2015.
[7] *The Telegraph*, 24 May 2015.

migrant men, women and children have been buried in unmarked graves in 70 sites in Turkey, Greece and Italy since 2014.

* * *

In autumn and winter when the winds are stronger and more frequent, corpses float around on the sea in the triangle between Tripoli, Zouara and Lampedusa and then are washed ashore, mostly of those who were attempting to cross the Mediterranean in search of a better life. Some, including children, get lost during the fatal journey and may remain unaccounted for. In Europe, for example, it is estimated that some 10,000 children had disappeared during 2014–2015.

In several regions of the world, including the Middle East and North Africa (MENA), sub-Saharan Africa, Central America and parts of eastern Europe and Asia, there have been in recent years unprecedented internal displacements as well as massive and unpredictable mixed flows of refugees, persons deserving humanitarian protection and poverty-driven irregular migrants. As already mentioned, these have been variously triggered by political and religious tensions, violent conflicts, persecution and insecurity, combined with economic dislocation and, in many cases, severe poverty. While these diverse flows have several features in common, they also differ in many important ways just as their geopolitical contexts do. Instead of lumping them together, I have thought it useful, for purposes of both insightful analysis and policy formulation, to treat them separately, albeit all in a global context.

In doing so, I have selected four main flows, which lately have also been receiving wide attention of the public and the policy-makers alike—two of them in Europe and one each in the Americas and Asia. Clearly, these are all urgent, and among the top, migration issues. However, given both its magnitude and its wider political and economic implications, I have discussed Europe's refugee and mixed migration crisis in more detail than the other flows.

Part I

The European Refugee and Mixed Migration Crisis in a Global Context

2

The Backdrop of the Crisis in Europe
MENA and Sub-Saharan Africa: Flights in Despair, Cruel Deaths at Sea

In 2012, when I was finishing a companion volume of this book,[1] the high hopes of the Arab Spring in the conflict-prone Middle East and North Africa (MENA) region were already receding with the rising trends of sectarian, tribal and local conflicts and tensions within and across countries. I had at that time expressed concern—not the only one to do so—that if the then ongoing sectarian Shia-Sunni and tribal conflicts could not be resolved within individual countries, these could easily suck in neighbouring ones, threaten the stability of almost the whole region, generating huge outflows of refugees and migrants as well as massive internal displacements, with serious geopolitical repercussions going beyond the region.

The Backdrop of the Crisis

Five years on, sadly, these misgivings have turned into hard realities, and things were looking increasingly even more ominous. Sharp divisions within the warring religious sects, often mingled with tribal/ethnic

---

[1]Bimal Ghosh, *The Global Economic Crisis and the Future of Migration: Issues and Prospects. What Will Migration Look Like in 2045?* Palgrave/Macmillan, Houndmills, England, 2012.

© The Author(s) 2018
B. Ghosh, *Refugee and Mixed Migration Flows*,
https://doi.org/10.1007/978-3-319-75274-7_2

rivalries, and the rapid rise of opposing local militias in the political/security vacuum have made the MENA region extremely unstable. The situation has been worsened by tensions between regional governments and their active or tacit alignment with one conflicting group or another within a country. These have made the conflict in the MENA region both multi-layered and multifaceted and increasingly more violent. Amid the ongoing fighting in Syria and Iraq, the emergence of the Islamic State of Syria, Iraq and Levant Organisation (dubbed ISIS or IS) has added a more alarming and grotesque dimension to the conflict which has not only now engulfed the region but has pulled in several world powers, sometimes acting for cross purposes and reigniting the old East–West tension of the Cold War era.

The "wars within wars" in the region are thus casting a dark and worrisome shadow on the global situation as well. Mostly, as a consequence of these upheavals between January 2015 and January 2016, Europe saw an inflow of a total of 1.2 million asylum-seekers and migrants, of which 1.06 million travelled by sea. Greece received nearly 911,000 of them and Italy over 157,000 during the period; and the flows, although seemingly somewhat subdued, had not ceased.

Several of the MENA countries such as Iraq, Syria and Libya were at the time of writing badly fractured, with swaths of territory controlled by different non-state groups, and their power bases were almost constantly shifting. An analogous situation was developing in Yemen, where the ongoing conflicts, as I discussed in detail in 2012,[2] have become more fierce, widespread and complex, with no clear battle lines. Internal sectarian fighting has drawn in big external powers, and in fighting a proxy war, they have made the situation more violent and complex. In the power vacuum created by the resignation of the Sunni-led government, and internment of the President, different groups—Sunnis, Shia (Huthi), Al-Qaeda and tribal groups—had stepped up their fighting, and thrown the country into complete chaos, prompting Ban Ki-moon, then UN Secretary-General, to say "Yemen is collapsing before our eyes". Several western governments soon closed their embassies and evacuated their nationals.

---

[2] Ibid.

At the end of 2014, Yemen already had 334,000 internally displaced persons. With the widening of the conflict and gathering intensity of violence, the number jumped seven times to 2.5 million—8% of its population—by the end of 2015. Three governorates—Taizz, Amran and Hajjah—accounted for some 900,000 of them due to gruesome fighting. Displaced from their homes, they lived with their relatives, with host communities, or in makeshift camps in miserable conditions. By the end of 2016, the number of internal displacements rose to 3 million, according to the United Nations; it reached the level of 3.3 million in April 2017, of which 1.3 million later returned to their governorates of origin. As of March 2016, the conflict had led to 6000 deaths, of which one-third were children, according to a UNICEF source. In January 2017, the UN reported that number had risen to 10,000.[3] At least one child was dying every 10 minutes because of preventable diseases. Water and sanitation system was collapsing, cutting off nearly 15 million Yemenis from access to these services. And an epidemic of cholera, largely a consequence of over two years of conflict, had killed thousands of people and many more had been infected. Nearly 80% of the country's population needed humanitarian assistance. As of March 2017, 2.2 million people, including nearly half a million children, were suffering from malnutrition. "Cemeteries are filling up with unmarked graves, the deaths of children unreported to authorities, their suffering invisible to the world", UNICEF remarked.

Over 173,000 persons had fled the country. At the same time, political vacuum and lax border control have been swelling the traditional inflows, mainly from Ethiopia, to the country; many of these migrants were using it as a transit post to reach Saudi Arabia and other Gulf countries. The ongoing violence and destruction, including bombing by Saudi Arabia, and the breakdown of law and order would continue to increase disorderly movements, both inside the country and outward. In October 2016, a fragile, temporary truce was initiated by Saudi Arabia, but it soon collapsed. In an urgent message to the UN Security Council, Stephen O'Brien, humanitarian chief of the organisation, said that if the conflicts continued, the country could collapse with menacing implications for the wider region.

---

[3]http://www.voanews.com/content/reu-unicef-yemen-humanitarian-aid/2817370.html.

The situation in both Syria and Iraq continued to be no less alarming. UNHCR estimated that by October 2014, in Syria and Iraq a total of nearly 14 million persons had already been internally displaced or moved outside their home country as a result of the conflicts. And since then, these numbers have kept on rising, especially in Syria after the indiscriminate Russian bombings that seriously affected the civilian population in Aleppo city and the surrounding areas. According to the UK-based Syrian Observatory for Human Rights, 4000 civilians had been killed by these bombings. And, as of February 2016, Syria alone had 6.6 million internally uprooted people (IDPs) and 4.8 million refugees outside the country. By March 2017, the number of refugees rose to 5.1 million, according to UNHCR. This implies that since the conflict began five years ago, the hostilities had uprooted half its pre-war population of 22.5 million, killed possibly between 450,000 and half a million people[4] and left much of the country in ruins. According to the United Nations, as of February 2016, a total of 13.5 million people, including refugees and IDPs, needed humanitarian assistance—more than three times the number (4 million) in 2012.

More gloomy news had also been pouring in. For instance, a recent joint UN/St. Andrews University study showed that over 80% of Syrian population was below the poverty line, compared to 28% prior to the conflict.[5] The country's food production dropped to an all-time low due to conflict-related instability and devastation. Between March 2011 and November 2015, the price of wheat flour and rice rose by 388% and 723%, respectively. Increasing numbers of civilian populations have become captives in enclaves as adjacent territories are controlled by opposing conflicting powers, making access to them for humanitarian supplies extremely difficult.

In October 2016, when Syrian forces, backed by indiscriminate Russian bombings, mounted a brutal offensive, and attempts at a

---

[4]The actual number and categories of deaths, as well as the responsibilities for them, remain a subject of controversy. At the upper end, an estimate puts the number at around half a million. See also in this connection Colum Lynch, "The war over Syria's war dead", *Foreign Policy*, January 2016. A most recent estimate (March 2017) by the Human Rights Observatory in Syria put the figure at over 321,000 deaths and 2880 disappeared, of whom more than 96,000 were civilians, including children.

[5]UNESCWA, *Syria at War: Five Years On*, UNESCWA, Beirut, April 2016. www.unescwa.org/news/syria-war-five-years. The 2016 UN/St. Andrews University study estimate.

temporary ceasefire to permit the distribution of aid were making little headway, there was widespread concern over a looming humanitarian crisis. By December 2016 as the Syrian government soldiers, with the support of Russian bombings, were making headway into the hitherto rebel-held areas, and human casualties were mounting among the civilian population, there was an exodus of people from those areas, with possibly more than 100,000 moving to the government-controlled part of the country within weeks. At the same time, in the absence of the possibility of distributing aid, the humanitarian situation was worsening by the day. Finally, at the end of 2016, at the behest of Russia and Turkey, a truce was signed by the parties concerned, excepting the ISIS, which regained control of Palmyra in the same week that Aleppo succumbed. But peace had not returned. And the situation took a new turn when, on 7 April 2017, the US government staged a missile attack on the Syrian airfields in retaliation to the use by the Syrian army of chemical gas in the rebel-held areas. The future, as the script was going to press, looked uncertain.

In Iraq, too, already by June 2015 the number of internally displaced persons had risen to 3.9 million, including 250,000 displaced from Ramadi, the capital of Anbar Province, along with more than half a million (520,000) refugees and asylum-seekers abroad. By April 2017, the total number of forcibly displaced persons rose to 5 million, of which 1.7 million had later returned to their areas of origin. As in Syria, shifting control of swaths of its territory and the consequent insecurity were aggravating the situation. In moving across provincial lines with lots of checks and control, displaced persons were often feeling like crossing borders as immigrants. The situation was both chaotic and fluid. In Mosul, for instance, as by March 2017 the Iraqi army was advancing towards the west after gaining control of the eastern part of the city, some 3000 ISIS militants were holed up among 750,000 civilians. In June 2017, as Iraqi forces began its assault on Mosul's old city in the last phase of the month-old battle against ISIS militants, the situation became vicious. The United Nations estimated that up to 150,000 civilians were trapped in the city, held by ISIS fighters as human shields, while the supply of food and water was perilously running low. According to UNICEF, 2016 alone saw 626 deaths among children, 20% more than in 2015, making it the darkest year for children so far.

At the same time, the country had to accommodate nearly 300,000 refugees, uprooted from conflict-ridden, neighbouring Syria. The US-led coalition has made it possible for the government to recapture much of the territory from the ISIS which at one stage had control over 40% of the territory. However, peace and stability remained elusive. Renewed sectarian violence could refuel the anger and resentments that led to the rise of the ISIS and its control of Sunni-dominated areas. In October 2016 when the Iraqi government, jointly with Peshmerga Kurdish soldiers and Shia militia, launched a campaign to restore Mosul which was under ISIS control, there were fears of large-scale human displacement, which, according to some NGOs, might have involved 200,000 people; and already in October at least 160,000 were displaced, although 30,000 of them had returned later. And, again in January 2017 when a new offensive was launched to capture the western part of the city, still held by the ISIS, there were fresh fears of massive internal displacements.

In May 2017, the UN was fearful that 200,000 civilians would be driven out of Mosul, adding to some 700,000 already displaced. Most of the new IDPs were likely to end up in displacement camps; some would, with government authorisation, move in with relatives in other parts of the country; and some others would try to get into Europe. As the Sunni population made up the majority of people in Mosul, there was also the danger that they may resent government efforts if they believed them to be driven by a Shia supremacy agenda. This could ignite new sectarian tension and create more instability. Meanwhile, tensions were also rising between Turkey, which wanted to take an active part in the operation in order to maintain its influence in the area, and Iraq, which was totally opposed to it.

Already by November 2014, with opportunities for entry in neighbouring countries like Jordan, Lebanon and Turkey (which had already accommodated a combined total of some 5 million people) nearly exhausted, refugees from Syria had almost nowhere to go.[6] In desperation, many turned to human traffickers who made them embark on a perilous journey through the Mediterranean in unseaworthy boats

---

[6]Nine in 10 Syrian refugees are currently being hosted by five neighbouring countries—Turkey, Lebanon, Jordan, Iraq and Egypt.

towards southern Europe. The UNHCR estimated that in 2014 over half of nearly 220,000 people who fled their country by unsafe boats across the Mediterranean came from strife-torn, refugee-producing countries, mainly Syria. In February 2015, some 2000 migrants who took such a vessel in Turkey were rescued off the Italian coast. But many never made it. Since before these incidents, reports of the deaths at the Mediterranean were already piling up and the scale of the horror was rapidly unfolding, sending shock waves in Europe and beyond.

Libya, like Syria and Iraq, has long been politically and militarily fractured. At the beginning of 2015, as violence escalated and the security situation rapidly deteriorated, several western countries evacuated their citizens from the country. The outflows of people, both nationals and migrants, also increased. Many of those migrants who were unable to escape with the help of their governments or on their own turned to human traffickers who were mercilessly taking advantage of the situation. According to reports from the field, many migrants were being forced by traffickers to embark on unseaworthy boats. As this script was being written, there was a fragile hope of peace as the UN-backed unity government consolidated its position in the country which has been fractured between two governments since 2014, with rival parliaments in Tripoli and the east of the country. However, many challenges remained (discussed further in Chapter 3).

In sub-Saharan Africa, too, widespread violence and conflicts were driving people, including women and children, to leave their home and hearth and seek safety elsewhere. For instance, in the four countries of the Lake Chad Basin—Cameroon, Chad, Niger and Nigeria— some three million people had been displaced since the beginning of the cross-border attacks and the rising fears of further insurgency by Boko Haram. In Nigeria alone, more than two million people had been internally displaced and 200,000 reported to be externally displaced. According to a January 2015 report by Amnesty International, since 2013 the number of killings by Boko Haram in Nigeria alone may have reached at least 5400 and was likely to be even higher. By September 2017, the numbers rose to 20,000 deaths and 2.6 million internally displaced persons. The ferocity of such violence can be imagined by the fact that in early June 2016 alone, the attacks launched by Boko Haram in Niger led to the forced internal displacement of some 50,000 people, according to the UNHCR. An estimate by UNICEF suggests that nearly half a million children will face starvation and 80,000 might die if they did not get treatment in the humanitarian crisis caused by Boko Haram atrocities.

In the Central African Republic, fierce communal conflicts, in which some 14 different armed groups were involved, had led to forced displacement of some 400,000 people since 2013, and lasting peace was yet to return. As of end May 2017, the conflict in South Sudan had forced more than 1.9 million people to become internally displaced and as of end March 2017 nearly 900,000 others to seek asylum in neighbouring countries. Already in 2016, a United Nations Commission found that in parts of the country brutal ethnic cleansing was taking place. It was a shattered country, with shards of armed factions, mostly formed on ethnic lines, brutally fighting for fast dwindling resources. And in February 2017 the organisation declared famine in South Sudan, calling it a man-made catastrophe and warmed that 100,000 faced starvations and up to 5.5 million severe food shortages.

Many of those who fled the country took shelter in northern Uganda, which has been generous enough to welcome them. The process had led to the formation of the Bidi Bidi resettlement centre, which, with nearly a quarter million refugees, turned out to be the biggest of several centres in Uganda's West Nile region—and probably also the biggest in the world (further discussed in Chapter 7, pp. 90–91). In South Sudan alone, as of February 2017, three million people had become homeless, with several thousands fleeing to neighbouring Uganda almost every day.

Along with South Sudan, three other sub-Saharan/MENA countries—Nigeria, Somalia and Yemen—are now all facing officially declared famine at the same time involving no less than 20 million people. This is an unprecedented situation in recent decades, and it was leading to forced displacements, both internal and external, of thousands of people. Repression in Eritrea was triggering seemingly relentless outflows of people. Gripped by a most violent ethno-political conflict, Burundi was burning, and the nation torn apart. As of April 2016, 230,000 people were forced to seek relief abroad and at least 474 and probably more had been killed.[7] By February 2017, the number of refugees had gone up to 300,000. Despite

---

[7] It is difficult to figure out the exact number of deaths. Independent research by Cara Jones, a US political science professor, for instance, has suggested the number might be between 800 and 900.

the efforts of the UN Security Council and the African Union, there were few signs of an end to the brutal hostilities and killings. Significant numbers of these desperate people from sub-Saharan Africa, together with those in a similar situation in countries like strife-torn Afghanistan,[8] were further swelling the already massive outflows of people from the MENA countries who were seeking a better and more secure life in Europe.

Many of these desperate people were striving to reach the shores of southern Europe across the Mediterranean, sailing from ports in Libya or Turkey. According to the IOM, in the first three weeks of the month of February 2015 alone, Italy had received a total of some 4300 migrants—3800 just between Friday 13 and Tuesday 17 February. The majority of these migrants were sub-Saharan Africans, although they also included a number of Syrians and Eritreans. Many among them were from strife-torn countries and potential asylum-seekers or had possible humanitarian protection claims. However, in the absence of other avenues of regular entry, they were taking the risky course of making the journey in rickety, unsafe and overloaded boats, often relying on human traffickers. In the process, many were meeting death in the sea or extreme hardship ashore. An IOM estimate suggests that in 2014 the majority of migrants who died in transit—65%—came from Africa and the Middle East.

In February 2015, more than 1600 migrants, mostly from sub-Saharan Africa and some 200 from Somalia, were rescued from a dozen unseaworthy, inflatable vessels in a stormy Mediterranean. This happened just days after 300 migrants, including children, were reported lost, presumed dead, a week earlier. The chilling conditions under which the tragedy happened were poignantly described by one of the three survivors saying ".... we left on a rubber dinghy with more than 100 [passengers].... On Sunday, around 11 a.m. our dinghy collapsed. Thirty fell into the water, while I held on with another 70. For hours I watched my fellow passengers die one by one, exhausted by the cold, the waves, and then, letting themselves fall into the sea. I saw them drift away, with their hands close to the surface. By then only three were left".[9]

---

[8]With relations between the two countries becoming strained, Afghan refugees in Pakistan are coming under pressure to leave the country. According to the UN sources, as of October 2016, some half a million of them were returning to Afghanistan creating a nightmare for the aid agencies, while a smaller, but significant, number of them were trying to move to Europe.
[9]IOM Press, 16 February 2015.

(a)

(b)

Total arrivals overview: countries of first arrival in 2015

	Sea	Land	Total
Greece	853,650	3,713	857,363
Bulgaria	–	31,174	31,174
Italy	153,842	–	153,842
Spain	3,845	–	3,845
Malta	106	–	106
Cyprus	269	–	269
TOTAL	1,011,712	34,887	1,046,599

Fig. 2.1 Migration flows in the Mediterranean region and beyond. **a**. Overview of migration flows to Europe (*Source* UNHCR). **b**. Total inflows in countries of first arrival in 2015 (*Source* IOM)

And as the future looked still more ominous with masses of desperate people waiting in Libya to take the same perilous journey, the European Union came under rising pressure to put an end to the terrible human tragedy (see Fig. 2.1), which it could hardly ignore.

3

The European Union's Response
A Saga of Criss-Cross Decisions

On 23 April 2015, the EU leaders somewhat belatedly considered a strategy to deal with the deepening migration crisis that was taking a rising toll of human lives and tended to make the Mediterranean what Pope Francis called a "human cemetery". They decided to strengthen the presence of Triton, the EU's border security arm, which had replaced, but with inadequate resources and limited powers, Italy's Mare Nostrum, by tripling its resources to improve the operations of rescue and relief of the migrants at sea, and to fight the human traffickers and combat irregular immigration. They also agreed to reinforce the EU members' solidarity and responsibility to help the front-line states facing the pressure of immigration and invited the EU Commission to submit specific proposals in pursuance of these objectives. Consideration was given to a proposal, backed by Germany, to resettle some 5000 refugees across EU states on the basis of a set of criteria such as the size of population, economic capacity, unemployment rates and the number of refugees already accepted by it. Some, including the European Commission, pushed for resettling 10,000 refugees in the Eurozone on a mandatory basis.

The EU, however, did not have a mechanism to handle a relocation operation of this kind, which aimed at a system of fairer distribution of refugees. The discordance among the member states in taking

© The Author(s) 2018
B. Ghosh, *Refugee and Mixed Migration Flows*,
https://doi.org/10.1007/978-3-319-75274-7_3

refugees is, of course, well known. Germany and Sweden had been more generous—with their pledges, as of March 2015, to take 30,000 and 2700 Syrian refugees, respectively. Most other member states, including France and the UK, had been less forthcoming.

Any plans of this kind were in effect a test of intra-EU solidarity and of the depth of member countries' commitment to burden (or responsibility) sharing as a logical corollary of free movement of people within the Union. The matter remains complicated by the fact that in the EU the power structure and authority to deal with migration are bifurcated. While border-free internal movement of people is a basic tenet, cherished and guarded by the EU at the community level, border control, including screening of asylum claims, is enforced by individual governments and remains a national prerogative.

In the event, fearful of the anti-immigrant feeling at home, member countries, including France and the UK, rejected the proposals. As a gesture of help to front-line member states in the south which were under pressure, they opted for a voluntary, as opposed to a mandatory, scheme, and without a target, and kept the possibility for emergency relocation.

The situation, however, remained uncertain and fluid, while migration inflows continued. Following the summit meeting, the EU Commission President Jean-Claude Juncker and the EU Parliament called the decisions inadequate as a response to the crisis. A resolution by the European Parliament called for a mandatory quota system for the distribution of an increased number of refugees among 28-member countries for settlement and for providing more humanitarian visas to asylum-seekers prior to their departure, which would allow them to travel to Europe by established means of transport and avoid using the perilous sea route, using the services of human traffickers.

On 13 May 2015, the European Commission came up with its "European Agenda on Migration", based on the earlier discussions, including at the EU summit, and the EU Parliament resolution on the Mediterranean migration crisis. It unveiled a plan to relocate up to 40,000 asylum-seekers across the EU to relieve the growing pressure of migrants and asylum-seekers arriving from Syria, Eritrea and potentially Iraq on its southern border countries of Greece and Italy. Member states would receive a number of asylum-seekers in keeping with a set of criteria such as gross domestic product, population, unemployment rate and the number of asylum-seekers already in the country. As an inducement, states would be granted EUR 6000 per refugee. It reaffirmed the proposal to triple the budget for life-saving missions throughout the Mediterranean and not just around the coastlines with a 30-mile limit. It also set a target of resettling 20,000 refugees from outside throughout the EU over the next two years, for which EU funding of EUR 50 million would be available. And to fight human trafficking, it put forward proposals to systematically identify, capture and destroy vessels used by smugglers by Common Security and Defence operations. Further, it proposed plans to engage with the migrants long before the migrants reach the Mediterranean and to support countries bearing the brunt and burden of those displaced by conflicts and human rights abuse.

These proposed measures were a step forward in dealing with the crisis and went beyond what the EU summit had considered. Not surprisingly, they elicited, in general, a positive reaction from international organisations, including from the IOM Director-General, William Swing, and the then United Nations Special Representative on Migration and Development, Peter Sutherland.

However, the measures did not seem to go far enough to avert the deepening crisis due to the seemingly relentless human flows showing no signs of abating any time soon.

Identification and Registration of Asylum-Seekers

Admittedly, saving human life from imminent danger should have the priority. It was therefore understandable that the EU's attention was focussed on fighting traffickers who were playing a nefarious role in worsening the crisis. However, despite a reference to the importance of "building strong partnership with key countries outside Europe" and support for development of the origin countries, there was little specific in the proposals that would address the root causes of the crisis in the countries of origin, including the role of the EU countries in a multifaceted programme of such action. And until this was done, the crisis, even if temporarily tamed, could continue (further discussed in Chapter 4). Finally, there was no certainty the proposals would be approved by the EU Council and implemented, especially since some of them were controversial among the EU member states: several east European countries, notably Hungary and Slovakia, flatly refused to accept the compulsory quota system for taking the newcomers.

In the event, when the EU summit met in June 2015, instead of producing a clear and unified response to the crisis, the leaders clashed over the EU Commission's proposal for mandatory relocation of 40,000 asylum-seekers across EU member states. Although the number was a small fraction of some 170,000 new arrivals in 2014 in Italy alone at the time (over 153,000 that Italy had already received in 2014), and more were coming, Matteo Renzi, the then country's prime minister had hoped that the acceptance of the Commission's proposal would establish a principle of burden-sharing. Yet there was vehement opposition especially from the EU's East European member states. At one stage of the acrimonious debate, Mr. Renzi told his fellow heads of government, "If this is Europe, you can keep it". In the end, they agreed to share 40,000 asylum-seekers—less than 10% of a total of 560,000 asylum applications received by the EU countries in 2014—but only on a voluntary basis. The summit also agreed to retain the plan to resettle 20,000 from outside the region. There was, however, no indication how these targets would be met. Even so, Commission officials expressed satisfaction that these targets were retained. Even Mr. Renzi called it "a first step towards a European migration policy".

However, in July 2015, the EU's plan to spread the burden of asylum-seekers arriving in Greece and Italy suffered a setback when members could agree to take only 32,000 of the new arrivals, which fell short of the target of 40,000. In June, it had already rejected the relocation scheme to be mandatory as proposed by the EU Commission. It was thus the second time in a month that the EU leaders watered down the EU Commission's proposals. France and Germany were fully supportive of the proposals, but several countries, notably Austria and Spain, were critical of the scheme on the grounds that they were already doing enough. Even so, Spain agreed to take 1200 as part of the scheme, while Austria flatly refused to participate in it. Countries such as the UK and Ireland have opt-outs from the EU's migration policy. However, Ireland agreed to take in 600 asylum-seekers, while the UK was firmly opposed to the scheme. The failure to reach the target of 40,000 was a blow to the European Commission officials and many others who had hoped that the reforms would mark the beginning of a more cohesive asylum system across the EU.

The only relieving feature was that the leaders agreed to take in 22,000 refugees exceeding the target of 20,000 from outside the EU. However, this relates to the scheme under which the UNHCR selects refugees for settlement and was only a modest increase on what most EU countries already did.

In August 2015, as violent protests erupted in the eastern German town of Heidenau where neo-Nazi and other right-wing demonstrators tried to block access to a newly opened asylum centre, Angela Merkel and François Hollande hurriedly got together to condemn the violence and to revive the European Commission's proposal for all 28 countries to agree to a binding quota agreement and share the burden—which had failed to take off in July due to opposition mainly, though not exclusively, from central European countries. In an emotional appeal, President Hollande said: "There are moments in European history when we stand (together) before an extraordinary situation. Today is such an extraordinary situation".[1] The two leaders called for the full implementation of EU asylum rules across the block, agreement on common definition of safe countries of origin to which would-be asylum-seekers could be returned and full establishment before the year-end of refugee registration centres in Greece and Italy.

On 3 September 2015, Alan Kurdi who was 3 years old, along with his brother Ghalib Kurdi (5 years old) and their mother drowned in the Mediterranean in their failed attempt to reach Europe. The image of Alan Kurdi's body washed up on a Turkish beach became a seminal moment in the refugee crisis and the global response to it.

---

[1] Cited in *Financial Times*, "Paris and Berlin urge EU unity on refugees", 25 August 2015.

By October 2015, the pressure of the flow of people towards Greece through the Aegean Sea had already been mounting fast. As the situation on the West Balkan route was creating widespread concern, the EU leaders agreed, at the urging of the UNHCR, to a plan of receiving 100,000 asylum-seekers. Despite strong opposition from Greek officials, it was agreed that Greece should provide temporary hotspots for accommodating 30,000 asylum-seekers and assessing their eligibility before sending them to other countries. Another 20,000 places for asylum-seekers would be provided by makeshift arrangements, including Greek people's homes. These extra places would be supported by the UNHCR and financed by the EU. The leaders were hoping that these extra places, coupled with what had already been agreed upon by the EU (a total of 160,000 places), would improve the situation. Sadly, however, it was a false hope.

The snag was that things were not moving as planned. As of October 2015, national governments had offered fewer than 1000 of the proposed 160,000 places, and only a dozen people had been actually relocated. Even by the beginning of 2016, less than 600 relocations had taken place. This implied that Greece would be stuck with a bigger load of asylum-seekers than anticipated. The reason for the slow progress in actual relocation was not just the lukewarm response of the EU countries. It was also at least partly due to the reluctance of the asylum-seekers to take part in the scheme either because they did not trust the EU officials and were fearful that they would be deported or because they were unwilling to move to the selected country of relocation. This was set to create an uncomfortable situation: the places in the sought-after country were likely to run out soon, leaving unused places in countries the asylum-seekers wanted to avoid.

The sheer number of arrivals every day was also a problem for proper registration, including finger-printing of the asylum-seekers. The infrastructure in both Greece and Italy was not adequate to cope with the task. Over 50,000 people entered Greece in the month of July 2015 alone, more than the country received during the whole of 2014. The Greek Prime Minister, Alexis Tsipras said in despair, "Greece is facing a crisis within a crisis", as it struggled to cope with the sudden influx, sparking fears of a humanitarian disaster (see Fig. 3.1). The EU plan for screening and relocation

3 The European Union's Response

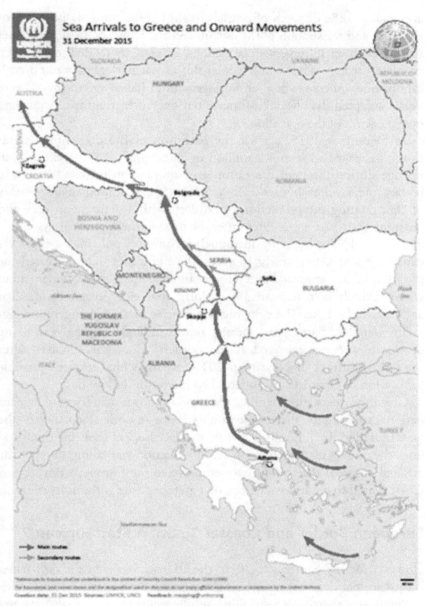

Fig. 3.1 Sea arrivals in Greece and onward movements (*Source* UNHCR)

also included the dispatch of officials to aid Greece and Italy in the identification and registration of the asylum-seekers. However, in all such cases sensitivity about infringement of national sovereignty tended to present a problem. In Italy, while some viewed this as valuable assistance at a critical juncture, others saw it as an infringement of Italian sovereignty. Greece finally accepted the offer of assistance but only after months of wrangling over the remit of the operation.

In December 2015, against the backdrop of the deepening migration crisis that had seen 1.2 million migrants and asylum-seekers reach Europe during the year, the European Commission unveiled a plan to replace the Frontex border agency, which had a limited mandate only of coordinating the protection of borders, with a permanent force and coastguard. It was a last-ditch attempt to save the Schengen system of free internal movement by introducing common policing at the EU's external borders. For nearly 15 years, the EU leaders had discussed the proposal of a common border force, but failed to overcome member states' strongly held resistance to yielding sovereign powers to monitor and control borders. The systemic deficiencies in the Schengen arrangements were laid bare by the massive new arrivals during the year, many of whom were unregistered at the borders. Concerns climaxed after the terrorist attack of November 2015 in Paris which revealed possible infiltration of terrorists into unchecked migration inflows.

Given, however, the member states' well-known anxiety to safeguard national sovereignty, there were doubts about smooth acceptance of the new initiative. In June 2016, when the EU leaders took up the question, the doubts turned largely true. The reaction was falling short of the original proposal that would have empowered the European Border and Coast Guard to enter the territory of a member state without its consent.

European Border and Coastal Guard: A Step Forward?

However, on 14 September 2016, the EU made a step forward when it took a final decision recognising integrated border control and management as a shared responsibility. While member states shall have the primary responsibility for border management, the new EU agency is endowed with a monitoring and supervisory role in relation to risk analysis and vulnerability assessment concerning the protection of the Community's common external border.

As part of this task, it shall establish a technical and operational strategy for integrated management of the common external border, and national action by member states must comply with it. The agency shall intervene to assist a member state in implementing the strategy at its request or when deficiencies persist or when a member state is unable or unwilling to do so. Such action shall be taken at the Union level based on the recommendations of the agency and the EU Commission and approval by the EU Council. If a member state refuses such intervention to avert a migration crisis, it will be placed outside the Schengen arrangement and face border control by its neighbouring states.

Integrated Border Management

The new border guard, which will embrace Frontex, will have a stronger mandate than its predecessor (which had only a coordinating role), with more staff and money. It will have liaison officers posted in all EU countries with external borders. Member states will be able to call on a reserve pool of 1500 extra guards in situations of excessive strain on their borders.

Some critics have argued that the new border guard will hardly make any real difference in the situation, and the European Council on Foreign Relations, a think tank, went to the extent of describing the guard as "new in name only". True, the agreement was not likely to restore full confidence in the Schengen system. And yet it was clearly a small but valuable first step towards the goal as it met at least partly the EU's urgent need to strengthen its common external borders "in a structural way", as Klaas Dijkhoff, Dutch minister for migration who oversaw negotiations for member states, put it.

The deepening of the crisis also led the EU to opt for two other measures at the beginning of 2016. The North Atlantic Treaty Organization (NATO) was invited to send ships to the Aegean Sea to help Greece and Turkey to track down smugglers bringing migrants to Europe and to pass the intelligence on such activities to Greek and Turkish coastguards. The suggestion for this unorthodox activity of the NATO came from Ms. Merkel following her meeting with Ahmet Davutoglu, then Turkish Prime Minister, in Ankara. The NATO's quick response, with plans for almost immediate deployment of five ships standing near Cyprus was a clear signal of political support for the EU as it faced the crisis.

However, analysts were doubtful if the measure would make much difference in the situation; at best, it might reduce some of the worst activities of human trafficking in the area. A main reason for this was the deteriorating situation in Syria where Russian bombing was generating large new outflows from Aleppo city and its outskirts, hitherto a stronghold of the moderate rebels fighting the Assad regime. Even more important, if the NATO operation was to be confined only to information-gathering, and not seising the traffickers and destroying their networks, as was announced, the question arises if this was the most cost-effective way of doing the task. Could it not have been done by strengthening Triton or the planned coastguard at much less cost under the aegis of the EU itself? Given the aggressive geopolitical stance of Russia in the Middle East and the strategic/military importance of the Aegean Sea route, some analysts were pondering if the NATO's new operation might not also be linked to a more active surveillance of the movements on this sea route. However, a European Commission spokesman said that it viewed the plan as "a sort of forerunner" to the proposed European coastguard. If so, it would make more sense.

There were also some sensitive aspects of the deal. Both the EU and Germany had long sought, with little success, closer Greco-Turkish cooperation in policing the straits between mainland Turkey and the Greek islands. Turkey has had concerns about formal NATO cooperation with the EU (of which it was not a member). But in the new circumstances it cautiously accepted the arrangement. Greece, for its part, was suspicious that Ankara might use the deployment of Turkish vessels to support its territorial claims in the Aegean Sea. In the event, Greece agreed to NATO involvement on condition that its ships should not be under either the Turkish or Greek command and that they would respect the territorial waters of the two countries.

The second EU measure concerned Greece's position in the Schengen system. As the west Balkan route was becoming overcrowded by migrants and asylum-seekers coming from Greece, it was putting strain on the diplomatic relations, rekindling the dormant conflicts and tensions between the Balkan states long embedded in history. There was a cascade of border walls being built—or threats to build them—to stem the inflows. Tit-for-tat border closures were making migrants and asylum-seekers trapped into small countries unable to cope with the arrivals, creating a humanitarian disaster. Given that Greece was unable or unwilling to manage the flows, a plan first floated by Slovenia, raised the possibility of member states sending troops to the Macedonian side of Greece to control or seal the border. Greek Prime Minister Alexis Tsipras was, however, strongly opposed to the plan which, as he put it, would turn Greece into a "black box of refugees". The fear was not groundless, given that, as already mentioned, the plans to relocate refugees from Greece and Italy were making little progress. However, many EU leaders were in favour of Greece serving as a refugee camp for the rest of the bloc, with the arrivals then distributed among the other states.

In February 2016, the EU summit decided to keep in abeyance the plan to seal the Macedonian border. However, Greece was given a list of some 50 measures to improve border control and asylum registration within the next three months, and was informed that the default in doing so would put Greece out of the Schengen system. Meanwhile, however, the processing of asylum applications, including finger-printing, had significantly improved in both Greece and Italy, with finger-printing done in Greece having covered 78% of arrivals, compared with just 8% in September 2015, and in Italy 87% of the arrivals, compared with just 38% in the same period. Greece had also moved quickly in January 2016 to build a series of reception hotspots on five eastern Aegean islands that in 2015 received over 800,000 migrants arriving by boat from Turkey. In Lesbos, which had more than 400,000 arrivals in 2015, the hotspots had started operating since November 2015 as the EU had suggested.

Some analysts thought that while Greece was definitely a troubled, porous state, it was likely that the EU was looking for a nice, legal scapegoat to allow a two-year time out from Schengen for member states which had already put in place border control measures until

May 2016 but wanted a longer period than that. As one analyst put it, a damning assessment that turns Greece into the scapegoat for the failure of Schengen is just what they need".[2]

The situation turned ugly late in February 2016 as Austria planned to limit the number of persons who could apply for asylum at the Austrian border to 80. Under the plan Austria would still allow people to travel through the country, although the number would be capped at 3200 a day. This led to a chorus of protests not just by Greece but also the EU in Brussels. The European Commission said that the move was incompatible with the 1951 UN Convention on refugees (of which Austria is a founding signatory) as well as with the EU's Charter of Fundamental Rights. Austria's plan also triggered fears that it would drive parts of the migratory flows from the western Balkan routes (though Macedonia and Serbia) eastwards through Bulgaria or Albania, neither of which had the capacity to shelter and feed tens of thousands of people. This could therefore create a major humanitarian crisis. In a worse turn of the situation, on 24 February 2016, Austria unilaterally agreed with the nine Balkan states to restrict the numbers of migrants crossing their borders, with a commitment to accept those deemed to need protection.

There was still another unsettled issue that was troubling the EU leaders, especially Angela Merkel. The EU had long been trying to persuade Ankara to take back willingly asylum-seekers who had travelled through Turkey to reach Europe. In exchange, the EU would open a massive resettlement programme for 250,000 refugees a year from Turkey as proposed by Diederik Samson, a Dutch politician, who floated the idea. However, meanwhile, in keeping with the usual twists and turns of events during the crisis, Athens was pondering the designation of Turkey as a safe third country. Greece did so as part of its drive to increase deportation of asylum-seekers, despite the doubtful legal and ethical validity of such a scheme. The Greek move seemed to have seriously upset Ankara. According to one Turkish official, this would scupper (at the time) the EUR 3.0 billion potential flagship deal between the EU and Turkey aimed at reducing the flow of migrants and asylum-seekers into Europe—a deal which was being strenuously negotiated over months.

---

[2]Christian Oliver, "Greece takes a fall for Schengen", *Financial Times*, 12 February 2016.

EU–Turkey Deal: A Last-Ditch Response

Despite all the uncertainties and misgivings, on Thursday, 17 March 2016, the EU and Turkey agreed on a deal aimed at containing the migration crisis. Under the audacious and highly controversial deal, all irregular migrants (failed asylum-seekers and those who had not applied for asylum) arriving in Greek islands from Turkey after 20 March 2016 are to be returned to that country. In exchange for each Syrian asylum-seeker returned to Turkey, the EU will accept and resettle up to 72,000 a year, an equivalent number of Syrian refugees (whose claims have been duly processed) directly from the refugee camps in Turkey. In addition, the EU will pay Turkey six billion Euros towards the refugee-related expenditure, facilitate, under certain conditions, visa-free travel for Turkey's nationals (and assimilated individuals) and speed up the process of Turkey's accession to the EU. The idea behind the arrangement was that it would lessen the attraction and thus the pull effect of the EU as a destination and smash the business model of human traffickers.

It was a highly controversial deal on several grounds, legal, ethical and operational, as discussed later in this chapter.

A New Marshall Plan for Africa?

On 11 November 2016, the German development minister Gerd Müller urged rich countries to launch what he called "a new Marshall Plan for Africa" to bolster the continent's economies through public and private investments, and create jobs, with a focus on education and training of youth and strengthen the rule of law. At the time of writing, Mr. Müller was yet to spell out all the details. However, the preliminary announcement seemed to suggest a more positive approach to addressing the root causes of irregular and unsafe migration through development of origin countries, even though slowing down African migration to Europe remained the primary objective. What appeared to be missing, however, was any specific reference to the need for well-calibrated openness on the part of rich countries in trade and migration that met the interests of both groups of countries. It should not be forgotten that development itself tends to generate some new migration, as explained below. However, if the economic development is employment-oriented and broad-based, it helps restrain irregular and forced migration driven by poverty and despair.

Irregular Migration, Unsafe Migration, Public Investments, Private Investments

Most, if not all, of the new migrants who may be enabled and encouraged to move as a result of development are likely to do so in search of better opportunities. And their decision to move is apt to be a matter of free choice, based on a rational assessment of costs and benefits involved: they are also less likely to move through irregular channels. While the plan rightly argued for job creation and for education and training of the youth, it follows from the above that there should have been more clarity about the crucial importance of broad-based development if it is to restrain irregular and disorderly migration driven by poverty and despair and as a matter of compulsion. It is therefore important to take note of the distinction between "poverty-driven migration" and "opportunity-seeking migration" to understand the changing composition of migration in such a situation.[3]

Clearly, while this long-term programme of deep engagement with origin countries is worked out, there should be no slackening of efforts to meet the immediate need of saving human lives and resettle those uprooted men, women and children who are desperately looking for a new home and a better life.

Valletta Action Plan

On 11–12 November 2015, there was a breakthrough when the EU Valletta summit somewhat belatedly adopted an Action Plan covering five priority areas: addressing root causes of irregular migration and

---

[3]For a discussion on the distinction between "survival migration" and "opportunity-seeking migration" see Bimal Ghosh, *The Global Economic Crisis and the Future of Migration,* Palgrave/Macmillan, 2013, Chapter 7, p. 251; *Huddled Masses and Uncertain Shores*, op. cit. Chapter 2, p. 35.

forced displacement; legal migration and mobility; protection of refugees and asylum-seekers; preventing and combating irregular migration, migrant smuggling and human trafficking; and return, readmission and reintegration.

In June 2016, the objectives and main features of the new initiative were defined. Although rescuing and receiving migrants and refugees were still a major concern, the new approach had several positive elements, including a shift of emphasis towards the collective responsibility of Europe and Africa in addressing poverty and underdevelopment as the root causes of irregular migration. A strategy paper, "Partnership Framework", which was to guide the new initiative, stressed the need for a "coordinated, systematic and structural approach matching the EU's interests with the interests of our partners".[4] As part of the initiative, the EU planned to sign bilateral agreements with a group of African countries, including Mali, Nigeria, Niger, Senegal and Ethiopia. It also promised to increase the resources of the Africa Trust Fund, which it had already agreed to set up with an initial capital of EUR 1.9 billion, by an additional EUR 500 million; furthermore, the EU dangled a pot of EUR 3.4 billion in guarantees for private investment, backed by a further EUR 3.4 billion from member states for countries willing to sign agreements with the EU on migration, with the possibility of raising EUR 88 billion through leveraging.

Malta Declaration

In March 2017, when the European Council met under Maltese presidency, arrivals by the eastern Mediterranean were falling sharply, marked by a decline by 98% in the last four months of 2016, compared with the same period in 2015. In striking contrast, inflows by the central Mediterranean were still high (further discussed in Chapter 4), with the number of persons dead or missing reaching a new yearly record since 2013. The attention of the summit was, somewhat belatedly, focussed on inflows

---

[4]European Commission, Press Release, 6 June 2016.

by the central Mediterranean route, which was a matter of direct concern to the Maltese government as well.

The declaration reaffirmed its policy of ensuring effective control of its external border, and of stemming irregular migration, and deepening long-term cooperation with a number of partner countries to address the root causes of irregular migration, in keeping with the Valletta Action Plan. However, the EU apparently had few operational tools in its policy kit to stem the inflows through the central Mediterranean route other than the action plan it had agreed with Turkey, seemingly with some success. The summit declaration thus focussed on a set of 10 specific measures, among other things, to stabilise conditions in Libya, ensure adequacy of its capacities and conditions for receiving and dealing with its inflows of migrants and those of its neighbouring and other transit countries to manage their borders and help reduce the migratory pressure on Libya. The UN-backed government in Libya will receive EUR 200 million to carry out the internal measures, including for strengthening Libyan coastguard and improving conditions in migrant reception centres.

However, as will be discussed in the next chapter, the plan has come under strong criticism by the UNHCR and rights groups on the ground that running camps in Libya was fraught with the danger of further abuse of the human rights and refugee rights of the detainees.

By 2017, the situation about the inflows to Italy was becoming increasingly unsustainable. More than 83,000 migrants had arrived in Italy by boat in the first half of 2017, a 19% increase over the same period in 2016, itself a record year. Although the final tally for 2017 may not necessarily exceed the record number of 181,000 in 2016, it is the accumulation of the new arrivals over the past three years that made the crisis reach a tipping point. In the past three years, Italy had received 580,000, according to the Italian foreign minister, Angelino Alfano. The Italian government was feeling that it had been abandoned by the rest of the EU while a backlash was fuelling the populist parties. Tensions were heightened when Austria revealed that it had stationed 750 troops on standby to control immigration flows via the Brenner Alpine pass on its border with Italy. Marco Minniti, then Italy's interior minister called the Austrian move an "unjustified and unprecedented initiative", with likely negative repercussions on cooperation between the two countries on security issues.

The situation led the government to send an ultimatum to EU member states in which it threatened to shut its ports for foreign boats carrying asylum-seekers unless it got more help in dealing with the crisis. The demand included a fundamental revision of asylum rules to ensure migrants are not forced to request asylum in Italy as the first country of arrival; additional funding for the Libyan coastguard to turn back migrant-carrying boats while they were in their territorial waters; and tighter regulations of migrant-rescuing boats operating in the Easter Mediterranean Route, Central Mediterranean Route, Mediterranean. This was soon followed by a meeting of Italian, French and German interior ministers to consider Rome's concerns. Although they failed to address all of them, they made headway on some of them, which they wanted to place at the top the agenda of EU's interior ministers.

In July 2017, in response to Italy's demand, the European Commission, for its part, unveiled a plan to help the country to manage the country's "ever more pressing" migration issue. The plan includes the allocation of EUR 35 million to help Italy deal with the recent sharp rise (19%) in inflows and EUR 46 million to support the Libyan authorities and the coastguard. It also promised to help Rome draft a code of conduct for NGOs operating between Italy and Libya which might require their vessels to comply with certain standards and carry certain specific equipment. Further, it called on member states to do what they had already agreed in relocating migrants in their respective territories, as Italy had urged in order to lessen its strain caused by the inflows.

Although the plan generally was well received, certain aspects of it came under criticism, as further discussed in the next chapter.

4

The European Union's Agonies

Fault Lines, Strategic Errors and Institutional Inadequacies

What Is New About the Flows? Causes and Characteristics of Mixed Migration

Migration to Europe across the Mediterranean is not new. What is new, however, is not just the volume of the flows, which is unprecedented since World War II, but also its complex composition and characteristics as well as the daunting policy challenges they present. As noted, in just one year over one million people had moved into Europe across the Mediterranean, over 4000 died during the journey and 10,000 children disappeared. It has seen rapid shifts in the routes and modes of travel and revealed a complex amalgam of political, economic and human factors as drivers of movement of masses of uprooted people, sharpening the problem of managing mixed migration. The inflows have thrown into focus several new issues or reignited the old ones. According to the preliminary indications, these trends and the related challenges were likely to continue unabated throughout the years of 2016–2017, and their consequences to extend far beyond. Discerning the salient features of these flows and the kind of challenges they entail is an important first step in developing an effective policy response.

If the sheer magnitude of the flows and the rapid shifts in the routes and modes of movement manoeuvred by the traffickers have added to the difficulty in managing the flows, their predominantly mixed composition—asylum-seekers, poverty-driven economic migrants and persons deserving humanitarian protection all bundled together—has made the situation much worse. Not only has it made the screening process more onerous and time-consuming, it has also made some states less welcoming to the new arrivals and a few, notably Hungary, used this as an argument or easy excuse for rejecting them all.

The issue of mixed migration has two aspects: (a) mixed motivation of the migrant and (b) mixed composition of the flows. The first happens when a person is motivated to move for a mixture of (often interrelated) reasons—for example, when political discrimination is combined with lack of equal access to economic opportunities. A person exposed to such a situation may be driven to move abroad not only to escape political discrimination and harassment but also to improve his/her economic opportunities, and be free from the feeling of "relative deprivation".[1] The second aspect—mixed composition—occurs when the malfunctioning of one channel of entry prompts a person to try and seek admission through some other channel or channels. For instance, if despite unmet labour demand in the destination country, its channel of labour immigration remains unduly restrictive, a potential labour migrant may try his/her entry through the asylum channel, should it look more promising. This is a situation of opportunistic "category jumping" leading to entanglement of channels: a situation somewhat distinct from the case of mixed motivation. These two factors have combined to shape the composition and characteristics of the present mixed flows in Europe, and in doing so, they have made their management more difficult.

---

[1] Knowingly or unknowingly people tend to compare their own economic situation with that of the others in the country. They may not necessarily be victims of poverty or unemployment but when they feel that some others are making much faster progress and doing it more easily because of their privileged position or inequities embedded in the prevailing economic and social system, a sense of relative deprivation may be a motivating factor of migration. See, in this connection, Bimal Ghosh, *Huddled Masses and Uncertain Shores: Insights into Irregular Migration*, Martinus Nijhoff Publishers/Kluwer Law International, The Hague, 1988, pp. 42–43.

Narrow and Fragmentary Approach, Inadequate Protection

The existing national and international laws are proving inadequate to meet the protection needs created by the new situation of mixed migration and its complexities. The narrow scope and strictly defined criteria of the existing refuge laws fail to give adequate protection to any of those who are in a refugee-like situation and deserve humanitarian protection but remain excluded. At the same time, the rigid classification of types of migrants under existing migration and refugee laws fosters a fragmentary and faulty approach to migration management. It ignores the real possibility that if one legal channel of movement does not work properly, almost invariably it affects the smooth functioning of some other channel or channels. Recent migration history shows many such examples of category or channel jumping, but this seems to have happened on a very large, probably unprecedented, scale in the current migration and refugee inflows to Europe.

The new mixed flows have highlighted once more these inadequacies of the current international instruments and mandates, notably the 1951 UN Convention on the Status of Refugees and its 1967 Protocol, to meet the needs and conditions of humanitarian protection of the fast-changing world.[2] The UN Convention, drafted at the end of World War II, was designed mainly to meet the protection needs and conditions of refugees from the communist regimes and omits several individuals, especially groups of individuals, even if they too are in refugee-like situations and in genuine need of protection. They include victims of: forced migration resulting from civil war, armed conflicts and generalised violence, massive violation of human and minority rights, and natural and man-made disasters (some, but not all of these are covered in the Cartagena Declaration and especially the OAU convention on refugees)[3]. Also, in many situations of forced movements, instances of individual

---

[2]See in this connection, Bimal Ghosh, *Human Rights and Migration: The Missing Link*, University of Utrecht/THP, The Hague, 2008.

[3]Full titles of the two instruments, respectively: 'Cartagena Declaration on the Problems of Refugees and the Displaced in Central America, 1988'. 'Convention of the Organization of African Unity on the Specific Aspects of the Refuge Problem in Africa, 1999'.

persecution (an essential criterion under the UN Convention) are not easily identifiable. Inadequacies of the UN Convention also relate to the exclusion of cases of persecution by non-state agents, from the uncertainty of protection in the situations of interdiction or interception of would-be asylum-seekers on the high seas or of those rescued at sea.

Many of the asylum-seekers in the current inflows fall into one or more of these categories and may not be eligible under the UN Convention. EU states, as those in North America and Oceania, have sought to respond to several of these humanitarian emergencies on an ad hoc basis by accepting them as temporary refugees or creating some special categories of protected persons. Yet, in the absence of internationally agreed and harmonised norms, protection remains unpredictable, fragile and insecure. It also makes the screening process more complicated and time-consuming as exemplified by the current experience in the EU.

At the same time, the rigid classification of types of migrants under existing migration and refugee laws fosters a fragmentary and faulty approach to migration management. It ignores the real possibility that if one legal channel of movement does not work properly, almost invariably it affects the smooth functioning of some other channel or channels. The situation also carries the risk that a potential migrant or asylum-seeker, driven by mixed motivations and composite push factors, may fall through the gaps between the rigidly defined, legal entry slots.

The way in which the conundrum of mixed migration can be addressed is discussed in the next chapter (Chapter 5) as well as in last chapter (Chapter 12).

This apart, one special requirement of eligibility for protection under the UN Convention is that the asylum-seeker must apply from outside the country of origin (the requirement is hardened by the insistence by some governments that the individual must also have valid travel documents).[4] Not surprisingly, this has propelled many desperate people

---

[4]Under Article 31(1), the Convention does provide an exemption when one comes directly from a country where one's life was threatened and can show good causes for violating applicable entry laws. In practice, however, it may not be easy for a potential asylum-seeker to prove the circumstances prescribed in the Article. Nor are destination countries always inclined to respect the exemption provided in the Article. The provision needs to be tightened and more effectively applied.

to make the perilous journeys to seek asylum in Europe, change the routes and modes of travel, and has helped the unscrupulous traffickers to profit from a flourishing market. As discussed later in Chapter 5, in-country processing, like offshore screening, has many shortcomings and pitfalls. Yet, it is possible that a timely and well-managed system of in-country processing in safety zones, and with adequate safeguards, within a few selected countries, would have been less costly in terms of human life and hardship and less overwhelming for the European Union than it has turned out to be. However, as will be discussed in Chapter 5, offshore processing in a third country such as Egypt, Turkey or Tunisia, though seemingly tempting, is fraught with perils.

Another characteristic of the flows that has made their management more difficult relates to the composition of the newcomers, which often included an entire family, with varying, and, not infrequently, urgent needs of children (roughly 28% of the flow), expectant mothers and elderly parents. The intensity of the flow is yet another aspect of the problem. The time gap between the arrival of a labour migrant and that of his/her family that, even under a most liberal family reunification regime, is normally observed was not available. And the EU countries, which were hardly prepared to accept these large inflows, were much less equipped to deal with such varying and urgent needs and conditions of the new migrants and asylum-seekers.

Strategic and Tactical Errors

The EU's member states have made a solemn and collective commitment to free internal movement but have been reluctant to give away (or pull together) their sovereign prerogative needed to manage migration at their external borders (further discussed later in this chapter). Many have traditionally pursued a short-sighted policy and relied on bilateral agreements with mostly autocratic governments in the MENA countries to shut out irregular immigrants. The dichotomy has weakened the EU's capacity to deal effectively with the flows at its external borders, with inadequacies and vacillation in policies, and a series of strategic and tactical errors in its operations.

First, in carrying out its operations to meet the crisis, the EU, largely due to the member states' zealous attachment to sovereign prerogatives, has always been more reactive and myopic rather than pro-active and circumspect. Also, partly, though not exclusively, because of the absence of an effective early warning system, it failed to take timely action at some of the crucial turning points of the inflows. Already at the beginning of 2014, there were several ominous signs, including human tragedies in the sea, portending a massive increase of migrants taking perilous journeys by the Mediterranean; soon thereafter the London-based International Maritime Organisation (IMO) reckoned that, if the prevailing trend remained unabated, half a million people could be expected to take the same perilous journey in 2015 and that as many as 10,000 might die in the process. And, at about the same time, an Italian official was reported as saying that up to one million desperate people were waiting in Libya to take the perilous journey.

A Shift from the Aegean to the Mediterranean Route to Europe

However, even when in 2014, overwhelmed by the massive level of the inflows and the rising expenses to run the Mare Nostrum rescue ships, Italy dismantled the programme, the EU took time to launch the Triton operation as part of its border agency, Frontex, and when it did, it was a much scaled-down operation, mainly on the basis of the *faulty* and callous assumption that if the journey was riskier, then fewer would attempt it. Subsequently, this was modified and at least twice Triton's mandate was widened and its resources augmented. Had this been done on time, many more lives could have been saved.

The EU action was also late in monitoring developments, and it turned out to be a tactical blunder, as it continued to focus its attention on the Italian shores and much less on Greece even when a large part of the flows had already been shifting to Greece and its islands, which shortly afterwards became more important as an entry point than Italy. The same thing happened when it failed to take timely notice of the eastward shifts in the migrant's land route after Hungary decided to build its border fence in September 2015. [An immediate crisis within the Balkan states was averted at the last minute by the EU intervention. But much bad blood had already been created.]

Later, repeating a similar mistake, the EU devoted almost all its attention to the migration crisis in Greece and the Balkans, which was no doubt urgent, but it forgot for quite a while to take into account the growing new inflows of mostly irregular migrants to Italy from sub-Saharan Africa through the central Mediterranean Sea or other possible routes. The lack of timely attention to these possibilities was causing a growing concern to the Italian government. And tension between Italy and the EU was growing, although by September 2016 some action was initiated by both the Commission and Frontex to remedy the situation, and this had to be further reinforced in July 2017 (discussed in Chapter 3).

More recently, the terrorist attack in Spain in August 2017 has once again highlighted the crucial need to monitor the shifts in the direction of the mixed migration flows. Pressures on Europe of these flows through the central Mediterranean route could be shifting further west from North Africa, especially Morocco to Spain, which still retains possessions of two enclaves, Ceuta and Melilla, on the Moroccan coast. As the EU steps up efforts to choke the flows, helped by smugglers and traffickers, through Niger and Libya, and Italy clampdowns on rescue missions by charities in the central Mediterranean, human traffickers and smugglers are likely to switch their operations through the shorter and safer route from Morocco to Spain. According to analysts, networks for ISIS recruitment of jihadists often straddled borders between Morocco and Spain.

The unrest in Morocco since October 2016 that has weakened stability in the country could further this jihadist danger and contribute to fuelling the migratory flows towards Spain. Morocco has also become an important launch pad for an increasing number of irregular migrants and potential asylum-seekers from West Africa. Some try to take advantage of the visa-free travel facility offered by Morocco for nationals of several West African countries. In 2016, Spain received 13,246 migrants and potential refugees. In 2017, already by mid-August the number of arrivals by sea was hovering around 11,849 and it was estimated that by the end of the year it could be significantly higher than in 2016, and even exceed the number of new arrivals in Greece. According to Juan Ignacio Zoido, Spain's interior minister, migrant arrivals, numbering 15,500 (including over 11,000 who were rescued from the sea) increased by more than 88% in the first eight months of 2017, compared with 2016 for the same period. This signals the need for the EU to be more alert and circumspect about the changing routes of the flows and the agility of the traffickers to adapt the strategies of their operations.

A related, major strategic and diagnostic error, which the EU was about to commit but narrowly escaped, concerns the EU's knee-jerk plan, pushed by Mr. Renzi, then Italian prime minister, to bomb the trafficking boats off the Libyan shores at the beginning of the crisis. As discussed above, there were of course practical problems and pitfalls in such action, including: the problem of securing the Libyan or UN authorisation for the interventions, likely danger of further destabilising a country where conditions were already unstable and creating human casualties and generating additional outflows of people. But, even more important, the plan was strategically faulty as it assumed that human trafficking is static, uniquely located in Libya and ignored the well-known agility of the traffickers to change their courses and mode of operation at short notice and their access to an extremely flexible network across countries and regions. At the same time, they find an easy market when people are in desperation and tend to be more gullible to false promises, creating a demand for traffickers' services.

EU–Turkey Deal: A Desperate Capitulation

The EU–Turkey agreement[5] had already become controversial even before it became operational on 20 March 2016. There are good reasons—legal, ethical and operational—why critics have expressed doubts about the success of this opportunistic deal. *First*, there are doubts about the legality of the arrangement which provides for blanket return

---

[5]Since the arrangement was not adopted as an act of European Parliament, it may not be considered as a formal agreement but a deal between the EU and Turkey or a joint statement. However, in this book I have used the two terms interchangeably for reasons of convenience.

of masses of people to a third country without ensuring proper safeguards for refugee protection under international law. Doubts about the compliance of the arrangement with the international and European human and refugee rights laws have been expressed, among others, by the European Parliamentary Assembly and the Greek National Commission for Human Rights. Under the plan, these individuals would be sent to a country which did not provide full protection to refugees. According to Turkish law, only persons fleeing from Europe can be granted refugee status as defined in the 1951 UN Convention. Although Turkey has given temporary protection to Syrians, it is not a fully fledged "safe" third country. The EU has tried to blunt this criticism by insisting that the screening will be done on an individual basis, although on a fast-track criterion of admissibility test, in keeping with a new law (LAW 4375/2016). The law requires the individual concerned must pass an admissibility assessment before an application for asylum can be considered on its merits. However, even if Greece, with EU help can ensure this in a credible manner (although it remained doubtful, see below), lawyers, including the Greek Appeals Committee, have tended to maintain their reservations about the process on the grounds that Turkey was not a fully fledged "safe third country".

Later, however, in response to this widespread criticism, Turkey, agreed to bolster legal protection to non-Syrian asylum-seekers. Although Ankara had resisted pressure from Brussels to reform its asylum system, on 27 April 2016, in a letter to the European Commission, Turkey pledged that all returnees from Greece will have their applications heard in full and within a reasonable time period. Syrians who enjoyed refugee status before embarking for Greece will also have a way to have that restored. The assurance to give Syrian and non-Syrian returnees similar status has blunted much of the criticisms by UNHCR and rights groups of the deal, although much depends on how the arrangement is implemented. It is also important to note that although Turkey offers a watered-down refugee status to Syrians, given that they are not fully covered by the provisions of the UN Convention, their rights remain limited. The EU was also anxious that Turkey made efforts to clear a backlog of some 140,000 applications so that the operation of the new arrangement can run smoothly.

Second, ethically too many are shocked that the EU has entered into such a deal at a time when Turkey had openly expressed contempt for European values, including respect for human rights, and has been undermining the independence of its judiciary and media. There were also allegations by Amnesty International that Turkey was forcibly returning Syrian asylum-seekers, and that its guards were even shooting at Syrian refugees stranded at the border, although Turkey denied them. Some asylum-seekers were also claiming that even after legislation was approved allowing them to work in Turkey, authorities remained reluctant to issue work permits. Many were questioning whether by allowing visa-free travel for over 80 million Turks in its territory or opening the path for (an unreformed) Turkey to become its member, the EU would not be betraying the values it has long cherished and championed, with its ethical assets demolished. This remains a delicate issue for the EU as it faces increasing pressure from Turkey for fulfilment of the commitment it has made, but finds it difficult to do so in view of widespread and multi-layered resistance from within the EU member states and the European Parliament. Some were critical of the deal also on the ethical ground that in making the deal with Turkey, the EU was trying to avoid its responsibility simply by "outsourcing" the problem instead of thrashing it through the EU's own collective action, with each member state playing its part.

Third, there was a huge problem of logistics. Despite the promised help from the EU and member countries, such as the planned dispatch of 4000 officers, including migration specialists, translators and others, to strengthen Greece's creaking asylum service, there was serious concern if its infrastructure can cope with the situation. At the beginning, Greece served as a main transit country, then as a holding pen for some 50,000 migrants and asylum-seekers; and suddenly under the agreement it became the main enforcer of the arrangement for screening and return of failed asylum-seekers to Turkey, while dealing with the backlog of some 50,000 migrants who were already in the country. The aim was to process up to 600 applications a day and 6000 actual transfers a month—highly ambitious targets. The target was to conclude each case within just 15 days.

But inevitably, delays occurred. The first returns from Greece, which were due to take place on 28 March 2016, were delayed until 4 April due to administrative difficulties over asylum hearings on the islands. The next deportations of 750 migrants to Turkey, previously scheduled to take place on the following day, were also postponed by a few days, raising concerns that the plan could stall. Furthermore, international aid workers on Lesbos expressed doubts over whether those returned had been offered an opportunity to claim asylum, given the absence of interpreters and legal representatives. All migrants have the right not only to claim asylum but also to appeal against rejections and there were many complex questions over the process itself, from the treatment of unaccompanied minors to provision of legal aid.

In the aftermath of the agreement, many of those who had not applied for asylum earlier were doing so, increasing the caseload of applicants. And this was happening at a time when, along the land part of the Balkan route, between 10,000 and 14,000 migrants were waiting in squalid camps at Idomeni on the border of Macedonia which had been closed since 9 March 2016, threatening to create a potential humanitarian crisis. Tension was running high as the migrants refused to move and were getting increasingly restless and desperate to force through the fences. Risks of violence with the Macedonian border guards were running high.

Not surprisingly, Greece had already come under criticism by the refugee aid agencies for its move to turn EU "hotspots" for screening and registering migrants into closed and grim detention facilities. At Moria, for instance, over 3000 asylum-seekers, including women and children, were stuffed into a fortress-like place of barbed wire and watchtowers, with little freedom of movement for the inmates. Worries were surfacing that vulnerable asylum-seekers would be held in detention under unacceptable conditions. Amnesty International called the conditions at Moria and another centre on the island of Chios as awful. In September 2016, due to a fire, believed to be voluntary, between 3000 and 4000 fled the camp in Moria, and 150 children had to be evacuated. Disturbing incidents in the overcrowded camp were not new, but never before was it necessary to evacuate so many children all at once. In protest at the move, three of the biggest aid agencies—the UNHCR, the International Rescue Committee and the medical charity *Médecins Sans Frontières*—suspended or scaled back some of their operations. As the plan of expulsion began to be implemented, the UNHCR complained that across Greece numerous aspects of the systems of receiving and dealing with people who might need protection were either not working or absent.

The stream of arrivals, although reduced, was out-spacing Greece's limited facilities for detaining and processing asylum applications. The conditions in processing centres on Greece's outermost islands such as Chios and Samos were deteriorating and some of the camps and shelters in derelict buildings had seen rioting and stabbings as migrants panicked about their future. On the mainland, tents hastily erected by the Greek military lacked adequate lighting and sanitation and the government relied on volunteers and aid agencies to supply regular meals to the inmates. The whole situation in both Turkey and Greece led Yanis Varoufakis, Greece's former finance minister, to warn against the two countries Greece and Turkey becoming "a large concentration camp for hapless refugees".[6] The arrivals and occupancy on the five Aegean islands far exceeded the capacity of the reception centres. The situation on the Greek islands was particularly disturbing. As of 3 October 2016, the average daily arrivals on the islands was 14,331, which was almost double the estimated capacity (7450) of the islands to receive them, according to the UNHCR.

The EU Commission said that it was addressing these concerns, assuring that it was working to send an extra 2500 staff to help transform the camps and processing centres in keeping with international standards. The EU also set up an EUR 700 million fund to help Greece cope with the crisis, and a new law approved by parliament sought to bring the country in line with the EU directives on asylum and refugees.

The Erstwhile Favoured Route May Close but Other Potential Pathways to Europe Remain Open

There was also a related issue: even if the EU/Turkey agreement lessens the pressure on Greece, the human tide, driven by the traffickers, was likely to be diverted to other European destinations, notably Italy, through the central Mediterranean Sea and other possible routes, as already mentioned above. In fact, Italy was already pleading for EU help

---

[6]*CNBC*, "Greece's Varoufakis addresses EU migrant crisis", 3 March 3016.

to ramp up the deportation of migrants following a sharp rise in the number of new arrivals across the central Mediterranean Sea. In 2014, the number of new arrivals reached 170,000, a fourfold increase over the total number registered in 2013. In 2015, there was a temporary lull in the flows due to weather conditions, with the total number decelerating to 154,000, while there was a sharp rise in the number of new arrivals in Greece. However, in 2016 the new flows to Italy started rising again. According to Frontex, in April 2016 the number of migrants reaching Italy *by sea* exceeded the total for Greece for the first time since June 2015. (Some 8300 migrants were detected on the central Mediterranean route compared with 2700 on the Turkey–Greece route.)

Italy's concern was already heightened when in April 2016 a boat carrying over 500 migrants, including Somalis, Ethiopians, Egyptians and Sudanese, sank on its way to the Italian shores. It revived the painful memories of the boat that laden with 800 migrants capsized off the Libyan coast almost exactly a year ago, triggering wide concern and a major policy initiative from the EU.

As discussed above, arrivals in Italy were rising fast. In November 2016, Italy received more new arrivals than it did in all of 2015, and the number reached over 180,000 by December (most of them from sub-Saharan Africa, led by Nigeria, according to the Italian interior ministry). At the end of 2016, new arrivals in Italy and Greece were almost evenly matched, numbering 181,436 and 173,561, respectively. In the past three years (2014–2016), Italy had received over half a million migrants.

Italy was also concerned that as the EU/Turkey plan goes into action, it may compound the problem by encouraging Middle Eastern migrants to switch routes and attempt to enter Italy and the EU through other routes. If, for example, Syrians do not want to stay in Turkey and want to enter Europe, they can go around and try to get to Italy through Libya. Even this was not all. There are at least two other additional pathways to Europe that migrants and traffickers could follow: the Greece–Albania–Adriatic route and the Black Sea–Ukraine–Poland route. The route through Albania may be tough because of the difficult terrain and snow-capped mountains, but human traffickers, drug smugglers and jihadists have proved adept in surmounting such obstacles and desperate migrants and asylum-seekers have been found to take even deadlier risks.

In fact, Italy had already initiated talks with Albania about containing an eventual surge in flows through this route and Tirana was reported to have dispatched special police units to its southern frontier with Greece.[7]

As for the Black Sea route, the closure of the Balkan route may drive migrants to reach Poland from Turkey after trekking across Ukraine. According to the *Financial Times*, Poland had been assessing this possibility at its eastern border and the country's third largest party had urged the construction of a fence at that frontier. Bulgarian borders with Turkey and Serbia were also vulnerable points. By September 2016, the EU Commission considered it necessary to extend emergency assistance of EUR 108 million to help strengthen vigilance of its external borders while Frontex, too, was strengthening its presence at Bulgarian borders.

When under pressure from Italy, the EU somewhat belatedly focussed attention to the central Mediterranean route and the arrivals to Italy started falling, the flow, as discussed above, diverted towards Spain through the western Mediterranean route.

The bottom line is that as long as the emigration pressure remains high, human smugglers and traffickers will take advantage of the situation and the flows will take the route or routes that provide the least resistance. And the clear implications are that the EU needs to be vigilant about all the potential routes of entry and, most importantly, fight the root causes of forced and irregular emigration in the source countries themselves.

The Implementation of the Deal

In March 2016, ahead of the deal's implementation, average daily arrivals in Lesbos, Chios and Samos, main islands targeted by traffickers fell from 700 to 300 individuals.[8] New asylum registration also fell

---

[7] According to a most recent Reuters report (20 May 2018) Montenegro may build a razor-wire fence to stop migrants passing through the country on a route to Europe from Albania.

[8] There was clearly a sharp fall in arrivals on the islands in anticipation of the deal coming into force. Estimates of average daily arrivals, however, vary depending on the exact period covered. ESI, for instance, estimated the average daily arrivals fell from 1148 during 1–20 March to 333 individuals during 21–31 March 2016. "Fire in the Aegean, scenario of failure, how to succeed", ESI newsletter, 11 October 2016. See also its enlarged PDF version.

in some countries—in Germany, for example, it declined to 21,000 in March 2016 from 200,000 in November, although it was far from clear whether this was entirely due to the new agreement. The September 2016 report of the European Commission, its third in the series, on the implementation of the agreement, optimistically observed that "despite challenging circumstances, the implementation of the agreement had continued to develop and accelerate". It also claimed that by August 2016, the numbers of daily arrivals were 97% lower than in August 2015. Critics, however, were less convinced. The European Stability Initiative (ESI), for instance, thought in October 2016 that the agreement might be about to collapse because of inadequate implementation and lack of the right focus, with possible highly detrimental consequences for Greece, the Balkans, the EU as a whole and the UN Refugee Convention.[9]

(According to the ESI, the immediate effect of the agreement, lasting three months or so, worked well. Crossings through the Aegean Sea fell from 115,000 in the first two months of the year to 3300 in June and July while drowning and deaths fell from 366 to seven during the same periods. Since then, according to the ESI report, the effect seemed to be have been tapering off, with the result that while there were 15,372 new arrivals on the Aegean islands during the six months since the initiation of the agreement (April–September 2016), only 578 were returned to Turkey (further discussed in Chapter 5).)

In any case, the EU/Turkey deal did have a restraining effect on the inflows to Greece and the rest of Europe. Given the fact that for many of these migrants and refugees Greece served as a staging post on their way to western Europe, the decline in the inflows was helped also by the closure of the Balkan routes and reducing their pull effect. Even Switzerland seemed to have benefited by the slowdown in the inflows. According to the projections by the State Migration Service (SEM), the number of new asylum-seekers in 2017 was expected to fall to 24,500 from 40,000 in 2015. The agency also expected the number to rise again to 32,000 in 2017 if the EU/Turkey deal collapsed.

---

[9]"Fire in the Aegean, scenario of failure, how to succeed", *ESI newsletter*, 11 October 2016. See also its enlarged PDF version.

The Net Result of the EU/Turkey Deal and the Outlook for the Future

Admittedly, the EU/Turkey arrangement, together with the blockade of the eastern Balkan route, did send an effective message which stemmed new inflows to Europe. Daily crossings from Turkey to the Greek islands fell from 10,000 persons a day in October 2015 to 43 a day by 2 March 2017. Overall, arrivals dropped by 98%. Death tolls, too, had fallen substantially (from 1100 to 70). However, the implementation of the scheme, apart from being controversial on ethical and political grounds, suffered from two drawbacks.

First, it has been inadequate and sluggish in clearing the huge backlog of cases. In the first three months following its initiation, only 578 migrants were returned to Turkey and 522 resettled from it; even nearly a year after—as of 2 March 2017—the numbers remained at 849 and 3565, respectively. This was clearly too little, and too slow, when judged against the EU's total commitments concerning resettlement from Turkey and even more so when compared with the load of nearly three million Syrians in the country. *Second*, as discussed above, the EU's concentrated attention to the Aegean flows and its preoccupation related to the deal with Turkey may have at least partly contributed to the delay in EU action related to the rising flows through the central Mediterranean route. Thus, while the arrivals in Greece were falling fast, those in Italy were going up. Likewise, though the death tolls went down at the Aegean Sea by 2016, it turned out to be the deadliest year on record for the central Mediterranean route. There were 434 deaths in the flows from Turkey to Greece through the Aegean Sea during 2016, but the number was more than 10 times higher at 4569 on the central Mediterranean route—or on average 14 people deaths every single day. According to the EU, by the beginning of September 2017, it could resettle about 10,000 (8834) Syrians from Turkey (out of a total of 22,500 from all countries), but the number of returns to Turkey had remained considerably lower.

The main positive thing about this highly controversial deal was that at a time when the migration/refugee situation was about to reach a breaking point, it allowed the European Union a much-needed breathing space to rethink its asylum and refugee policy and hopefully reform it to strengthen the common responsibility of the member states and address the root causes. Angela Merkel was courageous and ethical enough to uphold the ideal of refugee protection, but many felt that in sponsoring the deal she made the EU pay an unduly high price—the loss of credibility in its commitment to some of the very basic values on which it is built. And, as some critics have argued, it may also tacitly encourage Turkey's march towards authoritarianism. As already mentioned above, it is also important to note that the slowdown in the flows to Greece was not just due to the EU/Turkey deal: the closure of the Balkan route and the diversion of the flow through the central Mediterranean route also played a role (admittedly, the latter was partly driven by the situation created by the EU/Turkey deal.)

In any case, with the political changes in Turkey, and the rising reservations within the EU itself about allowing visa-free movement for Turks, and the country's full EU membership, the future of the agreement looked uncertain. The decision by the German Parliament recognising mass murders by Turkey of Armenians during World War I as genocide and the tension that followed between the two countries was not likely to help matters.

However, soon afterwards—in June 2016—there were reports of a likely breakthrough in the EU–Turkey negotiations on visa-free travel as Ankara showed signs of willingness to reform its broadly designed anti-terrorist laws. This has been a major sticking point holding up progress towards the implementation of the deal. Even so, in the aftermath of the attempted coup in July 2016 and the subsequent crackdown on the media and the arrests of opposition members of Parliament by the government once more made the situation uncertain, and it worsened with the chain of events that marked the process of constitutional change widening the Presidential powers. In July 2017, following the arrest of Peter Steudtner, a German human rights activist, by the Turkish authorities, Wolfgang Schäuble, then German finance minister, openly accused Turkey of arbitrary arrests and flouting common consular standards and likened Turkey to communist East Germany. At the time the script went to press, many remained sceptical about the future of the agreement. The most likely possibility is that the agreement will not be totally abandoned, but substantially amended.

The EU's Agreement with Libya

Despite criticism by UNHCR and rights groups, the EU's decision to use Libya as a detention centre for migrants using the central Mediterranean route also raises questions somewhat similar to those applicable to the EU/Turkey agreement. At the time of writing, it was not clear whether or to what extent the detention centres were to be used for screening purposes. As further discussed in the next chapter, given the unstable, almost chaotic, political conditions in Libya and the miserable conditions in existing camps, it is difficult to see how Libya could serve as a suitable country even for purposes of temporary detention of migrants, many of whom could well be genuine asylum-seekers. It is clearly worthwhile for the EU to help improve the conditions in existing camps. However, unless and until these conditions are significantly changed and political stability and freedom fully restored, concerns expressed by the rights groups about establishment of detention centres in Libya will continue to loom large.

Elusive Root Causes

Another source of confusion that bedevilled the EU's policy-making and operations was related to a lack of a clear understanding of the "root causes" of the crisis. Some member states may have used this as an excuse to avoid the immediate responsibility of accepting any new arrivals, as some critics have suggested. However, there was also quite a bit of confused thinking about the reality of the situation. As already noted, at least initially, for some member states the root causes were the machinations of the traffickers and the remedy lay in crushing their boats and networks. They ignored, or at least paid less attention to the fact that while the traffickers brutally exploited desperate people, they did not create the desperation that led people to flee in the first instance, although they may well have worsened it.

Others went only a wee bit further. Their focus was on the neighbouring transit countries outside Europe. Under this approach, Turkey should be given generous aid (and other concessions such as visa-free travel to the EU) on condition that the country would accept and settle large numbers of migrants, with the right to work, who would otherwise cross into the EU countries. And, additionally, a helping hand should be extended by the EU to countries such as Lebanon and Jordan that had already been "bearing the brunt and burden" of carrying large numbers of asylum-seekers. This should be done both by resettling a small number of those who were in the camps in these countries and by increasing refugee-related aid to them.

Some of these measures will no doubt help in distributing the burden over a wider area. Money will be needed, but some EU member countries were reluctant to chip in. A pledging conference was being held in London at the time of writing for US$9 billion; and John Kerry, then US Secretary of State, had suggested a 30% increase in refugee aid. Both the World Bank and the IMF had also stepped in and urged the rich countries to increase their aid in support of the refugee programmes. Jim Yong Kim, the World Bank President, estimated that the cost of international response had surpassed US$20 billion. If the response was good, and the money well spent, it would be useful, including for improving the living conditions currently lodged in camps in poor countries such as Jordan and Lebanon; otherwise, many of those lodged in camps would try to move to Europe, as some in Jordan had already expressed their intention to do so. The World Bank was planning to provide US$3–4 billion in zero-interest loans to Jordan and Lebanon to cope with the influx of asylum-seekers and refugees. The IMF was negotiating a bailout programme for Tunisia and rescue programmes for Jordan and Iraq to help these countries deal with the refugee situation (also discussed in Chapter 8). However, aid money alone will hardly be enough to manage the situation.

The EU's Shallow Response to the Root Causes: Need for a Deeper Engagement with Origin Countries

The EU was not totally insensitive about the fact that while aid to the countries hosting refugees and to improve conditions in refugee camps is important, it is not adequate and that the root causes, too, must be addressed. Faced with the increasing pressure of flows from sub-Saharan Africa, the EU has thus reactivated its old policy of signing return migration agreements with source countries. Nigeria, for instance, has become a focus of attention after a sharp rise in arrivals from the country since 2014. Italy saw a 37% increase in the number of arrivals of Nigerians in 2016 compared to the same period in 2015. However, as past experience with return migration agreements shows, the approach is inadequate and faulty. Many African migrants destroy their identification documents during their journeys, making it difficult to trace the origin country and enforce the agreement (see also Chapter 7, pp. 118/120). The EU is also conscious of the fact that if economic and employment growth fails to keep pace with the demographic expansion in Nigeria and almost across West Africa, pressures for irregular and disorderly migration in the near-term will be huge. It also has come to realise that if fences do not stop the flows, shallow readmission agreements do not solve the problem, either. Take-back agreements are likely to work when there is a concurrent increase in the origin country's economic, especially labour market, capacity to absorb new people, with a promising outlook of the future.

However, until November 2016, in most of the debate on the root causes of migration crisis little serious attention was given to the structural and endemic issues (leaving aside the issue of geopolitical and sectarian conflicts) which helped generate these huge disorderly, and mostly forced, movements. True, there were fleeting references to the push factors in the countries of origin; at one point, Angela Merkel, the German Chancellor, stated, "The money we inject in fighting the root causes of the flight would ensure that fewer people will be forced to leave country". There was also a proposal to spend one billion Euros to improve conditions in the origin countries, but, not surprisingly, it took the EU some time to flesh out a specific plan for the purpose, as discussed below.

At an initial stage, there was some discussion in the EU on a four-page document, *Migration Compact*, submitted by the Italian Prime Minister, Matteo Renzi, to the EU, which contains two interesting proposals in this connection.[10] First, it pleads for a much deeper and more systematic engagement of the EU with the origin and transit countries as a shared policy for development, including job creation, stability and migration. Second, it proposes issuance of "EU-Africa bonds" and "Common EU Migration bonds" to supplement the EU's funds that would be needed to implement the policy.

There are two attractive features of this latter proposal. It blunts the reluctance of individual member states to allocate additional resources from their national budgets in response to the migration crisis and effectively pools their individual commitments on migration to the Community level. True, in the context of the recent financial crisis in the Eurozone some member states, led by Germany, have strongly opposed the idea of Eurobonds involving mutualised commitment and liability, implicit in EU-bonds. However, the proposed migration bonds could have been expected to have less resistance as a special case and being limited to relatively small amounts of debt. Given that Angela Merkel was in the forefront of the call for solidarity among member states to deal with the migration crisis, and her great need to maintain tattered unity in the migration crisis, it had seemed that this time she would be supportive of the proposal, despite some eventual resistance at home. It had also been well received in Brussels, including by Donald Tusk, the EU Council President, who welcomed the idea of deeper engagement with the origin countries. In the event, however, the proposal was rejected by Ms. Merkel with unusual force and speed, presumably because of anticipated strong resistance and her waning popularity at home.

---

[10]To an extent, it is a follow-up to the Italian government's paper, "A shared policy strategy for growth, jobs and stability", submitted in February 2016. (See also Solon Ardittis, "Matteo Renzi's "Migration Compact" proposal: a step closer to a viable and comprehensive solution to the EU migrant crisis?" *New Europe*, 4 April 2016.)

However, given the circumstances, Ms. Merkel's negative reaction was not totally surprising for two important reasons. *First*, there was a rising wave of anti-immigrant feeling in Germany. In a survey by INSA, a pollster, 61% of respondents were less happy about accepting refugees after the sexual assaults and raids on New Year's (2016) Eve; 63% thought there were already too many asylum-seekers in Germany; and only 29% still agreed with her that the country could handle it. This was also reflected in the big gains of the anti-immigrant party Alternative for Germany (AfD) in recent regional elections. Significantly, as part of its efforts to assuage the public concern the coalition government agreed to include in the federal budget increases in social welfare spending for national Germans. Second, there was always a potential danger that the scheme, even if initially confined to refugee-related expenditure, could be a slippery slope towards pressure for issuance of Eurobonds in general. Any such co-mingling of Eurozone debt could weaken any incentives for southern countries to carry out much-needed structural reform, leaving Germany to shoulder the debt burden.

The Valletta Action Plan: A Small and Hesitant Step in the Right Direction

The EU's Valletta Action Plan was a small step in the right direction. It meets some of the conditions needed to be met for developing truly joint efforts and common commitment to address the root causes of forced and disorderly migration. Even so, the plan was still tilted more towards the concerns and objectives of the EU as destination countries than the needs and aspirations of origin countries. The emphasis still seemed to be on immigration control and readmission rather than on orderly migration based on regulated openness and genuinely reflecting reciprocity of interests. As an Italian official put it, "only through the control of migration can we imagine a partnership between Europe and Africa". The way in which such a plan can be more closely geared to addressing the root causes of irregular and disorderly migration is discussed in some detail in the next chapter (Chapter 5).

5

The Way Forward

Addressing the Mixed Migration Conundrum

As discussed in the previous chapter, the mixed migration conundrum has added to the EU's difficulty in managing the inflows. A twofold approach needs to be followed to respond to this complex situation. First, the scope of the 1951 UN Convention should be broadened and attuned more closely to contemporary realities (some of them are reflected in the OAU Convention and Cartagena declaration on refugees), though without overburdening it. The present restrictive political climate may not be very conducive to launch it now, but it should nonetheless remain a medium/long-term objective. Meanwhile, as an immediate and complementary measure, efforts should be aimed at strengthening, harmonising and codifying the wide variety of scattered arrangements that already exist in different countries for humanitarian as well as other forms of temporary protection for forced migrants. The EU's mixed migration problem has also demonstrated the perils of a fragmented approach in managing migration, given that the malfunctioning of one channel of entry tends to have adverse repercussions on some other channel or channels as well. While each specific channel of entry has its distinctive characteristics and needs to be managed accordingly, they are thus also interconnected. This underlines the need for the EU to adhere to a comprehensive approach and a strategy of coordinated action to better manage the Community's migration system as a whole and its components.

A New Start for Neighbourhood Cooperation and Joint Commitment or a Revisit to the Past?

It is intriguing to note that in an otherwise interesting recent article, *The Economist* called the new Valetta action programme one of "more aid to African and Middle Eastern countries that clamp down on migrants".[1] This is a typically wrong description of the way in which the EU can develop a true engagement with the origin countries. The objective should not be seen as "clamping down" on all types of migration but stop, or at least reduce, the pressure for disruptive and irregular migration while providing opportunities for safe and orderly migration to meet the labour market and demographic needs of the European countries. The two are interrelated. As I have often emphasised elsewhere,[2] when there is high emigration pressure in origin countries and unmet labour demand in the destination countries, and especially when the two coexist, undue restrictions at either end do not stop migration but only drive it to irregular channels.

As the EU's past experience shows, it is not enough to offer a few sweeteners or dole out some funds to win the origin countries' shallow acquiescence in a partnership plan. Sadly, however, the new approach does not give the impression of the EU moving sufficiently away from its old practice. As Denis Tull at the German Institute for Security Affairs in Berlin observed, "We should not pretend there is a common interest here. What is being called 'cooperation' by the EU is seen very differently in Africa". In fact, many in Africa perceive the new plan as

---

[1] "Misplaced charity", *The Economist*, 11–17 June 2016.
[2] See, for example, Bimal Ghosh, *Huddled Masses and Uncertain Shores: Insights into Irregular Migration*, 1998, pp. 34/35.

a repetition of the same kind of bargaining deal for cracking down on migrant smuggling as the Berlusconi government made with Muammar Gaddafi of Libya in 2008.

Rights groups were highly critical of the new arrangement on the grounds that it made Libya seem safe and also for the denial of humanitarian values, the deplorable conditions in camps and continuing dangers faced by its inmates. "Libya is not a safe place and blocking people in the country or returning them to Libya makes a mockery of the EU's so-called fundamental values of human dignity and rule of law", said the *Médecins Sans Frontières*. According to Amnesty International, the agreement would cause "horrendous suffering". The *BBC* quotes a migrant saying the following about conditions in Libya "It was a nightmare. If many people knew what was going on there, they would not dare to come. There is killing every day. I saw a man kill an innocent boy for no reason".[3]

Old habits die hard, and the EU runs the risk of becoming a prisoner of its past attitudes and ways of doing things. It must not fall into that trap. It should be keenly alive to the fact that old-fashioned development aid or doling out some money as specific grants to these countries (often run by autocratic governments) on condition that they would contain the outflows and accept return migration as in the past will not do. Money is no doubt needed to implement a sound policy reflecting a genuine commitment by both origin and destination countries to fight the root causes of forced and disorderly migration. But money alone cannot buy either reform or stability in the origin countries.

Nor will the traditional, shallow readmission or association agreements serve the purpose. An essential condition of success of the EU's new plan lies in ensuring that the African countries are genuinely convinced of their stake in the partnership and be truly committed to it. For this to happen, the EU needs to have a much deeper engagement with the origin countries to create conditions for orderly migration, help reduce the pressure for irregular migration and help counteract the generation of new refugee flows, on the basis of an interstate

---

[3] *BBC News*, "Migrant Crisis; Italy a haven from killings and kidnappings", 4 September 2016.

alliance built on common interests (as discussed in Chapter 12). The conditionality attaching to the partnership should be seen as reciprocal imperatives for the parties concerned to make the initiative a success and not a one-sided obligation (in return for money) for the origin countries alone.

The awareness and recognition of a common stake and the spirit of cooperation underlying the new initiative should make it distinct from the "stick and carrot" approach that characterised the failed initiatives of the past. Unless the EU learns from its past experience, it is likely to make the same mistakes. With a shared strategy, and mutual confidence-building, stability and orderliness in movement can be expected to take hold, though this will take time to produce lasting results. There is hardly a shortcut to a real and lasting solution or a recipe for a quick fix.

And in keeping with the conditions of a genuine partnership its template should be wide enough to include, in addition to aid and investment in projects, planned and calibrated openness in trade and labour migration as well as assistance in institutional development and related capacity-building in origin countries. These should all be interrelated elements of a coherent policy. It is also important to note that while these activities would of necessity be multi-sectoral and multipronged, the focus of the initiative remains in ensuring that future migratory movements become safer as well as more orderly and predictable, as against those that are irregular, disorderly or forced and driven by despair. It should not be seen or conceived as a vehicle for introducing wholesale economic and social reform in origin countries or exporting to them all the core ethical values of the EU must be avoided. Any such over-ambitious targets will not help, but only divert focussed attention away from the new initiative.

There is also room for improving the credibility of some of the financial projections made under the EU's plan. As mentioned, the EU has already promised to increase by EUR 500 million the resources of its EUR 1.9 billion Africa Trust Fund, in addition to a guarantee of EUR 3.4 billion for private investment. However, as of October 2016, member states were reported to have added just over EUR 82 million to the Fund, and even by August 2017, the contribution amounted to no more than EUR 200 million. Doubts have also been expressed about the rosy projections of future private investments in migrant-producing African countries.

As part of its new initiative, the EU decided to host an investment forum in Lagos, Nigeria's financial capital, in November 2016. However, there was considerable scepticism about the prospects of much private capital flowing to these countries at least until all guarantees were in place, and a degree of stability had returned. At the time of writing, the final and concrete outcome of the consultation was not known.

Finally, a plan like this, when launched with a lot of fanfare, runs the potential risk of being over-ambitious, which, as already discussed, must be avoided, if it is to serve the specific purpose of better management of migration. While it must fit into a country's overall development and its underlying strategy, the plan must at the same time be targeted at specific economic sectors, demographic groups and geographic areas that are sensitive to alleviating the pressure of migration through irregular and unsafe channels driven by poverty and despair. Any over-ambitious targets will not help, but only divert focussed attention away from the new initiative.

The Template of New Partnership Should Be Different from That of the EU/Turkey Agreement

It will be wrong to perceive the new partnership agreements with African countries as being analogous to the recent EU/Turkey one, as some analysts have done. Although both seemingly share, and are motivated by, a common objective of reducing the excessive pressure of migratory inflows to EU and the burden it entails, there are also significant differences not only in their methods of approach and modalities of action but also in their objectives and ethical implications.

As discussed, the EU/Turkey agreement has been criticised as an attempt at outsourcing the EU's migration problem that already exists. By contrast, the new partnership should be more forward-looking and aim at tackling the root causes of the problem of irregular and disorderly movements in the origin countries themselves with the active support of the EU and its countries. Also, unlike the EU/Turkey accord, the partnership agreements should be proactive in providing opportunities for new entries that meet the needs and interests of both the EU and the origin countries in Africa. The twofold approach, based on a policy of regulated openness, should make future movements safe, orderly and more predictable. These are far beyond the reach of the template underlying EU/Turkey agreement.

The ethical and political dimensions of the new partnerships also sharply differ from those of the recent EU/Turkey agreement. The ethical and political reservations about the latter stem from two main standpoints. First, under the *non-refoulement* principle enshrined in the 1951 UN Convention on the status of refugees, it would be ethically wrong for the EU countries (as signatories of the 1951 UN Convention) to send back migrants to a country until it is considered to be a fully fledged "safe country" in terms of the protection of human and refugee rights. The second set of reservations is both political and ethical. Subject to a number of conditions, the EU/Turkey agreement provides for visa-free access for over 80 million Turks to the EU territory. Furthermore, even if the outcome is uncertain, Turkey continues to be engaged in the process of accessing EU membership. On both political and ethical grounds, many will continue to be critical of these possibilities unless and until there are significant internal changes in Turkey. Neither of these two reservations applies, at least at this stage or in the same degree, in the proposed new partnership arrangements with the selected African countries, although liberalisation of trade and visa regulations is clearly not excluded.

Thus, as noted, it was not surprising that the approach adopted in Malta virtually seeking to outsource to Libya the problem of inflows through the central Mediterranean route to Europe has come under sharp criticism from the rights groups, including the UNHCR and Amnesty International. They expressed concern that running camps where migrants were detained would expose them to further abuse, and given the political instability in the country, it was hardly likely that even with financial and technical assistance, the UN-backed government which has limited control over the country would be in a position to improve the dismal conditions and abuse to which the migrants were currently exposed.

Others have been critical of the fact that the declaration aims at controlling migration but says nothing about the protection of the rights of asylum-seekers and their resettlement. An affiliate of the European Council on Refugees and Exiles (ECRE) fumed to state that the approach in effect violates the principle of *non-refoulement* as it requires third countries to forcibly block the passage of people who are in clear need of international protection. The EU seems to have been largely inspired by the immediate (and largely perceived) success of the EU/Turkey agreement. But in reality, as discussed above, the EU/Turkey deal was hardly an ideal template to forge EU's partnership with origin, transit and destination countries to better manage the migratory flows. The contextual political and security conditions in Libya made the EU's deal with that country even worse and more worrisome.

As Sigmar Gabriel, German foreign minister and vice chancellor, put it, the existing conditions on the ground already show "horrible and catastrophic conditions". "The idea to set up camps… would be in total disregard of circumstances for the people".[4] Pope Francis was even more critical: the holding centres had become "concentration camps", he said in exasperation. As already noted, Oxfam Italia, too, has been highly critical of the Italian government's deal with Libya and has urged a change in the EU policy, including assistance in training Libya's coastguard. The Libyan government was under investigation by the International Criminal Court because of attacks by its coastguards on migrant boats and humanitarian vessels. For the rights' groups, the arrangement by Rome and Brussels with the Libyan government was similar to Italy's "dirty deal" with Muammar Gaddafi's pledge to stem the flows of migrants to Italy in exchange for investment. Italy, which has contributed aid to Libya on a bilateral basis as well as via the UNHCR, IOM and NGOs, has, however, denied the allegations that it has any deals with militias on a bilateral basis or traffickers but was engaged in a dialogue with the Libyan government and cities for giving local population economic alternatives and has also rejected criticism that it was ignoring migrants' human rights.

In August 2017, on the eve of the country's general election Angela Merkel, too, sought to defend the partnership arrangements with Libya and sub-Saharan African countries sending refugees and irregular migrants. The underlying objective, she said, was to keep more refugees

---

[4]*Reuters*, 2 May 2017.

in Libya and other origin countries under the protection of UN organisations so that genuine asylum cases could be handled closer to their home countries and to give migrants opportunities to enter Europe.[5]

The idea of detaining migrants, including potential asylum-seekers, has, however, remained highly controversial. The doubtful legality of the arrangement is compounded by the terrible conditions in Libyan detention camps. In Germany, Katja Kipping, leader of the Left Party, disparaged the arrangement by saying that Germany and Libya had formed a "big coalition against human rights". The comments made by the President of Médecins Sans Frontières, Dr. Joanne Liu, were equally stern. The centres she had visited in Tripoli in September 2017 were filthy and chaotic, seething with reports of rapes, beatings and other abuses, she said. It is "the most extreme incarnation of human cruelty I've ever seen. It's manufacturing suffering at industrial levels", she added. According to analysts, it is the political chaos and institutional disarray in Libya which largely explained the sudden sharp decline in the flow of migrants to Italy in 2017 through the central Mediterranean route. The UN-backed government led by Faez al-Sarj has very little authority and relies on powerful private militias. "The line is very blurred between militias and the interior ministry", said Mattia Toaldo at the European Council on Foreign Relations. The situation explains the criticisms that armed groups had been contracted to stop migration and run detention centres.

In short, it is quite understandable that overwhelmed by the experience of 2015/2016, the EU would be anxious to explore ways of stemming the migratory inflows and avoid the same experience as it did. And the EU's efforts to help Libya in improving its capacity to better manage migration and control its borders are to be welcomed. However, it can hardly find a quick solution to the problem by outsourcing it via international organisations. Given the highly chaotic political, including law and order situation in Libya and the doubtful integrity of its police force, it is also unrealistic to think that international organisations can give "protection" to hapless migrants as Ms. Merkel claimed recently.

---

[5] *Financial Times*, "Libya migrants' sufferings revive memories of 'dirty deal' anger", 9/10 September 2017.

In such a situation, the involved international organisations, too, run the risk of allowing themselves to be scapegoats for failure to give adequate protection to the detained migrants.

EU Initiative in Niger and the Potential Pitfalls

In line with its arrangement for detention of refugees and migrants in Libya, the EU is also giving special attention to other transit countries, notably Niger, and is helping them control their borders and tame the inflows into Europe. A vast majority of West African migrants and potential refugees transit through Niger to reach Libya and then to Europe: in 2016 alone the number exceeded 300,000. This is a long, hard and perilous journey through inhospitable desert areas that often takes a heavy toll of human lives. It would therefore seem logical for the EU to focus attention on Niger as part of its Partnership Framework for Africa to tame the inflows to Europe. In 2016, Niger received EUR 140 million from the EU Trust Fund for Africa aimed at protecting borders and controlling migration and EUR 470 million for development, economic reform and good governance. In 2017, Italy, too, signed a bilateral agreement with Niger providing EUR 50 million with the aim of strengthening the country's border controls and drive down migrant entries.

Until recently, Niger had been a relatively stable country; it managed well the Tuareg rebels in the north who had created havoc in neighbouring Mali, just as it handled deftly post-Gaddafi turbulences in the region. And its response to the EU's initiative has been positive, although it has stated that it needed one billion Euros to deal with migration alone. There are also some fledgling signs of a decline in the flows from Niger to Libya. For these and other reasons, the EU has been quick to claim its initiative a success.

Analysts, however, are not fully convinced for several reasons.[6] First, there are indications that the locations that have been under formal

---

[6]"European anti-migration agenda could challenge stability in Niger", Hans Lucht, DIIS Policy Brief, 19 June 2017.

monitoring are now being avoided by traffickers in view of increased vigilance by police, and the military and the flows are now diverted to more dangerous, shadow routes which are difficult to monitor and of which the government may have remained in the dark. Second, although the government in Niamey has embraced the EU intervention, it has created uneasiness in the historically volatile and often rebellious Agadez region in the north, the economy of which relies significantly on incomes from human smuggling and trafficking. Under the EU initiative, border control has been tightened and various anti-migration measures introduced to tame cross-border movements, which have also affected the related income flows. However, alternative jobs and other economic opportunities that had been promised were yet to be seen.

According to some analysts, this has been feeding popular resentment against the EU initiative in Niger, with the risk that it would be seen more as externalising the EU's own border control than one dedicated to sustainable development of the country, which does not shun regular and safe migration that serves the interests of both Niger and EU countries. Unless this matter is carefully handled, the resentment among the youth in the Agadez could explode, threatening the stability and territorial integrity of Niger. The potential threat is compounded by the fact that Niger is also under pressure from the Boko Haram insurgency in the Diffa region and the Al-Qaeda-linked terrorist attacks on the Malian border. Concerns also exist about the arbitrary and ruthless manner in which Niger's security forces responded to the Boko Haram attacks. This has seriously alienated the civilian population in the region, and if such actions are replicated in Agadez, it could reignite large-scale rebellion and seriously threaten the country's stability. Recent attacks (October 2017) reported to be planned and executed by jihadist militants that led to the death of Nigerian and four US soldiers point to another potential source of instability in Niger.

A crucial point that emerges from the preceding discussions is that to be credible the partnership agreements must not be planned or perceived as an anti-immigrant intervention by the EU in the origin countries, but as a cooperative effort to avoid the evils and human sufferings associated with forced and irregular migration and to promote sustainable development and good governance in origin countries' objectives, which do not exclude, but embraces, orderly, safe and regular migration that meets the common interests of both the origin and EU countries.

Hiatus Between Regional Solidarity and National Sovereignty: Can These Be Harmonised?

Painful Decision-Making: The EU's Wavering Stance, Vacillating Decisions

The EU's agonies in coming up with a robust and unified response to the crisis as well as many of the operational problems and strategic mistakes I have just mentioned were the results of the EU member's knee-jerk reactions to the crisis and the absence of a robust and unified migration and refugee policy of a self-confident European Union. The EU Commission has tried its best to come up with some relatively bold and proactive proposals but has been constrained in moving forward and making them effective because of the divisions among the member states to accept and put them into effect.

Institutional inadequacy, including widely diffused power structure and decision-making process, constrained the EU to craft a timely and robust policy and operational response to the situation. Between May and December in 2015, the EU held more than a dozen meetings, including several at the summit level, to address Europe's unprecedented refugee/migration crisis. This was preceded by rounds of informal consultations within the EU. As narrated above, despite the urgency of the situation, the EU had to engage itself in long, arduous and convoluted deliberations on the possible intakes of new arrivals. It turned into a jigsaw puzzle due to division among the member states and their wavering decisions on the targeted numbers of asylum-seekers to be taken by the EU—which shifted from 5000 to 60,000 and then finally to 160,000—as well as on their distribution among the member states and on whether this should be voluntary or mandatory. In effect, as already noted in Chapter 4, by the end of September 2016, it could help settle only a small number (less than 600) migrants under the EU/Turkey agreement, and even by 2 March 2017, the number was around 3565.

As for relocation, despite the best efforts of the EU Commission, the process, launched in September 2015, was no more promising. Relocations from Italy and Greece totalled around 2280 as of June 2016 and less than 14,000 (13,456) as of 2 March 2017, according to the EU sources. Some states have continued to question the EU's right to impose a compulsory quota system for intakes of refugees. In a show of national sovereignty, Hungary had called a referendum on the issue (the negative outcome was invalid due to a low participation of less than 50%).

The same schism between member states' collective commitment and their stubborn adherence to sovereign prerogative has shaped the EU's attitude to external border protection and the role of Frontex in ensuring it. Despite the clear need for reinforcing the common external borders, they decided to limit the authority of the EU border agency, Frontex, allowing it only to coordinate the protection of external borders, rather than enforce it on its own. As noted, in December 2015, Brussels at last was planning to create a standing European border force to take direct control of the EU's external borders even in the face of opposition by a member state. It was a bold move and the single most important attempt at pooling national sovereignty since the creation of the single currency. The EU Commission was struggling to put the proposal in action but was facing difficulties due to the resistance from some members. As discussed above, when a decision was finally taken, once more member states' adherence to national sovereignty interceded and the original proposal had to be watered down.[7]

The difficulties in managing new flows have also highlighted many of such structural weaknesses of the EU. They have created doubts about open borders and free internal movement, one of the proudest achievements and hitherto a most coveted tenet of the European Union. Border controls have been re-imposed by a number of EU member states, and several others have threatened to do so. Under the current rules, a member state is allowed to apply it, but only for six months and under special circumstances and with the authorisation of the EU Commission only up to two years. However, several member states had announced or

---

[7] "Brussels plans new force to police external borders", *Financial Times*, 11 December 2015.

threatened that they would like to reimpose them on a permanent basis unless the inflows are better managed. The situation has exposed serious cracks in the member states' commitment to shared responsibility in managing migration at the Union's common external borders. There have been repeated and public manifestations of tensions between the member states in the south and those in the north and the west, as well as between states in the west and those in the east and at times even within each group. This has coincided with, and also fuelled by, a growing unhappiness with the way in which the EU has been handling the refugee crisis (Fig. 5.1).

Acrimonious arguments have on occasions been followed by legal actions or threats of them challenging the decisions already taken by the majority. Poland, Hungary, the Czech Republic and Slovakia adamantly refused to participate in EUR 240 million relocation schemes which had been designed to relieve the pressure on countries like Greece and Italy. Hungary had refused to pledge places for the refugees; Poland

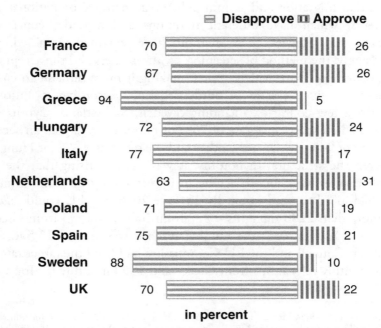

Fig. 5.1 Growing unhappiness with the EU's handling of refugee flows (*Source* Spring 2016 Global Attitudes Survey. Pew Research Center)

had pledged places, but refused to accept relocation; and the Czech Republic stopped complying in 2016. In July 2017, after the failure of its repeated attempts at persuading the three countries to accept the majority decision, the EU Commission went forward to enforce it by preparing for legal action against the hold-out countries, while keeping the door still open for the three countries to change their positions.[8]

In the case of Poland, tension with the EU was running particularly high because of the added, though unrelated, issue of the Polish government's proposed law to curb the independence of its judiciary. Hungary and Slovakia had asked the European Court of Justice to overturn the EU's mandatory decision of 2015 to distribute the burden of relocation among its member states, but as the Court rejected the appeal, Hungary attacked the Court decision saying it was "politically motivated" and "openly legitimatised the power of the EU above the member states". Brussels, for its part, said it was ready to escalate a separate legal procedure to force dissenting countries to comply with the EU decision. Given that migration and asylum policies are handled by national governments, which have different traditions and attitudes concerning migrants and refugees, these divisions have remained ingrained. Not surprisingly, the method of screening asylum-seekers and the acceptance rates of refugees have widely varied, making it more difficult to ensure a fair and unified system of burden sharing. According to Eurostat, in 2014 a few countries, including Sweden, Switzerland, Cyprus and Malta, had an acceptance rate of 70% or more. Bulgaria had an acceptance rate of 94%, while at the other end the rate was 9.4% for Hungary.

Given the structural dichotomy, it was not surprising that the EU member states were found lagging in implementing the commitments they had jointly agreed upon. By 15 June 2016, the EU could *relocate* not more than 2280 migrants—777 from Italy and 1503 from Greece. Even by 2 March 2017, the number reached was around 13,546. The European Council and the EU Commission had fixed the target rates of 3000 monthly relocations from Greece and 1500 monthly for Italy. But

---

[8]By that date only 24,647 refugees had been relocated from Italy and Greece, a fraction of the 98,255 legally envisaged under the EU Council decisions (and 47,905 formally pledged), leaving a gap of some 73,608.

the actual relocation rates proved to be much lower. Only two member states—Malta and Finland—were on track to meet their obligations for both Italy and Greece. At least three states—Austria, Hungary and Poland—were still refusing to participate in the scheme at all and many others (e.g. Bulgaria, Croatia, Czech Republic and Slovakia) were doing so on a very limited scale. The EU Commission projected that at the current pace of relocation only 57% of the persons eligible under the EU Council decision would be relocated from Greece and 44% of those eligible in Italy. In order to meet the September 2017 targets set by the EU Council for relocating all eligible applicants, the current rates of relocation of 1000 per month needed to be raised to 3000 a month for Greece and from 750 a month to 1500 a month for Italy.

By early September 2017, as a result of the EU Commission's continuous persuasion, the situation showed some improvement, with the total of 27,695 persons (19,244 from Greece and 8451 from Italy) relocated. However, with around 2800 persons still to be relocated from Greece and new applicants arriving every day from Italy, more needed to be done. Malta and Latvia fulfilled their allocations for Greece, and several others (Finland, Lithuania, Luxembourg, Sweden) were close to doing so. Malta and Finland were about to do so for Italy. Austria just started relocating from Italy. While all these countries were laggards, Czech Republic, Hungary and Poland continued to defy the collective commitment.

Until the spirit of solidarity, based on a sharpened recognition of common interest, is reinforced across the member states, a fair sharing of the burden will always remain an onerous and incomplete process. Some EU leaders have expressed concern that the Schengen agreement that ensures free movement across most of EU states may have to be written off; some others have suggested that Schengen should be reformed. And to save the Schengen system, some would like even to throw Greece out of the system for failing to properly register the asylum-seekers on arrival.

The reality is that it will be increasingly difficult for the EU to maintain the Schengen agreement on free internal movement alongside the Dublin Convention assigning responsibility for the asylum-seekers to the state first receiving them unless there is more solidarity on burden-sharing among all member states which benefit from open borders for movement of people. The agreement to relocate asylum-seekers from Greece and Italy is a step in the right direction but it should not be just a one-shot operation or a temporary derogation of the Dublin Convention. It will make sense to make the arrangement a permanent one under which when a member state's acceptance of asylum-seekers reaches a certain threshold, the surplus would be relocated in the other member states in the same manner as being planned under the new agreement. The determination of the threshold should also be based on a set of agreed criteria.

Unless this is done, countries facing massive inflows of asylum-seekers or unwanted migrants will always be tempted or indeed constrained to shirk the full responsibility for them by defaulting to register them properly. Throwing Greece out of the system, as some have suggested, will not help.

In relocating the asylum-seekers, full consideration should be given to their preference of the country of settlement on the basis of language, existence of ethnic network and cultural affinity and other factors that would facilitate their integration in the host society. However, once an asylum-seeker is relocated and becomes entitled to social benefits in a country, the individual will lose those benefits by moving to another country on his/her own. While safeguarding the person's freedom of movement, this will prevent welfare shopping and safeguard the integrity of the burden-sharing system. On attaining the status of a refugee, the person, of course, must enjoy full freedom of movement within and outside the country.

In May 2016, the European Commission had finally put forward a plan to enforce the principle of burden (or responsibility) sharing in order to save the Schengen system of passport-free travel within the Schengen area and lighten the strain of the front lines when they are overwhelmed by sudden influx of masses of people. It had considered a centralised plan that would require EU countries to sign up to an automatic system obliging them to take in a share of all those arriving on EU soil, virtually tearing up the responsibilities of the first country of arrival under the Dublin Convention. Under the plan EU countries that refuse to take asylum-seekers under an automatic quota system will face a charge of EUR 259,000 per asylum-seeker. The Commission proposal builds on the EU's emergency scheme to relocate 160,000 refugees and becomes applicable when a country receives more than 150% of its fair share of asylum-seekers—a threshold fixed on the basis of population and national income. This was a bold and positive measure to strengthen the principle of intra-EU solidarity. The proposed measure, however, looked like a threat of sanctions against a defaulting member state, and the question remained as to whether it would not have been wiser to allow an element of flexibility by inserting a temporary escape clause for a member state under a set of well-defined exceptional circumstances.

In the event, the proposal was watered down. It finally decided in favour of maintaining the present arrangement but with an emergency clause that would provide relief to a country faced with a sudden influx of refugees. It was also decided to make the new European Border and Coast Guard Agency operational. However, even at the end of February 2017—five months after it was officially launched—joint investment and collective engagement in ensuring the full operational capability of the Agency were still needed—there were shortfalls in terms of both personnel and equipment, especially for the Rapid Reaction Pool—to enable the Agency to provide timely support to member states at external borders and help them avoid future crises.

The EU needs to beef up its assistance to its member states suddenly facing heavy influx of potential asylum-seekers in order to ensure speedy and fair processing of the claims and avoid unduly long detention of those without genuine claims and speed up their return. This would enhance the credibility of the EU asylum system, and by doing so, this may be expected to discourage those without genuine claims from trying entry through the asylum channel leading to its clogging and would also make the take-back programme work better.

Human Displacements and Strategic Planning for Military Intervention

Will the proposed approach be sufficient to deal with the refugee flows from the conflict-ridden countries? Not really. Those responsible for migration policies in the EU or elsewhere can do little about the conflicts, chaos and widespread insecurity in the Middle East and the African continent that are among the main causes of the refugee or refugee-like flows, although the EU's foreign policy can certainly play a proactive role in dealing with the underlying issues, and the EU's Valetta declaration rightly makes a reference to this.

Clearly, however, there is one, so far neglected but important, area where those responsible for migration policies in the EU and elsewhere can make a significant contribution. Military operations, be it in the form of civil war or internationally approved military interventions, almost invariably cause human displacements, internal or external or both and, as we all know, their negative consequences could be destabilising and heartbreaking.

However, experience shows that these migratory consequences are hardly taken into account as part of strategic planning in advance even in the case of a legitimate and widely discussed military operation. Governments are more used to dealing with them on a post facto basis. As they then improvise to cope with human displacements under great urgency and pressure during or after the military operation, action becomes uncoordinated, haphazard, sometimes even chaotic, and people suffer. This has happened time and again—as in the aftermath of the interventions in Bosnia in 1992, Iraq in 1991 and 2003, Libya in 2011 and now in Syria and Yemen. This is an area where those concerned with migration policy and management can play a useful role by stepping up efforts to ensure that in the strategic planning of any legitimate military operation the likely effects on internal and external migration are fully taken into account, and anticipatory measures thought through.

The Outlook: The Birth Pangs of a New Policy or the Agonies Over a Stillborn One?

In sum, the history of the European Union is closely intertwined with a history of tension between regional solidarity and national sovereignty, between common commitment and unilateral action. As in other policy areas, notably that of banking and finance, the EU's performance related to asylum-seeking and migration has been affected, as already

5 The Way Forward

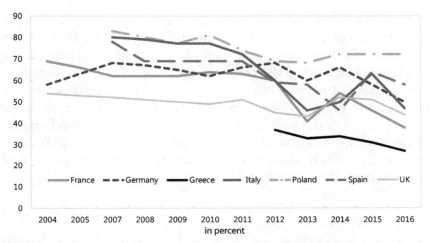

Fig. 5.2 Declining positive views of the EU (*Source* Spring 2016 Global Attitudes Survey. Pew Research Center)

noted, by this tension and shaped by a series of fragile compromises resulting in small and hesitant steps rather than bold action for a qualitative change or a sustainable solution, including a deeper engagement with the origin countries. It is unlikely, however, that the EU can continue to move ahead postponing bold action and just by muddling through the problems or constantly float in a state of transition. Nor can it stand at a crossroads for ever. As already noted, according to a recent survey by Pew Research Center, majorities in every 10 countries covered overwhelmingly believe that the European Union had been doing a poor job of handling the refugee crisis, including 94% of Greeks and 88% of Swedes.[9]

The refugee crisis has contributed to a weakening of the confidence in the future of the EU itself (Fig. 5.2) although there are again some fledgling signs of a positive change. The current migration/refugee crisis is symbolic of the kind of challenge it will face in future and find increasingly difficult to avoid or postpone by taking half-hearted measures.

---

[9]Pew Research Center, "European opinions of the refugee crisis in 5 charts", 16 September 2016. http:/www.pewglobal.org/2016/06/07euroskepticism-beyond-brexit.

The crisis should serve as a wake-up call and spur the EU member states to unified action, worthy of the challenge it faces. It is not too early that the President of the European Commission, Jean-Claude Juncker and, following the recent elections in France and Germany, both Emmanuel Macron and Angela Merkel (though weakened by her personal and her party's declining popularity) have been giving some close attention to the ways in which this can be achieved. The London-based journal, *The Economist*, has optimistically called the EU's fumbling, painful efforts to cope with the crisis as the birth pangs of a new policy. It needs not be a stillborn one.

6

Asylum-Seeking and Externalisation of the Screening Process: Why so Controversial?
The EU's Stance and the Global Experience

Externalisation of processing asylum applications is not a new policy option used by states to address asylum-seeking and refugee issues. Different destination countries have taken recourse to it in different periods of time to deal with the specific migratory flows. Depending on the surrounding circumstances, they have used either or both forms of externalisation: processing the claims of entry inside the migrant's country of origin itself or at a conveniently located offshore centre. And offshore processing has sometimes entailed interdiction, which may involve removal of the potential asylum-seekers after they have reached the destination country or their interception on their way to it. A number of countries had used either or both of them in the past and some have kept the practice of external processing open while some others have been thinking of opting for it.

Offshore Processing: The EU's Vacillating Stance

In the EU, the discussion on externalisation has been floating around for quite some time. In the late 1990s, as the member states were focussing on restrictive immigration policies, externalisation of asylum procedure received some special attention. In 2003 in its "Vision Paper", the UK strongly advocated that asylum-seekers in the European Union should be taken to the transit and processing centres outside of the EU. More recently, with the rising waves of migrant inflows in 2014, there was a revival of interest in the issue. The discussion focussed on the possible establishment of offshore processing centres, most likely in North African countries, which were being used as transit posts by many migrants from Africa and elsewhere. In 2014, during their respective EU presidencies, both Greece and Italy expressed themselves in favour of locating such centres in North Africa, and the then Italian Prime Minister Matteo Renzi proposed their establishment under the auspices of the United Nations in Libya. The idea seemed to have found a favourable reaction in the EU's Justice and Home Affairs Council. Several other options for external processing were also floating around, including conducting feasibility studies on the launch of an external processing scheme.

However, there was no effective follow-up at the time. The main reason for the flagging interest was the absence of an agreed system of burden or responsibility sharing among the EU member states, which were more used to bilateral partnership to stop the inflows of irregular migrants. As the former EU commissioner for home affairs Cecilia Malström observed, in order to make the external processing work, the EU needed to have a prior agreement on how the accepted refugees were to be distributed among them. As also discussed in Chapters 3 and 5, the absence of a clear system of burden sharing and the member states firm commitment to it were found to bedevil all EU's efforts to establish a Common European Asylum Policy. More recently, as already mentioned, the EU has discussed the possibility of supporting the settlement of some of the asylum-seekers temporarily sheltered in countries outside the EU countries. However, the idea of external processing as such, though not dead, had been lying somewhat dormant, with more attention given to the distribution and relocation of asylum-seekers inside the EU. Even so, as the EU faced serious difficulties in moving ahead with its scheme of relocating migrants within its territory, there seems to have been a revival of interest in external processing as a means of keeping the migrants and potential asylum-seekers away from its shores.

6 Asylum-Seeking and Externalisation of the Screening Process

This is already foreshadowed in a recent statement by the Austrian foreign minister suggesting that the EU should follow the Australian model of offshore processing in dealing with new inflows of migrants[1] and the EU's decision in Malta to establish detention centres in Libya and Niger (as discussed in Chapters 4 and 5). At the time of writing, it was not quite clear if these detention centres would be used for final processing of asylum applications, but the indications are visibly in that direction.

Not surprisingly, the idea floating around in the EU to establish external processing centres in North Africa has caused widespread concern. The UNHCR has expressed reservations on grounds of safety of the asylum-seekers. Ensuring their safety and fair treatment in the processing centres or camps becomes problematic if they are located in countries under oppressive regimes, with a poor human rights record, and the facility is run by them. The token presence of one or more representatives of an outside agency like the UNHCR during the screening process alone can hardly mitigate the problem. The government of a destination country may have some good reasons to keep the asylum issue away from mob frenzy within the country, but externalisation hardly solves the problem as it tends to carry with it doubts about transparency and integrity of the screening process itself. The EU has also been warned that if interdiction at sea involves pushing individuals back with nowhere to go, it breaches international refugee law. The European Court of Human Rights has already ruled against such policies, including a deal struck by Italy and Libya to push back boats in the Mediterranean. Also, the European Council on Refugees and Exiles has argued that forced transfer of asylum-seekers already on EU territory to external processing centres would in effect be a contravention of the right to asylum-seeking guaranteed under the EU Charter of Fundamental Rights.

---

[1]DW *News*, 5 June, 2016. www.dw.com.

Experiences Elsewhere: Australia and the USA

Australia has long relied on external processing as a tool of managing migration/refugee inflows, including in particular as a deterrent to unauthorised entry of those arriving by boat. It is the only country in the world to enforce mandatory offshore detention of potential asylum-seekers. The policy known as the Pacific Solution, launched in 2001, provided for intercepting and transferring all asylum-seekers to Manus Island, Papua New Guinea and Nauru. In 2008, following its wide condemnation as being harsh and inhumane, the policy was abandoned, and the unauthorised immigrants were moved to Christmas Island, an Australian territory. However, in 2012–2013 as new waves of boat people overwhelmed the reception capacity of the island—some 20,000 of them arrived in 2013—the government revived the offshore policy of screening the new arrivals. In September 2013, the then new Liberal-National coalition government, led by Tony Abbott, further tightened the policy and rolled out Operation Sovereign Borders—a panoply of hard-line measures of interdiction and repatriation. Under the command of a military general, the navy began turning back the boats to Indonesian waters and all asylum-seekers who reached the Australian shores were transferred mostly to Manus Island and Nauru for screening, with successful asylum applicants being transferred to Papua New Guinea, Cambodia or other willing countries.

The US Experience in the Caribbean

The US government has made extensive use of policies of interdictions at sea and offshore processing in dealing with the huge outflows of Haitians by boat that followed the overthrow in 1991 of the Haitian President Jean-Bertrand Aristide. It opened the Naval Station at Guantanamo Bay and set up a Migrant Operations Centre for screening asylum claims. By 1992, 12,500 Haitians were held there.[2] In 1994, the US government

---

[2]Zara Rabinovitch, "Pushing out the boundaries of humanitarian screening with in-country and offshore processing", MPI, 16 October 2014.

expanded the facilities at the centre for detention and processing of the Cubans interdicted at sea, in concert with in-country processing system operating in Havana. The Obama administration maintained the centre at Guantanamo Bay for detention and verification of asylum applications. Successful applicants were held until resettlement places are found in third countries; none was to be settled in the USA.

Perils of Trying to Push the Problem Away

When Externalisation Breaches Human and Refugee Rights' Laws

Externalisation of the asylum procedure be it in the form of offshore or in-country processing remains a delicate and highly controversial issue. True, it helps avoid desperate people taking risky, often deadly, journeys and falling victims to human traffickers. It also relieves some of the strain on the border control agencies and reduces the backlog of cases that slows down the screening process in the destination country. However, both forms of externalisation also entail some very serious pitfalls.

Interception and forced transfer of potential asylum-seekers as part of externalising the problem of verification have come under criticism by human rights organisations and experts on the ground that these undermine vulnerable individuals' right to seek asylum and tend to infringe on the principle of *non-refoulement* enshrined in international refugee law. Under the 1951 UN Convention Relating to the Status of Refugees (CRSR), "the state has a duty to abide by the principle of no rejection at frontiers without fair and effective procedure for determining status and protection needs" (UNHCR, EXCOM 1981, 1997, 1998). The situation, however, varies, depending on the location of interception and of subsequent placement of the individuals concerned. As mentioned above in the EU context, if interdiction at sea involves pushing individuals back with nowhere to go, it breaches international refugee law.[3]

---

[3]See, in this connection, Bimal Ghosh, *Elusive Protection, Uncertain Lands: Migrants' Access to Human Rights*, IOM, Geneva, 2003, pp. 22–23.

In a like manner, if interdiction at sea is combined with forcible repatriation to origin country, with no, or only inadequate, access to asylum-seeking opportunities, as it happened under the then US policy in Haiti in the early 1990s, the individuals' right to seek asylum is curtailed. The US courts have upheld the US administration's repatriation policy on grounds that the section of the US law which prohibits such repatriation does not apply outside US territory. The matter, however, has remained controversial. As Judge Sterling Johnson was clearly uncomfortable with his own judgement[4]: "It is unconscionable", he wrote, "that the United States should accede to the Protocol (of the UN Convention) and later claim that it is not bound by it". For its part, the UNHCR has warned that interception of persons in international waters and their repatriation to their home country where they can be persecuted could be in direct contravention of the principle of *non-refoulement* enshrined in international refugee law, and if they are likely to be tortured there, this would breach the international anti-torture convention. Amnesty International has alleged that Australia had breached provisions of the anti-torture convention in repatriating asylum-seekers to Sri Lanka where they were imprisoned and tortured.

Threats to Life, Liberty and Welfare at Offshore Centres

Offshore processing is not just a matter of establishing a facility outside the destination country; it also raises the question of human rights, including security, and living conditions of the asylum-seekers in the detention and processing centres, especially when they are located in a third country. Australia's policy to revive in 2012 the use of regional processing centres in Papua New Guinea, Nauru and other willing countries—despite the dismantling of the policy in 2008 due to complaints of dangerous inhuman conditions at the centres—became

---

[4]Explaining the judgement, he referred to "a controlling precedent [Bertrand V. Saval] …which indicates that the Protocol's provisions are not self-executing". Bill Frelick, "Haitian boat interdiction and return: First asylum and first principles of refugee protection". *Cornell International Law Journal*, vol. 26, Issue Symposium 1993.

controversial because of similar reasons—reports of poor conditions, abuse and deteriorating mental conditions of the detainees. Most of the centres are run by private for-profit contractors. A government-appointed commission had highlighted claims of abuse of children and did not consider the arrangements appropriate or safe for the detention of those seeking protection. In 2014, an Iranian detainee was beaten to death by guards during a riot at the Manus Island centre in Papua New Guinea. And a report by the UN Special Rapporteur on torture found the detention of asylum-seekers, including children, at the centre in violent and dangerous conditions that constituted an infringement of their human rights. In 2015, disregarding such criticisms, Australia maintained the detention centres and went further in passing legislation which makes it illegal for employees at detention centres to disclose information about conditions in the centres, including child abuse and infringement of human rights.

In April 2016, Papua New Guinea asked Australia to close its detention centre on Manus Island following a Supreme Court ruling that the detention on the island was illegal. This happened hours after an asylum-seeker living at Australia's other main offshore processing centre on Nauru set himself on fire in protest over his continued detention on the tiny island. There have been other incidents of self-harm by inmates at Nauru centre who lost hopes of resettlement after more than two years on the island. As Ian Rintoul of the Refugee Action Coalition crisply put it, "People are at the end of their tether with no hope of resettlement, no education for children and no prospects".[5] However, Australia's High Court upheld the government's authority under Australian national law to enter into agreements with the government of Nauru and service providers in relation to detention of asylum-seekers transferred from Australia to Nauru. The UNHCR reacted by maintaining that the court decision does not change Australia's obligations under the 1951 UN Convention and other international human rights instruments that set out the international standards on the treatment of asylum-seekers and refugees.

---

[5]Cited in "Australia urged to close detention centre", *Financial Times*, 28 April 2016.

An associated problem of externalisation to a third county concerns the need to secure the consent and cooperation of the host country concerned. A weak or failing state may be unable or unwilling to ensure the safety and protection of the asylum-seekers even if it agrees to do so, just as negotiation may be tough when the potential host country is dominated by an authoritarian regime. As history shows, such regimes are apt to use their consent and offer of cooperation as a lever to gain undue economic, political or military advantages.

In-Country Processing and Its Mixed Bag of Merits and Drawbacks

In-country processing, too, has a long history, dating back to the Cold War era. In keeping with its foreign policy objectives, the USA was anxious to welcome as refugees the political dissenters who would like to flee the USSR. The 1951 UN Convention on the Status of Refugees, however, requires a persecuted person to be outside the country to seek asylum.[6] It was, however, not easy at that time for such persons to leave the country even when they were permitted to do so. The USA could solve the problem by opting for in-country processing under its Immigration and Nationality Act which empowers the US President to designate countries where in-country processing can be used to verify the eligibility of their nationals for refugee status.

In 1979, the USA made an extensive use of in-country processing in Vietnam as part of its Orderly Departure Programme to stem the disorder and perils of the journey by boat of thousands of people following the Vietnam War. Between 1970 and 1979, over 523,000 persons were admitted through the process as refugees, parolees and immigrants. As mentioned above, in the 1990s the USA used in-country processing along with offshore processing for asylum-seekers from Cuba and Haiti and other Caribbean countries. And more recently, in the fall of

---

[6]It should be noted that Article 31(1) of the Convention does provide for exemptions from the requirement that the asylum-seekers travel with legal documents for those countries where their lives are threatened and there are good causes for their entry without such documents.

2015, following the exodus of mostly unaccompanied children from three Central American countries (discussed separately in Chapter 10, pp. 167–186) the USA launched in-country processing at its embassies in El Salvador, Guatemala and Honduras.

If, as discussed, in-country screening like offshore processing has certain advantages, it also suffers from several limitations. The possibility of avoiding unsafe journeys is considered to be one of its main positive features. In reality, however, this is not always the case. Unless the processing centres are conveniently located and discreetly accessible, individuals seeking asylum could expose themselves to a real danger of retaliatory violence. Individuals who are vulnerable and fearful of persecution are unlikely to feel safe to move to a processing centre for multiple interviews and be within the sight of the security officials of the country they were trying to escape from. In Haiti, the US embassy, used as the reporting centre, was located within the easy sight of security officials who could monitor those who sought to flee. In a hostile and violence-prone environment, many might wish to avoid taking advantage of the programme, which will defeat its purpose or at least diminish its usefulness.

Also, generally, intercountry processing does not provide any arrangement for safe and fair treatment of asylum-seekers during the screening period, although the US programme for Honduras provided for a resettlement shelter to minimise such risks. With multiple interviews, security and medical checks, the process could be long and risky for the applicants. In the context of Central America, some critics have therefore argued that the programme may be more suitable for orderly immigration than for the protection of vulnerable people, who are fearful of persecution and are seeking to escape and for whom time is of the essence.

In-country processing also raises some other sensitive issues. In order to obtain identity documents or those relating to exit visas, individuals may need to interact with officials of the home country they are seeking to flee. It could create tension that can flare up. Also, establishing a programme involves delicate bilateral negotiation between governments of destination and origin countries since it unavoidably touches on the sensitive question of discerning the responsibility for the flight of people. The destination country, in particular, will need to be tenacious and tactful to ensure that the departure arrangements are safe and discreet. It needs to tread the ground with care to avoid straining the bilateral relationship with the origin country government.

7

Refugees and Asylum-Seekers: Eroding Rights, Less-Friendly Welcome

Corrosive Effects of Rising Terrorism, Worldwide

Rising anti-immigrant sentiment, linked largely to conflicts, economic slowdown, security concerns, and the scale and composition of new flows have not only affected the rights and entitlements of migrants and naturalised citizens, but their conflated impact has also adversely affected asylum-seekers and refugees. Alongside the erosion of some of their hard-won rights, they are also set to face a less-friendly welcome. If the inclusion of irregular economic migrants in mixed flows was already hurting their reception, the actual and potential infiltration by the terrorists has made the situation worse in Europe, as in the USA. In Europe, the alleged involvement of some of the foreign-born persons in the robbery, rape and attacks on women on the New Year's (2016) eve had a particularly negative effect on the public attitude towards refugees and migrants in general.

The 2016/2017 annual report of Amnesty International presented a disquieting picture of widespread violation of human rights. It was particularly critical of the suppression of the rights of migrants and refugees during 2016 as it noted that no less than 36 countries had repeatedly violated their international obligations by sending asylum-seekers to countries where they were apt to face the risk of persecution.[1] "In their determination to increase the number of deportation, European governments are implementing a policy that is reckless and unlawful", the report harshly observed. It also cited EU statistics showing that the return of Afghan asylum-seekers sowed a marked decline in accepting applications from 68% in September 2015 to 33% in December 2016.

True, there have been sporadic and isolated gestures, both private and public, showing human compassion and solidarity, but the overall picture of the refugee and asylum situation in the past two/three years has certainly been bleak and troubling. Pope Francis has called the situation Europe's "anesthetized conscience". It may sound a bit hyperbolic, but it does reflect hard realities in Europe and beyond.

The trend is discernible in relation to family reunification systems as well. Despite the importance of family reunification, as reflected in the UN human rights treaties, the case law of the European Court of Human Rights and the European Union law, the trend now is towards imposing greater restrictions including for refugees, which was causing concern among human rights groups.

A rare, if relatively feeble, exception to this generally depressing situation is to be found in a less affluent country—Uganda. The country, which only a few decades ago under the brutal regime of Idi Amin (1971–1979) ruthlessly threw out thousands of migrants of South Asian origin, recently welcomed some half a million refugees from conflict-torn South Sudan as part of what has been called one of the most generous refugee policies in the world. At its well-organised refugee settlement centres, new arrivals are registered, vaccinated and given a medical check-up and a hot meal by a variety of NGOs and international agencies. They are then given a plot of land, materials and supplies to build a house and dig a pit latrine and are encouraged to integrate as quickly as possible into Ugandan society.

Sadly though, even in Uganda things were getting difficult. Newly arrived refugees now get smaller plots of land, with quality of soil not

---

[1] https://www.amnesty.org/en/latest/research/2017/02/amnesty-international-annual-report-2016/17.

always good and firewood was running out, prompting newcomers to stray further in search of trees to cut, and putting strain on the environment as well as on relations with host communities. Monthly food rations, distributed by the World Food Programme (WFP), have been already cut in half to 6 kg per person. Many have started wondering what would happen when all the empty land was allocated and how long the goodwill towards the refugees could last. As, with misgivings for future, the worrying commandant at Impevi refugee centre asked: "What happens, when we are full?"[2]

In Germany, Chancellor Angela Merkel continued to be courageous in welcoming genuine refugees, despite rising opposition in the country and several EU member states. In August 2017, she again expressed her willingness to support the UNHCR initiative to expand the current plan to resettle 22,000 refugees in the EU from outside the Union to 40,000 annually, starting in 2018. Throwing her support behind the plan, she stated that "Germany was ready to take its share" and that an extra 40,000 people would "not overstretch a continent with more than 500 million". However, the plan was likely to be controversial among those EU member states strongly hostile to refugee inflows. Even in Germany, and Ms. Merkel's own party, there was a growing resistance to any increase in the inflows of refugees. With reduced support in German Bundestag, she had to agree to limit the number of refugees to 200,000 a year in her efforts to form a coalition government.[3] The entry, for the first time, of the anti-immigration and anti-refugee populist party AfD was making the German Bundestag jittery and cautious over the refugee issue. The overall public attitude in Europe was clearly more restrictive than welcoming towards refugees and asylum-seekers.

---

[2]"Exodus from South Sudan creates world's biggest refugee settlement". *Financial Times*, 9 June 2017.

[3]At Ms. Merkel's insistence, it was, however, agreed that in the case of a new refuge crisis, the government and the Bundestag could revise the figure upwards or reduce it.

Anti-refugee Sentiment, Restrictive Policies

Many Europeans—a median of 59% across 10 European countries—are concerned that the influx of refugees will increase the risks of terrorism, including 76% in Hungary, 71% in Poland and 61% in Germany, according to a recent (2016) survey by Pew Research Center (Fig. 7.1).[4]

The situation was hardly different in most other EU countries. According to a recent Ifo poll, in both Italy and France 60% of people do not want more refugees. If misogynistic assaults and aggressive misdeeds as in Cologne and elsewhere in Europe on New Year's (2016) Eve have sharpened the anti-refugee feeling, the fact that foreign-born persons and those of immigrant origin were also the main perpetrators of the several murderous acts such as the ones in March 2016 in Brussels and in December 2016 into a Christmas market by a Tunisian asylum-seeker in Berlin, has further deteriorated the environment. In Germany, 61% of the respondents to an INSA/Bild poll (May 2016) said they have become less happy about accepting refugees since the assaults on New Year's Eve (more details later in this chapter). An even more direct link between refugees and security risks was found in people's minds in an Ipsos poll in August 2016, which showed that 71% of Germans believed that terrorists come with refugee flows.

A related factor contributing to the anti-refugee sentiment lies in the fact that growing numbers of Europeans now believe that diversity makes their county a worse place to live, with the negative feeling shared by more than 50% in countries like Greece and Italy, according to a Pew Research Center survey cited above (Fig. 7.2). Finally, the rise of anti-immigration populist parties and groups is yet another factor pushing the mainstream parties in most of western Europe to reduce the flows of asylum-seekers not only in countries where they were already in power but also in those which are set to have national or regional elections in the near future.

---

[4]Pew Research Center, "European opinions of the refugee crisis in 5 charts", op. cit.

7 Refugees and Asylum-Seekers

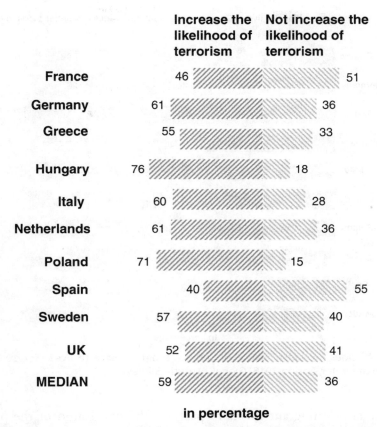

Fig. 7.1 Growing concern over the links between refugee flows and terrorism (*Source* Pew Research Center, Spring 2016. Global Attitude Survey. http://assets.pewresearch.org/wp-content/uploads/sites/12/2016/09/Refugees_2.pngs)

Austria has a long history as a sanctuary country. In the period following World War II, Austria accommodated refugees fleeing the clampdown on the 1956 anti-communist uprising in Hungary and welcomed refugees resulting from the 1968 Soviet-led invasion of Czechoslovakia just as it absorbed the outflows of refugees from Poland as a result of the imposition in 1981 of martial law to crush the Solidarity movement. Much has changed since then. The rise of the anti-immigrant Freedom party has been transforming the political and electoral scene of the country. The victory of Norbert Hofer

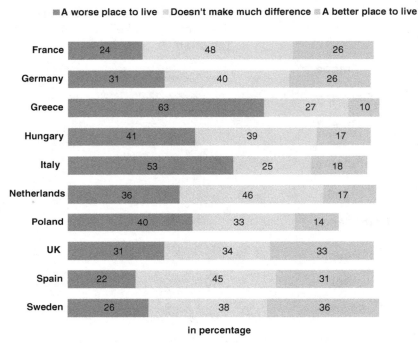

Fig. 7.2 Does diversity make your country a better place to live? (*Source* Pew Research Center, Spring 2016. Global Attitude Survey)

of the anti-immigrant Freedom party in the first round of the presidential elections was a clear sign of the changing situation. He was defeated in the final round, but only narrowly, signalling this new trend. Although his defeat was confirmed in the fresh election of December 2016 (ordered by court because of some irregularities in the previous one), the Freedom party has been consistently attracting more than 30% of voters in recent years, and the relative decline of the establishment parties had seemed to suggest that it would be difficult to keep the party out of power after the next national election due by September 2018, but with the recent dissension inside the ruling coalition government the election was advanced.

The victory of Eurosceptic Sebastian Kurz of People's party and the likelihood of his forming an alliance with the far-right Freedom party portended to further strengthen the anti-immigrant policy orientation in the country.

In a recent interview, Mr. Kurz was quite outspoken in airing his views: "Europe's refugee crisis brought people to Austria who sometimes brought ideas that have no place in our country".[5] It should be noted, however, that his party's pro-EU stance stands in striking contrast with the anti-EU policy approach of the Freedom party, which could have been a sticking point in his coalition talks with the Freedom party. However, in the event a coalition government with the Freedom party was formed.

Even so the outgoing government, fearful of the rising anti-immigrant sentiment and its electoral implications, had already passed tough asylum laws and imposed some of the strictest border controls in the EU. In May 2016, the new asylum law drew criticism from the UN human rights commissioner; in addressing the Austrian parliament in Vienna on 28 April 2016, Ban Ki-moon, then UN Secretary-General, was unusually outspoken in expressing grave concerns about the rising trends of restrictive asylum policies and growing xenophobia in Europe and elsewhere, in violation of norms and state obligations under international and European laws.

In some EU countries where the failure to ensure timely management of the migration/refugee crisis has strengthened the anti-immigration sentiments, populist parties have been quick to take advantage of the situation to enhance their popularity and election prospects. In Italy, for example, the populist Five Star Movement had typically shied away from taking strong positions on immigration. However, days after setbacks in municipal elections, it aligned itself more closely with the far-right and staunchly anti-immigrant Northern League party. And, Rome's Five Star mayor, Virginia Raggi demanded a halt to migrant/refugee arrivals in the city. It also joined forces that obliged Italy's centre-left government to delay a vote on a law granting citizenship to immigrants' children born in Italy.

---

[5]Interview with the *Financial Times*, 19 October 2017.

In Norway, social media have been critical of the government's ultra-strict attitude towards asylum-seekers and refugees as it deported an Iranian woman who had lived in Norway for eight years but was expelled in March 2017, separating her from her 13-year-old son. In Iran, she was given 80 lashes for allegedly consuming alcohol. She has since intended to take the Norwegian government to court, with the support of Amnesty International, for denying her the right under the UN Refugee Convention to protection from being returned to a country where one may run the risk of facing inhuman treatment or torture.[6]

Even in Sweden, a bastion of liberal values and reputed for its long-standing openness to foreigners, things were changing. In the wake of the 2015 migration/refugee crisis, it has adopted a much more restrictive immigration policy that slowed the flow of asylum-seekers from 163,000 in 2015 to fewer than 30,000 in 2016. In April 2017, after an Uzbek hijacked a truck through a crowded street killing four people and injuring 15 others, Stefan Löfven, the prime minister, defiantly declared, "We are an open, democratic society, and that is what we will remain".[7] And yet some were wondering if the openness can survive the new reality of terror, security and heightened vigilance.

In fact, with the rising popularity of the far-right Sweden Democrats party, with roots in neo-Nazism, the government has come under increasing pressure to stem the refugee flows by rolling back some of the rights and benefits so far granted to refugees, as mentioned below.

The political mood in the Visegrad group of countries (the Czech Republic, Hungary, Poland and Slovakia) was particularly hostile to inflows of refugees and their rights. Though disparate in several ways, these countries had a new-found unity in their rhetoric denouncing immigration and refugee inflows. In the Czech Republic, President Milos Zeman has called the refugee influx to the continent an "organised invasion" and characterised integration of Muslim refugees as being "practically impossible"; in Poland, Jaroslaw Kaczynski, chairman of

---

[6]*Euronews*, 22 September 2017.

[7]Cited in "Sweden faces new reality of heightened security and violence", *Financial Times*, 10 April 2017.

the ruling Law and Justice party, has warned that they may carry very dangerous diseases; and in Hungary, which has been in the forefront of efforts to close the EU's gates, Prime Minister Viktor Orban has called asylum-seekers' interference with the country's border fence "terrorist attacks" and the EU's refugee policy a "Trojan horse" for importing terrorism. In the aftermath of the terrorist attacks in France in January and November 2015, several of these countries, including Hungary, Poland and Slovakia, announced their intention of imposing faith-based restrictions on the admission of asylum-seekers. These were among the myriad visible signs of Europe's rescinding welcome to asylum-seekers.

The restrictive asylum policies and practices of the EU countries are also reflected in the level of approvals of applications relative to the number of asylum applications received. According to the Eurostat data, in 2015 six major receiving countries approved only around 20% of the total number of applications they processed that year (since the screening procedure often take years, many of those granted asylum may have applied before 2015).

Less-Friendly Welcome

If, at the time of writing, there were these trends of restrictive asylum and refugee policies in Europe, there was also almost a steady flow of news confirming new policies of less-friendly welcome to asylum-seekers together with the erosion of some of the rights or entitlements of refugees. On 26 January 2014, despite protests from the international human rights organisations and others, the Danish Parliament adopted a bill requiring individuals seeking asylum to turn over to the state possessions amounting to above 10,000 Danish crowns (US$1450) to pay for the costs of processing and providing social assistance. The measures also include extending the time required for refugees to be entitled to family reunification from one year to three years. Dissenting voices from small left-wing parties were heard, including from Red Green Alliance, but the bill passed with an overwhelming majority. It was supported by the opposition party, Social Democrats, indicating a shift to the right in Denmark's political landscape.

Switzerland, too, already has a law that permits confiscation of assets from an asylum-seeker in possession of more than 1000 Swiss francs. Under the Swiss system, anyone who leaves voluntarily within seven months can get the money back. Anyone accepted as a refugee with the right to stay and work is also required to surrender 10% of pay for up to 10 years until 15,000 Swiss francs are repaid. As the system attracted attention in the context of the new Danish law, the Swiss authorities defended the system saying that this was a decades-old law to cover the cost of processing asylum claims and providing social assistance. They also mentioned that this affected only a small number of persons—only 112 out of 45,000 applicants in 2015.

As noted in Chapter 4, in 2017 Switzerland had seen a significant drop in the number of new asylum-seekers since 2015 (a drop of 66% between November 2015 and November 2016), which led to the closure of a number of asylum centres. Even so, in 2017 it decided that Eritrean asylum-seekers who entered the country through irregular channels should no longer be eligible to seek protection, although until the summer of 2016 there were no such restrictions. The new measure, possibly indicative of a new restrictive trend, has come under criticism by rights groups as well as by the UN Special Rapporteur on Migrants' Rights. However, given the decline in the number of new asylum-seekers, Switzerland has agreed to accept an additional 2000 refugees recognised by UNHCR over 2017–2018.

In Germany, following the assaults on women by a number of foreign-born persons on New Year's Eve (2016), German Chancellor Angela Merkel has thrown her support to a proposal to tighten rules that would permit convicted refugees, even those given suspended sentences, to be expelled from Germany. The proposed new asylum policy also extends the waiting period for family reunification to two years for those with "subsidiary protection" status (those who do not qualify as refugees but cannot be expelled as they risk torture or the death penalty on return to their home country). According to the law introduced in 2015, for those asylum-seekers who were granted only "subsidiary protection", family reunions were suspended until March 2018. Some considered change in the law violated the German constitution which provides for special protection of the sate for marriage and the family which should apply to these individuals, too. This had become a sticking point in the Merkel's coalition talks with other parties to form a new government. Two conservative parties and the liberals involved in the talks wanted to keep the ban in place, while the left-leaning Greens party was insisting on lifting the ban. Furthermore, in keeping with new policy trends in Germany, three North African countries—Algeria, Morocco and Tunisia—have been placed on its "safe country" list, implying those who are from these countries will have much less chance of winning refugee status.

In Sweden, as mentioned above, with the changing political environment, marked by the rise of the far-right Sweden Democrats party, the government has felt constrained to cut back some of the rights and benefits accorded to refugees. With nearly tearful eyes, Asa Robinson, deputy prime minister, announced that, with effect from April 2016, most refugees would enjoy only temporary protection, and their rights to bring family members to Sweden would be curtailed.

Perceived Links Between New Refugee Flows and Threats to Security

Most of the recent terrorist attacks were home grown and not by the newly arrived asylum-seekers or refugees. Sadly, however, much of the current discussion, in Europe as elsewhere, on migration and refugee flows is, as noted above, bedevilled by a widely perceived public concern over the links between the migration/refugee flows and security threats by terrorists. And, anti-migration populist leaders seek to take full advantage of this.

This prevalent mindset hardly helps people to appraise where one of the real and main threats to security lies. Although most of the recent terrorist activities were home grown, it needs to be remembered that many of their perpetrators had an immigrant origin. This shows the inadequacy, even failure, not of the immigration policies as such, but of the integration policies of the host countries which left these migrants, marginalised and resentful, in the dark corners of the society, as in the outskirts of Paris and Brussels. I have called this conundrum

"*Perils of Reception without Integration*" (discussed in Chapter 8). All concerned need to be mindful that making a country's integration policy is a joint responsibility of the host society and the newcomers.

Asylum-Seekers: Harsh Treatment, Difficult Living Conditions

The waning warmth of welcome for new asylum-seekers is also reflected in the treatment meted to them in transit posts or detention centres, some of which (separately from established offshore processing centres, discussed above) are also used for preliminary verification of their eligibility for accessing refugee status or just for crossing the border on a transit country.

The treatment of asylum-seekers and conditions in detention and processing centres in Europe as elsewhere has come under criticism. As noted, the Pope has expressed concern over the appalling living conditions in detention centres in so many places in Europe. In September 2015, there were complaints by human rights activists of gross negligence by Hungarian authorities of the large numbers of uprooted people who had arrived in the country travelling through the Balkans. They accused the government of serious mismanagement in housing, feeding and processing applications of asylum-seekers. The Human Rights Watch went to the extent of asserting that the authorities were keeping migrants "like animals, out in the sun without food or water 2015".[8] The UNHCR expressed concern that the Czech Republic was holding migrants in "degrading" and prison-like conditions. Worse still, in a number of countries asylum-seekers' shelters have come under violent attacks. In Germany, for example, during the first half of 2015 the number of such attacks exceeded the total of 173 for the whole of the previous year (Fig. 7.3).

As already noted, in Greece the conditions at the overcrowded detention centre, with barbed wire and watchtowers, have come under sharp

---

[8] *World News Report*, 1 September 2015.

Fig. 7.3 Germany: Attacks on asylum-seekers' shelters, January–March 2015 (*Source* German Federal Criminal Police/FT)

criticism. An appalling situation was developing as children as young as 11, arriving by boat from Turkey, without their parents or adult relatives were routinely being detained in filthy police cells on the island of Kos. According to field reports, they had been held for weeks at a time in cells smeared in faeces, alongside adult criminals. They were provided one meal a day, in addition to fresh fruit and water that were supplied by charities and aid agencies; at least on one occasion, children in detention went without food for two days. They were not allowed to go outside and were handcuffed if they were to be moved to a different location. Following three visits to the island to help refugees, Tim Ubhi, the clinical director of Children's E-Hospital in Britain, described the conditions of a cell as "horrible". "It is like a medieval dungeon—there is no other way to describe it",[9] he said.

Greek authorities, which had been battling to cope with the masses of refugees and migrants by boat from Turkey, said that the children claiming asylum who could not be placed with relatives were automatically kept in police custody for their safety until they could be put under the supervision of a suitable legal guardian. Under the UN Convention on the Rights of the Child, children were entitled to special protection and help and as refugees should not be placed in detention with adults. Given the circumstances in Kos, the UNHCR has reached an agreement with the authorities that children in such conditions would in future be placed in the care of an NGO, which would run its own centre for them, with funding provided by it. In November 2016, following the deaths of two inmates in the centres on Lesbos island, the asylum-seekers set fire to the centre. As winter came, many of the migrants, including children, were exposed to freezing cold. For instance, around 1000 migrants, many of them children, were in unheated tents on the island of Samos, according to a January 2017 UNICEF report.

In September 2017, the Council of Europe severely criticised the conditions of asylum-seekers' reception centres in the country, which they considered were "inhuman, degrading and inacceptable". The centres were overcrowded, short of food and drinking water and were exposed to frequent police brutality, according to the Council. Of the 3000 asylum-seekers below 19 years registered in 2016, only 500 had separate accommodation; the rest was kept together with the adults.

In Serbia, too, asylum-seekers and migrants, stranded due to the closure of the Balkan route to western Europe, were facing a grim situation

---

[9] *The Independent*, 14 October 2014.

in the cold winter of January 2017. For instance, behind Belgrade's railway station 700 of them, already sick and tired, were found sleeping in and around abandoned buildings, anxious to avoid the police or border guards because of their fear of being turned away.

In the first two months of 2016, Hungary accepted only 34 of 1745 asylum applications. As part of harsher asylum policy, it was considering, in defiance of the EU norms, proposals for automatic detention of all asylum-seekers aged 14 and more in fenced-off transit zones and penned them in shipping containers as camps to prevent them from disappearing or moving freely.

It was also erecting a second wall on its southern border with Serbia to fortify the transit zone. Meanwhile, roughly 7000 asylum-seekers remained stuck in neighbouring Serbia, and the vast majority of them were likely to be turned away. Although some EU countries use containers as emergency accommodation for asylum-seekers, so far none has used them as normal detention camps during the whole period of processing their claims. On 7 March 2017, the Hungarian Parliament formally adopted the proposal, which prompted the UNHCR to express deep concern as it violates Hungary's obligations under international and EU laws and would have a terribly negative physical and psychological impact on all asylum-seekers, especially children, who had already greatly suffered. However, the EU's reaction to the situation has been relatively subdued, with Dimitris Avramopoulos, EU migration commissioner, saying that his officials would work with Hungary "to ensure that EU rules are complied with".

Pressured by the EU to get tough on refugees and migrants in order to quickly identify their protection needs and speed up the processing of asylum claims or their return to the countries of origin, Italy has been unduly harsh in its treatment of rescued migrants held in its hotspots. This has come under sharp criticism, especially by human rights groups. According to Amnesty International, the Italian authorities have increasingly resorted "to arbitrary detention, intimidation and excessive physical force". They are alleged to be acting "to the limits and over what is permissible under international human rights laws". The result is that traumatised people after harrowing journeys have been subjected to flawed assessment and in some case appalling abuse as well as unlawful expulsions.[10] The Italian authorities have, however, denied the use of excessive physical force. In 2017, the Italian government took a positive step to ensure better protection and integration of the unaccompanied child migrants. The country receives large numbers of unaccompanied child migrants—in 2016, the number rose to 35,846, the equivalent of the combined total of arrivals in 2014 and 2015. A new law in 2017 requires transfer of children in a specific reception centre within 30 days following their arrival and their subsequent placement in a family.

In France, children and women in camps were abused and raped, according to the UNICEF and Gynaecology Sans Frontières. The UNICEF report also mentioned cases of young girls being sexually abused in exchange of a promise of free passage to Britain and that such abuses were not limited to France. Following the demolition by bulldozer of the migrant village in the Calais Jungle, thousands of migrants and potential refugees moved to northern Paris where they slept under road bridges and on the roadside in squalor, with almost no access to water, sanitation and food. Even after the demolition of the main migrant village, Calais was still proving attractive to some migrants and potential asylum-seekers who were taking shelter in makeshift settlements, which, however, lacked even the basic necessities of life.

The government, however, was unwilling to provide any facilities that could encourage any new settlements. France's highest court called these shortcomings "a serious and unlawful infringement on a fundamental freedom" and has ordered the authorities to rectify them. The government then agreed to provide drinking water, toilets and sanitation and open two reception centres.

Even in refugee-welcoming Germany, the initial treatment of the newly arrived asylum-seekers could be rough and tough. In the country's federal system, the 16 regional states must integrate the refugees once the federal officials have fingerprinted them. With an estimated 90,000 asylum-seekers in 2015 in a population of 3.5 million, the state of Berlin was little prepared to cope with the situation. Asylum-seekers were required to register with LaGeSo, the state office for health and

---

[10] Amnesty International, "Hotspot Italy: How EU's flagship approach leads to violation of refugee and migrant rights", London, 2016.

social affairs, when they got to Berlin. But it proved to be an uphill and demeaning task. For instance, the hapless people, even pregnant women and babies, were sleeping on the pavement in freezing cold, hoping to make it to the head of the line on the following day; they had to depend on a voluntary organisation, Moabit Hilft, for food, clothes and advice. A humanitarian crisis had seemed to be building. The desperate situation received national attention only when Claudia Roth, a Vice President of Germany's parliament, wrote an open letter to Berlin's mayor, Michael Muller, saying the refugees "at LaGeSo are deprived of their human dignity", in violation of the German constitution.[11]

As discussed below, failed asylum-seekers generally face a grim situation in Europe. However, until recently Germany had been relatively generous in dealing with them. They were given a special "tolerated status", which gave them access to health care, and a small handout in cash. But, this is now changing. In February 2017, amid rising public concerns about the huge influx of migrants and refugees, Angela Merkel made new proposals tougher than those presented a month ago to speed up the removal of failed asylum-seekers within a limited time from the detention centres. These include toughening and accelerating asylum screening and repatriation regulations for those holding up procedures, and boosting the return of potential refugees to other EU countries under the EU's Dublin Convention. Included in the 16-point plan is the establishment of a new Centre for the Support of Returns in Berlin. A soft touch was added to the plan by adding an extra EUR 40 million towards voluntary return and repatriation and EUR 50 million towards reintegration of returnees through promotion of education, training and job opportunities in their home countries.

The plan faced criticism from human rights groups as well as from some of Germany's 16 regions which are responsible for implementing refugee laws. Six of them were reluctant to send back Afghan asylum-seekers since they might not be safe in their home country. And Günter Burkhardt, director of Pro Asyl, a refugee rights group, argued that accelerating asylum procedures would lead to a "violation of standards".

---

[11] Cited in "All down the line" *The Economist*, 19 December 2015–1 January 2016.

In Switzerland, too, there have been some concerns about the treatment of asylum-seekers. In the Canton of Geneva, for example, there were protests in January 2017 for detaining asylum-seekers in underground bunkers and the absence of a humane approach to their reception and treatment.

In Basel, at a federal asylum centre managed by a private company, Societé ORS service, the asylum-seekers were subjected to a regime of collective punishment, bullying and inadequate meals between November 2015 and the end of 2016, according to a report in *Basler Zeitung*. The employees at the centre were reminded of the confidentiality clause in the service contracts and were warned about possible dismissal if they made public statements concerning the internal working at the centre. The federal authorities have, however, denied the allegations, while the state migration service, SEM, admitted there had been only one complaint and that necessary remedial measures had been taken. The newspaper also recalled that five years ago there was a similar allegation against the ORS service which managed a centre in Lucerne and that the final report of the investigation that followed was critical of the oppressive management, arbitrary sanctions and inadequate meals offered at the centre. In Turkey, despite a sharp increase in enrolment rates, 380,000 refugee children, more than 40% of the total, have no access to schooling, according to UNICEF. They may well become a lost generation.

Finally, it needs to be recalled that faced with a seemingly relentless flow of migrants, including potential asylum-seekers, towards its member states the EU itself decided to divert the flow to Turkey and Libya despite the real risk that they could be exposed to abuse and flagrant violation of their human and refugee rights and the reservations expressed by the UNHCR and rights groups on that score (discussed in Chapters 4 and 5).

Restrictive Policies, Tough Treatment: A Global Trend?

In absolute numbers, the USA has resettled more refugees than any other country—about 3 million—since 1980. And the number of refugees annually resettled by the USA, although a small part of the global refugee flows, has generally increased with the rise in the global refugee population. However, these trends are now set to be reversed under the new US administration, which in turn are likely to boost Europe's new restrictive asylum and refugee policies and practices discussed above.

Soon after the November 2015 ISIS attacks in Paris, 53% of Americans said they did not want to accept Syrian refugees at all. Some 31 US states had stated their unwillingness to cooperate in the resettlement of Syrian asylum-seekers/refugees in their territories, and at least eight had refused to take any new refugees. Although this does not prevent the Federal Government from admitting the asylum-seekers, it complicates their resettlement in non-cooperating states if they decide to withhold the state-level assistance needed for the success of the scheme.

The anti-immigrant rhetoric used by the Republican party during the US presidential election campaign caused widespread concern in human and refugee rights groups. The very fact that the extremely negative views about migrants and refugees in general, and those of the Muslim faith in particular, were enjoying considerable support did not bode well for the future reception and treatment of asylum-seekers and refugees in the country.

Soon after his inauguration, by a new Executive Order which came into effect on 27 January 2017, Mr. Trump sought to close the US borders to refugees into the USA for 120 days pending additional vetting to ensure that those approved for admission as refugees do not pose a threat to the country. "We want to ensure that we are not admitting into our country the very threats our soldiers are fighting", he declared. He also ordered that the Syrian refugees be indefinitely blocked from entering the USA and that Christians and those of other minority religious faiths be given priority over Muslims. He thus introduced religion as one of the tests for admitting refugees, as had been some of proposed by the Central European leaders. US courts have thwarted the order but the President's order to halve the number of refugees admitted to the USA in 2017 still holds.

President Trump then issued a revised Executive Order which also provides for temporary shutting down of the US refugee programme. The revised order was due to come into force on 16 March 2017. However, this, too, was blocked by US courts following legal challenges by several US states. This led the US administration to make a judicial appeal, but that, too, was turned down. When the matter finally went to the US Supreme Court, it decided, pending a review of the whole issue of travel ban in October 2017, to temporarily uphold broad restrictions on the entry of refugees, thus blocking the entry of an estimated 24,000 refugees from across the world to settle in the USA. The order also capped the annual total of refugee admissions to 50,000, down from 110,000 under the Obama administration. Since, however, the Court lifted the ban on the six terror-prone predominantly Muslim countries for persons "with a bona fide family-based relationship" to a US citizen or a formal relationship to an American company or organisation, refugees satisfying these requirements would be allowed admission. But the cap does not apply to refugees who can claim a bona fide relationship.

However, estimates suggest that a large percentage of refugees who come to the country have no family ties in the USA. Refugee agencies also interpreted the Supreme Court's interim decision as meaning that refugees who have long-standing connection with one of the refugee settlement agencies would qualify to enter the USA. The administration officials contradicted this. At the time of writing, there were still considerable uncertainties about the situation.

On 2 August 2017, two Republican senators, Tom Cotton and David Perdue, introduced a new immigration bill, which reportedly had the support of President Trump. The bill, which seemingly seeks to cut low-skilled immigration, also provides for reducing the admission of refugees from 100,000 to 50,000 a year "in line with a 13-year average". However, as *The Economist* observed, this seems to be a "cherry-picked average".[12] It reckons that if the bill's authors had taken a 30-year average, the annual level would have been 75,000. During this 30-year period, only four times has refugee admission in the USA been below 50,000. To view the issue in its proper perspective, it is also important to recall that the US intake of refugees, like that of many other countries hosting refugees, has varied over decades, depending on the rise and fall of world refugee flows. In 1975, for example, in the wake of the Vietnam War, the USA admitted 125,000 Vietnamese refugees. In 1979, given the tense refugee situation, President Jimmy Carter doubled the

---

[12]"Attitudes to Immigration: Still Yearning", *The Economist*, London, 12–18 August 2017.

US intake of refugees from Vietnam, Cambodia and Laos from 7000 per month to 14,000, or 168,000 in the year, despite significant public reticence. As narrated in the Introduction of this book, since 2012 we have been witnessing a similarly desperate situation, perhaps on a still larger scale, due to a dramatic rise in the number of refugees worldwide.

In 2016, in keeping with the dramatic rise in the global refugee population the USA under the Obama administration raised its intake to 98,000. However, even this increase was much lower than in previous times of high refugee settlement in the USA and did not keep pace with the dramatic rise in the global refugee population. As of August 2017, the USA had resettled about 28,000 refugees, and looking ahead the Trump administration has proposed a refugee settlement annual ceiling of 45,000 to US Congress.

According to a recent study by PWC Research Center, if the number of refugees worldwide, including the 2017 annual increase, renewed as in 2016 and if few refugees entered the USA for the rest of 2017, the USA would be accepting just 0.2% of the world total—far less than the historic average of 0.6% and lower even than the share admitted in 2001 and 2002 following the September 11 terrorist attacks (see Fig. 7.4). One positive feature of an otherwise disappointing situation is that the USA promised to pay US$857 million to UNHCR for 2018—the biggest contribution to the organisation. However, this amounts to just 11% of the US$7.5 billion that the organisation needs to deal with refugee crisis.

A similar, less charitable, wind has been blowing in several other parts of the world. Already in 2001, under the premiership of John Howard, Australia had embarked upon a hard-line asylum policy, which denied the access of asylum-seekers arriving by boat to the services, rights and residency available to those arriving and seeking protection through the UNHCR programme of resettlement. That policy has now turned almost into a blanket ban on any asylum-seekers who arrive by boat and their detention on remote South Pacific islands. And both the ruling Liberal and opposition Labour parties have beefed up their rhetoric on anti-migration, anti-asylum policy. In several other parts of the world, too, the situation for asylum-seekers remains tough and from all indications it is getting worse, although there are some rare exceptions.

(a)

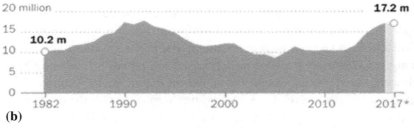

(b)

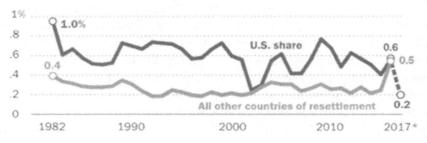

Fig. 7.4 **a**. Refugee population worldwide. **b**. Share of annual resettlement of refugees in the USA and all other countries

Degrading and dangerous conditions prevailing in mixed migration detention centres have become a matter of serious concern in countries like Libya. Based on investigations between November 2012 and 2014, a recent study, issued by Mixed Migration Hub, revealed a most disturbing picture of detention centres for asylum-seekers, refugees as well as young migrants in Libya. There were allegations of serious infringements of basic human rights, including arbitrary detention, violence and brutality at the centres, most of which were under the control and supervision of government authorities or militia forces (discussed in Chapter 5).

According to the study, the harsh and inhumane way the detainees were treated was a major contributing factor that drove many of them to seek safety in Europe through the Mediterranean even at the risk of their lives. A recent UNICEF investigation, based on personal interviews with 122 migrants, both women and children, revealed that 75% of the children and 50% of the women were physically abused, harassed and exploited almost routinely during the journey and following their arrival in Libya. There were also myriad complaints about arbitrary detention as well as about scarcity of food and inadequate measures related to health and hygiene in the camps. In April 2017, IOM issued a lurid field report narrating how some of these migrants while in transit become captives of a network of human traffickers engaged in the slave trade. They are physically abused, beaten and raped, subjected to extortion in different stages of the trade. Findings of a recent field investigation by IOM into the conditions of 13 detention centres reveal that in nine of 13 centres, migrants enjoyed access to outdoor space for less than half a day and only irregular access to drinking water in three centres. Also, out of nine centres 3 had either no ventilation systems or ones that work only irregularly. However, seven out of 13 centres had some health services and nearly all of them had referral services to hospitals for sick migrants.[13]

Likewise, a recent joint report by Oxfam Italia and others denounced the daily instances of brutality against migrants in Libya by local militias, smugglers and criminal gangs and has urged the Italian government to cancel its deal with Libya for retention of refugees and migrants. According to a more recent (September 2017) joint UNICEF/IOM report, 77% of migrant children and young persons, mostly from

---

[13] *IOM News*, 20 June 2017.

sub-Saharan Africa, experienced direct or indirect sexual abuses on their way to Europe by the central Mediterranean route.[14]

In May 2016, the attempt by the Kenyan government to close one of the world's largest refugee camps that was opened more than 25 years ago and was hosting over 250,000, mainly Somali refugees, is another example of the restrictive trends. Kenya's high court has, however, ruled that "the decision specifically targeting Somali refugees was an act of group persecution, illegal, discriminatory and therefore unconstitutional". The government has rejected the verdict and was preparing to lodge an appeal. Meanwhile, between May 2016 and January 2017 some 51,727 Somalis have been repatriated, including 33,600 with the help of UNHCR, from the camp where the number had peaked at 580,000 in 2011.

In 2015 even Lebanon, which has been hosting some 1.6 million registered and unregistered refugees, the highest number in the world as a share of the country's total population of 4 million, imposed visa requirements to restrict the flow of asylum-seekers. Syrians can apply for one of the six types of visas for entry: business, medical, tourist, transit and short stay but there would no longer be refugee entry visas. According to Human Rights Watch, not only does this make it harder for the Syrian asylum-seekers to enter the country but also makes those already there fearful of possible deportation, as they are now required to renew their permit every six months. Lebanon does not allow formal or organised refugee centres, with proper facilities in order to avoid encouraging refugees to settle down permanently in the country. They are required to rent their accommodation, which is hard for the poorest refugees. Thus, more than 40% of them live in insecure and exposed places such as garages, unfinished buildings and informal camps, dispersed in 1750 different locations. Most of them remain short of supplies to keep the inmates, including children, warm, dry and healthy in the bitter winter cold when the temperature can drop below zero degree.

---

[14]*Harrowing Journeys*, IOM/UNICEF, 9 September 2017.

Many in Lebanon are getting fearful about the risk of the presence of terrorists among the Syrian refugees. According to press reports, recently the mood turned darker after the army raided a camp near Lebanon's border town of Arsal in search of militant infiltrators. From among some 400 Syrian refugees who were rounded up, about 150 were kept in detention and four of them died.[15] While according to Lebanese army investigators, the deaths were due to "health conditions", human rights activists said their bodies bore the marks of being beaten and burnt. Traditionally, Lebanese agriculture and construction have benefited from cheap Syrian labour, and now from the refugee aid money that comes in and is spent in Lebanon. However, many Lebanese now perceive refugees as a security risk as well as a burden on the economy, already weakened by the Syria war, and want them to leave. Unlike Lebanon, Jordan has not blocked unrestricted entry, but the country recently announced it would no longer provide health care for the 623,000 registered refugees.

In Pakistan, according to the Human Rights Watch, over 600,000 Afghan refugees, both registered and unregistered, were forced out of the country in 2016 as a result of the recent anti-refugee policy stance of the government. Most of the Afghan refugees have lived in Pakistan for several years, and some were born there. However, with the deterioration in Pakistan's relations with Afghanistan, refugees are reported to have come under increasing suspicion and harassment and are being constrained to leave the country. The report, however, was contradicted by the government as well as by the local UNHCR representative. They maintained that the outflow was driven by a combination of several factors, including the recent call from the Afghan government for refugees to return home.

In Japan, too, asylum-seekers are reported to face a grim situation upon arrival.[16] Some are locked up for years, while their claims are processed. A Nigerian asylum-seeker who arrived in Tokyo in 2007 alleges he spent about 30 months under lock and key. According to Japanese

---

[15] "Lebanon's mood towards refugees darkens", *Financial Times*, 2 August 2017.
[16] *The Economist*, 14 March 2015. http://www.economist.com/news/asia/21646255-worlds-refugee-problem-grows-japan.

media, there were no full-time doctors in the country's three detention centres (only a few hours' visits a day by part-time doctors). In March 2014, two asylum-seekers died in detention. Following a visit to Tokyo, Antonio Guterres, then UN High Commissioner for Refugees, called the country's asylum system rigid and restrictive. And, the chairperson of the Japan Association for Refugees, a non-profit organisation, described Japan's system of collecting information about asylum-seekers from their countries of origin as being primitive and added that many applications were being needlessly rejected. In the decade to 2013, Japan, a signatory to the UN Refugee Convention since 1981, gave asylum to just over 300 refugees; in 2014, the number fell to zero; and in 2016, it took just 28 refugees, one more than it took in 2015. The tiny number of successful claims, despite a 44% rise in asylum claims to over 10,900, underscores its unduly restrictive asylum policy and practice. Also, due to rigid conditions attaching to entry, relatively few potential asylum claimants reach Japan in the first instance. As the chairperson of the Japan Association, Eri Ishikawa, put it, "The policy measures really prioritise immigration control rather than [offer] refugee protection".

However, the Japanese government strongly rejects the criticisms of its asylum system. It points out that the country is the fourth largest contributor to the UNHCR and that if the approval rate was low, the problem lay with the criteria enshrined in the international convention. In any case, over half of the Syrian applicants have been granted special permission to stay on humanitarian grounds. Also, with the help of the UNHCR, the justice ministry was reviewing its asylum system. Some are hopeful that the final recommendations would make the system fairer and more transparent. Others are less hopeful. Mieko Ishikawa, director of Forum for Refugees Japan, a network of refugee associations, feared that it might make things worse by giving more power to immigration officials for weeding out claims. All in all, the experience so far in Japan highlights once more two things: the scope and criteria of the existing 1991 refugee convention are proving too narrow relative to today's needs. At the same time, a trend is gaining ground towards an unduly rigid and restrictive interpretation and application of it.

Recruitments by Both Fundamentalists and Criminals in Refugee Camps

One worrisome fallout of the deplorable conditions in refugee camps and shelters is that, as the refugees agonise and despair over their hardship, it makes it easier for fundamentalist recruiters to approach the inmates, especially the younger ones, and seduce them using offers of help and support, including taking food and presents to them, helping in filling out forms and dealing with official bureaucracies. It is worth noting that Fayçal Cheffou, who has been charged with terrorist murders in the Brussels bombing, had been banned from visiting a refugee camp in 2015 following concerns that he was trying to radicalise asylum-seekers.

Just as refugee camps could be recruitment points for jihadists, they can also be a hunting ground for criminal gangs engaged in the drugs trade. Both try to take advantage of the despair and vulnerability of asylum-seekers, especially in camps and shelters where conditions are harsh and revolting. They do so sometimes in collusion with the security guards themselves. For instance, security guards at the refugee centre in Neukölln, a district of southern Berlin, were trying to recruit young migrants as drug dealers and had to be sacked. As Neukölln's commissioner for migration, Arnold Mengelkoch, observed, it was not an isolated incident. Criminal gangs were known to be on the hunt for new employees for their drugs trade. So far, influx of foreigners in Germany has not led to an uptick in crime—in fact, figures released in June 2016 revealed an 18% drop in the number of crimes committed by immigrants between January and March 2016 and indicated that they were no more likely to be involved in criminal activities than Germans.

However, authorities in Berlin were getting worried that newcomers were already being sucked into the city's thriving underworld activities. Many of the newcomers in camps fled war and violence in their homeland, still reeling from the long and hazardous journey. Frustrations over harsh conditions in camps, delays in integration, lack of knowledge of German and an uncertain future make them vulnerable to the allure of organised crime, when, using their native language, gang members or their agents seduce them by making seemingly tempting offers.

Rigging Contracts and Sealing Funds Meant for Asylum-Seekers

Another worrisome, but little noticed, danger faced by the asylum-seekers in some EU countries concerns the rigging by crime gangs of the contracts for housing, feeding and caring of the asylum-seekers and grabbing illicit profits by diverting resources allocated for the asylum-seekers and profiting from it. Given the sudden rise in the migratory inflows, EU governments have been scrambling to outsource these services to private individuals, companies and non-profit organisations. One estimate shows that in 2015, Italy was spending EUR 800 million per year for this purpose, with EUR 35 a day allocated per asylum-seeker, including a daily allowance of EUR 2.50, which hosts were supposed to pay directly to them. According to Italian prosecutors and watch groups, criminal gangs have succeeded at rigging the awarding of the contracts for managing the service-providing centres. Reports by Italian officials suggest that a criminal organisation that had come to dominate the business of making illicit profits by hosting the asylum-seekers was based in Rome. Organised crime groups could get a foothold in the business allegedly by colluding with local politicians and government officials. As Ignacio Marino, the mayor of Rome put it, "In recent years corrupt politicians and officials have taken advantage of the migrant drama. We are working to restore legality and transparency".[17]

Also worrisome is the backlash created by the involvement of crime gangs and corrupt officials in hosting the asylum-seekers. Not surprisingly, it has provided fuel to the anti-immigrant groups seeking to block any form of public assistance to the new arrivals: "We must stop the departures and landings, and block all the contracts", said Matteo Salvini, leader of the anti-immigrant Northern League.[18]

---

[17]Cited in: "Mafia divert funds from asylum-seeker reception centres, say officials", *Financial Times*, 25–26 August 2015.
[18]Ibid.

Do Charities Rescuing Migrants in the Mediterranean Collude with Smugglers?

Another worrying aspect of the fluid migration/refugee situation became public when the EU's border agency, Frontex, expressed concern that some rescuing NGOs were giving clear indications to migrants before departure on the precise direction to be followed in order to reach their boats and that criminal networks were smuggling migrants directly on NGO vessels. It is a fact that the number of rescues triggered by a distress signal fell to one in 10 in October 2016, compared with two-thirds in the summer. And this coincided with a significant increase in number of rescues carried by the NGOs in the central Mediterranean—from 5% at the beginning of the year to more than 40% of the rescues in October. Frontex also suggested that this change in activity may also be due to the fact that the lights used by rescue boats were acting "as a beam for the migrants".

NGOs, however, have angrily rejected the accusation that they were colluding with the smugglers and have argued that they were actively searching for boats in distress and spotting them earlier to help avoid deaths at sea which had increased due to smugglers' changing tactics and their use of increasingly unseaworthy boats following the EU's earlier crackdown on smugglers, including the smashing of more expensive boats.

What in reality seems to have happened was that as charities became more alert and active in searching for boats in distress, some unscrupulous smugglers were trying to take advantage of easier accessibility to NGO rescue boats and their prior knowledge of the location of those boats. As Frontex itself recognised, the recent increase in the number of rescues by NGOs without distress calls may also be due to the fact that NGOs were operating closer to Libyan territorial waters than in the past. One more reason for the situation may well have been, as Ruben Neugebauer of Sea Watch, a German charity running rescues, suggested, migrants themselves may have been reluctant to put in distress calls as they were fearful that Libyan authorities, once alerted, might push them back to shore.

* * *

Frontex also criticised the charities for their unwillingness to help with probes into human smuggling by refusing to collect leftover evidence from rescued boats and that some rescued migrants even claiming they were warned by NGOs not to cooperate with Italian law enforcement officials or with Frontex. The charities reacted by saying, "We have an obligation to save their lives, not perform the duties of security agencies", as the NGO, Save the Children, put it.

It is not surprising that at the cusp of an extremely stressful situation, there were some tensions between the EU's border agency and the NGOs running the rescue operations. However, the problem was not as serious as the language used by Frontex, or some media reports at the time may have suggested. The EU Commission admitted that NGOs had played a vital role in saving thousands of lives in the region and had in most cases acted in support of, and in close coordination with, governments. And in any case, as noted in Chapter 2, with the help of the EU, Italy was now set to sign a code of conduct with the NGOs involved in rescue operations which might require their vessels to comply with certain standards and carry certain specific equipment. This can be expected to ease the tensions.

What About the Conditions of the Failed Asylum-Seekers?

In Europe, life could be hard for those asylum-seekers who failed the test. They are likely to fall into the cracks of the EU asylum system and be pushed into limbo. Many EU governments seek to avoid the long-winded, expensive process of deporting failed asylum-seekers. It is also difficult to do so, when they have no travel documents or have destroyed them. Any attempt for a failed asylum-seeker to move to another EU country does not work either since under the EU (Dublin Convention) rules (designed to avoid asylum applications in multiple countries) the individual would be transferred back to the first country of arrival where the asylum application was processed. In practice, however, this does not work. In 2013, EU governments had sent requests for such transfers involving 76,000 people to other member states, but only 56,000 were accepted, and of these just 16,000 resulted in actual transfers.[19] Consequently, in order to avoid the responsibility attached to the first country of admission, many governments, not infrequently with the connivance of the would-be asylum-seekers themselves, avoid registering them, allowing the failed asylum-seekers to roam about within the EU as they find expedient on their wits—except that there would hardly be a place where they would be welcome. A failed asylum-seeker thus lives in a legal no-man's-land: unable to work, unable to claim any social benefit and, bereft of any travel documents, also unable to leave. They can rely only on charities and their will and wits to live.

---

[19] *Financial Times*, "Failed asylum-seekers caught in no man's-land", 11 June 2015.

8

Economic Effects of Migration/Refugee Inflows in Europe

When Economic Gains Coincide with Humanitarian Imperatives

At the time of writing, it was estimated that over one million migrants could surge into Europe in 2015 and more would follow in 2016. Many of them, though not all, are bona fide asylum-seekers (and potential refugees) or persons deserving humanitarian protection. Under international human rights and humanitarian laws, they are in principle entitled to protection and help, regardless of economic or other considerations. And yet, it is not difficult to see why European leaders were finding it difficult to take a firm decision on the matter. The scale of the flows, unprecedented since the end of the World War II, was not the only reason. The mixed composition of the flows, comprising bona fide asylum-seekers, persons deserving humanitarian protection and poverty-driven labour migrants, was adding to the problem of screening the mixture, and the task was made even more complicated by the potential threat of terrorists infiltrating into the flows. The EU's response to the challenge was also made difficult by its own diffused political structure and the decision-making process and by the absence of a coherent and well-coordinated migration and asylum policy. Above all, European leaders agonised over the economic implications of the inflows, which were yet to be fully determined.

© The Author(s) 2018
B. Ghosh, *Refugee and Mixed Migration Flows*,
https://doi.org/10.1007/978-3-319-75274-7_8

Unfortunately, the absence, at the time of writing, of detailed, complete and updated data concerning the composition of the newcomers, including age structure, skill profiles and gender, made it difficult to work out any precise estimate of the economic effects of the new arrivals. Much also depends on the conditions and costs of reception both on arrival and on long-term settlement of all these people. An additional difficulty stems from the fact that different receiving countries have different capacities and readiness to respond to the new situation. Given these constrains, only some tentative indications can be provided on the likely economic impact of these inflows on the receiving countries in Europe.

At a time of high unemployment and low growth in Europe, feeding and sheltering these masses of people will certainly add to the strain on governments' budgetary resources, just as it will increase pressure on its physical infrastructure and social services. This could also prompt populist warning about the threat they would pose to jobs and earnings of local workers. However, the picture may not be as gloomy as it may appear at first sight.

First, it is important to remember that although the arrival of over one million additional people within the time span of one year (with more to follow) seemed an overwhelming event, they would represent roughly one-fifth of 1% of the EU's population. The OECD estimated the new arrivals in 2015 would correspond to less than 0.4% of the labour force of the European Economic Area and Switzerland in 2016. Even for Germany their share would be no more than 1% of the total labour force in 2015. In the wake of the fall of Berlin Wall some 1.3 million people moved into western Europe in 1989–90. During the Bosnia crisis alone, when western Europe was much less prepared, it had to handle the problem of some 630,000 internally and externally displaced people, although most of the externally displaced ones needed, and received, only temporary protection. In the years following the end of the World War II, it had the experience of dealing with much larger flows, running into millions. Admittedly, then too, the surrounding conditions were vastly different. People then came as labour migrants to respond to the labour needs for reconstruction of war-divested Europe. Those needs were clear and largely predetermined, and both governments and employers were anxious to receive the workers; there were also some significant rotations of movements.

This is surely not the case with the current, mostly unwanted and sudden inflows; and today's newcomers represent, as noted, mixed flows, including asylum-seekers, and those needing humanitarian protection. Still, it is interesting to note that limited field investigations suggest that a significant number of the migrants, especially those who arrived in the first phases, do have middle-level skills and some were white collar workers who were forced to leave due to extreme insecurity, violence and fear of persecutions. An increasing number of middle-class Syrians has been leaving the country carrying skills with them. Reports suggest more than 40% of Syrians have completed at least upper secondary education (as further discussed later in this chapter, there was a change in their educational profile with subsequent arrivals). The fact that many of them could spend relatively important sums of money to finance the long journey also suggests the likelihood that they may have been engaged in an occupation or gainful activity. And given the arduous and hazardous journey they completed, there can be no question about their determination or entrepreneurial drive. Many Syrian refugees in Turkey are showing drive in setting up small businesses taking advantage of the relative ease of doing business in the country. Since 2011, 4000 businesses have been set up by Syrians or Syrians with Turkish partners. In 2015 alone, they set up 1600 businesses, with 590 more established in the first three months of 2016, according to the Economic Policy Research Foundation of Turkey, a think-tank (further discussed later in this chapter).

All this augurs well for their effective integration into the labour market and the prospects of a positive impact on the economies of receiving countries. Indeed, according to two economists at the World Bank, Massimiliano Cali and Samia Sekkarie, Lebanon, which at the time had received 1.1 million Syrian refugees (nearly 25% of its population), was on its way to score its highest growth since 2010.[1] In Jordan, the new inflows accounting for 10% of the country's population did not seem to have had a negative impact on the formal labour market, although it

---

[1]Massimiliano Cali and Samia Sekkarie, Much ado about nothing: The economic impact of refugee "invasions", 16 September 2015. https://www.brookings.edu/blog/future-development/2015/09/16/much-ado-about-nothing-the-economic-impact-of-refugee-invasions.

increased informal employment.[2] Research elsewhere also suggests that those inflows of low-skilled refugees (and for that matter, low-skilled migrants) do not necessarily depress wages of the natives and could help local workers to move into better jobs with higher wages. For instance, studies by Mette Foged at the University of Copenhagen and Giovanni Peri at the University of California showed that the inflows of refugees to Denmark between 1991 and 2008 encouraged local low-skilled workers to upgrade themselves to high-wage jobs.

However, as will be discussed below, these positive indications do not tell the whole story, and they need to be tested against the realities on the ground, including in particular the conditions and quality of social and labour market integration. It is also relevant to note that, contrary to the optimistic assessment by Messrs. Cali and Sekkarie, the official World Bank figures show that Lebanon's economic growth rate declined to 1.5% in 2015 and 1.8% in 2016, and project a sluggish growth rate of 2.5% annually over the medium term, if the spillover of the Syrian crisis into Lebanon persists.

There is little doubt that the immediate cost of resettling the refugees would be heavy, although it would vary from country to country. Germany had initially set aside EUR 6 billion on the assumption that it may have to accept up to one million asylum-seekers in 2015, and Wolfgang Schübel, the then finance minister, said the cost was manageable. (Some other estimates suggested, however, that Germany may have to spend EUR 10 billion in 2015 and EUR 12 billion in 2016.) Subsequently, Mr. Schäuble estimated on a tentative basis that the cost in 2016 might reach EUR 20 billion. A later estimate, made available in December 2015, indicated an allocation of EUR 17 billion for 2016. This is in line with the estimates made by the OECD which indicated an annual additional public expenditure of 0.5% of Germany's GDP in 2016 and 2017, while for Austria and Sweden the expenditures would amount to 0.3 and 0.9%, respectively, in 2016.[3] Turkey, which is not a

---

[2] Also, in 2013, but for the crisis in Syria, with higher exports to its neighbouring country, the growth rate for Jordan's economy could have been higher by one percentage point. Nasser and Symansky, IMF 2013.

[3] OECD, "Migration Policy Debates", no. 8, November 2015. www.oecd.org/migration.

member of the European Union, but has temporarily housed more of the new flows of potential asylum-seekers than any other country, claimed to have already spent $7.6 billion as of September 2015, which is roughly in line with the OECD estimate of 0.8% of the country's GDP for the year as a whole (it would get EUR 6 billion from the EU's aid package under the March 2016 EU/Turkey agreement, discussed below).

Most of the accepted asylum-seekers will need accelerated training, especially language training, for their integration into the labour market. This needed to start without delay, as the German employers had already suggested, and it will add to the immediate cost. Children will need schooling, which, according to one teachers' association, will require an additional 25,000 teachers. By June 2016, state funding for the language courses had already reached EUR 559 million.

Although the EU countries' immediate costs for resettling and integrating the new refugees would be heavy, it is also important that this is seen in a proper perspective, especially in relation to the amounts the European countries have been spending on border control and raising protective walls, often with little effect, and the large sums of money paid by migrants for circumventing them and securing entry. One estimate suggests that EU-28 spent EUR 13 billion between 2000 and mid-2015 on border control and costly evictions of unwanted migrants. And during the same period migrants themselves paid at least EUR 16 billion to traffickers, while the human costs in terms of deaths rose to 30,000, according to the same source.[4]

Both Germany and the rest of western Europe are now better prepared to accept refugees than in the past. And yet, both politically and logistically the preparation fell far short of what was needed to settle the new refugees. More so, for countries in eastern Europe, which are less used to dealing with large-scale refugee flows as an emergency. This could lead to high social cost even in Germany. In Berlin and Hamburg, for example, the housing situation to resettle was so precarious that the authorities were planning legislation to confiscate privately owned empty apartments. In Hamburg, this would apply to

---

[4]Migrant Files, http://www.themigrantfiles.com.

commercial apartments as well. Press reports suggest that there have also been cases where local governments terminated rental contracts of tenants in social housing to shelter refugees. In the Bavarian city of Furth, the requisition of a gymnasium meant the children would for now have to do without physical education. In big cities, Germans and newcomers were jostling for accommodation as housing shortage grows, despite the decline of the ageing German population.

All these could generate social tension and even xenophobia, as reflected in recent attacks—375, including 72 arsons, as of September in 2015 alone—on housing sites to lodge the refugees. Similar attacks on housing centres for refugees have also been reported elsewhere in Europe, especially in small towns. In Purmerend, a town in the Netherlands, for instance, the mayor called the police after protesters to prevent disturbances at a meeting in the city hall to discuss offering shelter to 750 refugees in a new centre or two former schools (see also Chapter 7, Fig. 7.2).

The new arrivals were creating social tensions, which could easily spark unrest and violence. During the New Year's (2016) Eve celebrations in Cologne and other cities of Germany, there were scores of incidents of rape, robbery and violence against women. The number of women filing complaints soared on the following days to more than 500 from 170 at the beginning. Most of the miscreants were of migrant (Arab or North African) origin. This in turn led to noisy demonstrations by right-wing, left-wing and women's rights groups. The right-wing demonstration led by PEGIDA (Patriotic Europeans Against Islamization of the West) was confronted by left-wing demonstrators, with the right-wing protest ending in violent clashes with police. The incidents chilled the atmosphere in the city as it prepared the next month's week-long carnival.

There may also be other sources of tension, linked to the refugees' integration into the labour market. In Germany, the employers have generally been more positive about the economic impact of refugee inflows and were calling for immigrants to have the right to apply for apprenticeship in German industry. However, IFO, the conservative economic think-tank, warned that the minimum wage of EUR 8.50, introduced in 2015, was likely to dissuade some employers to engage low-qualified refugees because of their low productivity and suggested cuts in the minimum wage to avoid possible increases of unemployment (running at the time of writing at above 6% amid slow growth). If, however, the government planned to move in that direction, those who had been pressing for a rise in the minimum wage would be upset and a bitter political controversy could ensue.

As for the effect on the German economy, analysts at several financial institutions including Commerce Bank, Credit Suisse, Deutsche Bank and UniCredit estimated that as a result of the mini stimulus from extra expenditure, there could be a small increase of 0.2–0.3% in growth over the next 12–18 months as a result of the multiplier effect mainly on non-tradeable goods. According to KfW, the German state-guaranteed development bank, refugee-related expenditure could push the country's growth by 0.25% or 1/8th of total growth of 2% in 2016. The IMF estimated the contribution of increased expenditure on food, shelter and integration projects should lead to an increase of 0.3% in growth by 2017 and added that in terms of GDP growth per person, the increase must be much smaller owing to the 2% increase in the country's population. Some others made a more conservative estimate of the growth from refugee-related expenditure. Mark Dowding at BlueBay Asset Management, for instance, thought that growth due to additional public expenditure might be of the order of 0.1–0.2%. The OECD, too, considered the additional growth could be of the order of 0.1–0.2% in 2016 and 2017 (the estimates by the EU Commission are separately discussed below).

However, the effect on public finances was expected to be more mixed. Germany ran a surplus of EUR 21 billion in the first half of 2015, and it had been foreseen that it would still be able to stick to its zero-deficit target in 2015. However, as Thomas Schäfer, finance minister of the state of Hesse, put it, with an estimated refugee-related expenditure of EUR 17 billion in 2016, the risks had increased greatly, making it difficult to assess the future outlook. An independent panel of economists (who advise the German Stability Council) said that the effect of the refugee influx on state finances depended on how quickly the new arrivals were integrated into the labour market. In the event, as in 2014, balanced budget was maintained in 2015, and in March 2016, the coalition government announced its forecast of the same for 2016 and until 2020. However, the previous expectation of a budget surplus of EUR 13 billion for 2016 had to be dropped. It was also agreed to boost the social welfare expenditure by EUR 2.3 billion in 2017 in response to public anger about the refugee-related expenditure of EUR 10 billion foreseen for 2017. This implied a planned increase of 1.8% in federal budget spending in 2016 and a rise of 5.4% in 2017. These increases could have reduced German fiscal manoeuvrability for future discretionary policy action, including expenditure. This is because Germany has imposed on itself a constitutional obligation to maintain fiscal balance over the economic cycle.[5] However, any such concern has turned out to be unfounded. Thanks to several favourable economic factors, Germany posted a budget surplus of EUR 12.1 billion in 2015 and EUR 6.2 billion in 2016; and, as this script was going to press, it announced, a near record budget surplus of 18.5 billion since German reunification in 1991 in the first half of 2017.

Any fiscal shortfall in Germany could have affected the attitude of other Eurozone countries to the budgetary discipline they have collectively agreed on in Brussels. As Holger Schmieding at Berenberg Bank had said, countries in the Eurozone could have cited the refugee-related spending as a justification to exceed the agreed fiscal targets. Since then, Italy and several other EU states had already sought flexibility in applying the EU fiscal rules on the ground of refugee-related additional expenditures, and both Spain and France seemed set to miss the fiscal targets. The situation would have put Germany, which has been insistent in enforcing fiscal discipline in the Eurozone, in a political and economic dilemma. This has not happened.

Between 2009 and 2014, southern European countries sent half a million migrant workers to Germany. Although in theory qualified refugees may compete with potential migrants from these countries, in reality this is not likely to be a major problem at least in the short term, mainly because of differences in both types and levels of skills between the two groups. In fact, unemployment fell to just 3.8% in June 2017. It was also believed that, as expected, high government spending on housing and integration for more than one million asylum-seekers was already having a small but positive short-term effect on the economy.

---

[5] *Financial Times*, "Berlin eases anger over migrants with welfare increase", 24 March 2016.

Medium- to Long-Term Impact

The medium- to long-term economic impact of the refugee influx in Europe, especially the fiscal and demographic effects, on the region is clearly more positive, though not fully automatic. Research across countries shows that, following the lapse of an initial period, immigration generally makes a net fiscal contribution. Estimates made by Bonnin and others showed that in Germany a net constant annual immigration flow of 0.25% of the resident population can reduce by 30% the tax burden of the future-born Germans, in the case of an even distribution among them of the net contribution made by the immigrants.[6] Recent studies in several other countries also showed that while humanitarian migration had a negative fiscal effect during the first 10–15 years, it turns positive with the entrants' progressive labour market integration.

The majority of the new migrants are young. According to Eurostat data available at the time of writing, 81% of the 689,000 migrants who had applied for asylum in the EU countries through August 2015 were younger than 35, and of them 55% were aged between 18 and 34 years of age. More recent data covering 1.2 million asylum applicants (asylum applications should not be confused with asylum granted) showed that 73% were men; 40% of them were 18–30 years old; and 11% were between 14 and 17 years old. They want to work, and if they are effectively integrated into the labour market, they are unlikely to make heavy use of social welfare funds and may well be net contributors to them. Christian Bodweg at the World Bank's human development sector for Central Europe and the Baltics argues that many of these migrants have the potential to not just alleviate declining numbers of workers but also boost innovation in the countries of the region.

Credit Suisse estimated that as a result of the inflows of young refugees the contribution of labour to potential output growth for the Euro area would double from 0.2 to 0.4%, raising potential output growth

---

[6]Bonnin, H. et al., 2000, "Can immigration alleviate the demographic burden?", *Franz Archiv*, 57(1).

from the previously projected 1.1–1.3% a year from 2015 to 2023. HSBC economists arrived at a similar 0.2% yearly increase to growth, with a potential addition of EUR 300 billion to Germany's GDP by 2025.

These benefits need to be seen in the context of the ageing population of the EU countries. According to the European Commission's projection, by 2060, there will be just two working-age persons for each person over 65 years of age, compared with the current dependency ratio of four-to-one. This has led the OECD to claim that the long-term benefits of the refugee inflows were "likely to be substantial" (Fig. 8.1).

This may well have been a little too optimistic, to which several caveats needed to be added. *First*, there is the question of access to labour markets; the waiting period for asylum-seekers, who are of working age, vary between European countries (see Fig. 8.2). While in countries like Norway and Sweden there is no waiting period, it could be as long as 12 months in other countries such as the Czech Republic and the UK. The initial costs for supporting the asylum-seekers could be high for those countries where the waiting period is relatively long.

Second, although, as noted, many of the refugees are of working age, some are not. Those who are too young, or too old to join the labour force, would add to the dependency ratio and welfare cost over the coming years. In 2015, out of the then over 800,000 new arrivals in Greece through Turkey, 28% were children. The fact that during the recession years European (and other OECD) countries had already seen a relative increase in the inflow of such persons with low employment potential makes the problem more serious. Taking into account the composition of the flows by country of origin, the age structure of asylum-seekers, labour market participation rates and the lagged effect of family reunification, the OECD high scenario estimates indicated that (as already noted above) the new arrivals would correspond to less than 0.4% of the labour force of the European Economic Area and Switzerland in 2016. Even for Germany their share would be no more than 1% of the total labour force.

8 Economic Effects of Migration/Refugee Inflows

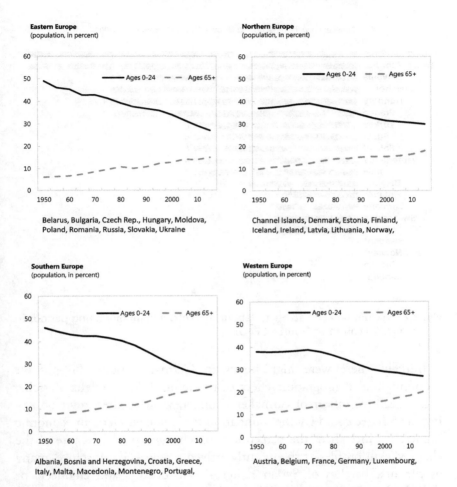

Fig. 8.1 Ageing in Europe (*Source* UN Population Division/Pew Research Center, 2015)

It is true, however, that over time refugees progressively improve their employment potential. On average in the EU, the participation rate of those who entered as humanitarian migrants increases with duration of stay up to about 75% for men and 50% for women (EU Labour Force Survey ad hoc module 2008). According to the German Bundesbank, the rate of labour force participation of the new arrivals would be just under 55%, as against 75% for the native-born.

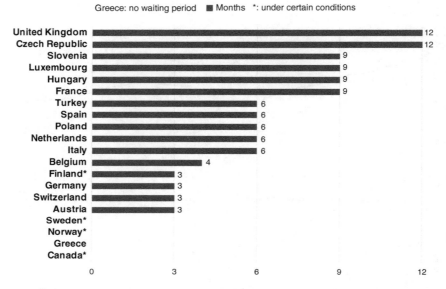

Fig. 8.2 Asylum-seekers' access to labour markets: minimum waiting periods in selected OECD countries (*Source* OECD)

Initially, there were high hopes in Germany about the positive economic and demographic effect of the refugee flows. Dieter Zetsche, chief executive officer of carmaker Daimler, went to the extent of saying the refugee could lay the foundation for "the next German economic miracle".[7] Since then, the perception has changed partly because of the changed skill profiles of the recently arrived refugees. For instance, many of the first batches of Syrian refugees were doctors and engineers or skilled otherwise, but most of those who came later lacked skills. A recent report by the Institute for Employment Research found that only 45% of Syrian refugees have a school leaving certificate and 23% a college degree. This largely explains their low rate of labour force participation.

Third, even the newcomers' improved labour participation rate does not necessarily guarantee that all of them will find employment.

---

[7]Cited in "Germany struggles to find employment for refugees", *Financial Times*, 23 June 2017.

More recently, the German migration office estimated that after five years only 10% of immigrants had a job, and the figure reached 50% only after 10 years. Recently arrived refugees are assumed to converge to such higher levels progressively as they start to settle and learn the host country language. The German Institute for Employment Research projects an unemployment rate of 70% in the first year following the recognition of an asylum-seeker as a refugee, falling to 40% in the third year. A most recent study revealed that in Germany 55% of refugees find employment after 5 years. Current statistics from the Federal Labour Agency showed that the employment rate among all refugees stood at only 17%. It should be noted, however, that the number of refugees seeking work had increased from 322,000 in July 2016 to 484,000—an increase of 50%—by mid-2017, with the number of officially unemployed (those not only have no work but also are not enrolled in any language or skills training programmes) standing at 178,500, which makes an unemployment rate of 36.8%.

Sweden needs an inflow of 64,000 immigrants per year to avoid labour shortage and sustain its social welfare system, according to the country's public employment agency. However, it assumes that all these foreigners will have the same rate of employment as Swedish workers. In reality, this is unlikely to be the case. In Sweden, foreigners are 2.6 times more likely to be out of work. And after 10 years, only half of asylum-seekers have a job. Recent figures show that while the country had an unemployment rate of 6.3%, it was close to 15% among foreign-born Swedes. It was worse among people from Asia and Africa, with unemployment rates of 21 and 29%, respectively. The OECD estimates that in the first five years of resettlement only one in 5 (20%) is likely to have a job. After 10 years, the rate rises to 56%.

Much of course depends on the quality of integration (further discussed below). And although for educated and skilled refugees the prospects for employment are relatively good, the situation is different for the uneducated and unskilled ones. Many of the refugees, especially from Afghanistan and even Iraq, probably belong to the latter group, given the high rates of youth illiteracy in these countries. As mentioned above, even in the case of Syria, many among the more recently arrived asylum-seekers in Germany lacked skills.

IMF points out that in the past immigrants from the same or similar countries (Syria, Afghanistan, Iraq and Pakistan) of origin as the current asylum-seekers found more obstacles to labour market integration than other migrants.

It is also important to note that while the EU may be short of medium- and high-skilled workers—a shortage of 32 million over the next 10 years—it will have a surplus of 23 million of low-skilled workers during the same period, according to one estimate. In Germany, according to a survey by the Munich-based Ifo Institute, published in November 2015, 59% of those surveyed said the chances of employing them for unskilled jobs were low. For low-skilled jobs, the refugees' employment chances were seen to be substantially poorer; 63% of employers saw little possibility of hiring refugees as trainees. For jobs with higher skills, the *negative* figure rose to 78% and for management roles for jobs 97%.[8]

There are, however, some fledging signs of improvement in the refugees' employment prospects. A study by Ifo Institute found 22% of companies had hired refugees in 2016, compared with just 7% in 2015, although many of them were being employed as interns, support staff or apprentices, with only 8% hired as skilled workers. At the same time, authorities were speeding up the asylum procedure so that the asylum-seekers did not have to wait too long to know their status and were also getting better in recognising foreign qualifications. However, bureaucratic delays and complexities, including those related to the determination of the person's residence status, continued to be among the major hurdles to employment of refugees.

Other factors, such as the geographic location of refugees, may also play a part. If, for example, refugees are settled in areas of high unemployment, they may find it more difficult to find jobs, and their arrival may make the situation worse.

Fourth, there remains the question of the levels of skills and productivity of the newly employed refugees. A separate study by experts at the OECD itself has shown that the effects of immigration on growth and

---

[8] "German companies mainly see refugees as unskilled workers". Ifo, Munich. November 2015.

productivity, though positive, are generally quite small. An increase of 50% in net immigration of the foreign-born between 1986 and 2006 generated, on average, an increase of three-tenth of a percentage point variation in productivity growth".[9] (This study was based on the immigration flows for 22 OECD countries between 1986 and 2006.)

And, in all probability, labour productivity of the new refugees will be low, relative to the resident labour force. Even the skilled refugees will need to go through some retraining and vocational re-adaptation, which will take time, before they can achieve the same level of productivity as resident workers.

Finally, while the refugee inflow would improve Europe's dependency ratio and public funding of social welfare for the coming years, it does not offer a long-term demographic solution to the ageing of the European population. This is because of the well-known trend that after a few years of their arrival, most newcomers tend to adopt the cultural mores and practices prevailing in the host society and the fertility rate of women aligns itself to that of the local one. Also, to fully counterbalance the worsening of the dependency ratio and keep it at the current level (1:2.9) OECD countries will need an enormous flow—according to past (2001) UN estimates, with 1995 as the base year, some 154 million by 2050, and far more thereafter.

Contribution Through Self-Employment and Entrepreneurship

What about the new arrivals' contribution through self-employment and entrepreneurship?

A recent survey by KfW[10] revealed that in Germany migrants in general start around 170,000 new businesses each year and are more active

---

[9] Ekrame Boubtane et al., "Immigration and economic growth in the OECD countries 1986–2006", CESIFO Working Paper no 5392.

[10] "Migrants start 170,000 new businesses each year", KfW, Press Releases 2017-04-04/Group. www.kfw.de/gruendungen-durch-migranten.

as entrepreneurs than the local population; they make up 20% of entrepreneurs, but 18% of the country's population. Since migrants venture into self-employment more often than the national average, they make a significant contribution to start-up activity. This is particularly pronounced among educated migrants: the overall rate of entrepreneurial activity among graduates averaged 2.3% between 2009 and 2015 but that of graduate migrants averaged at 3.1%.

Not only do the migrants start business more frequently, but they do so also with higher intensity in three main ways. First, over the period 2009–2015 of all new businesses, 42% were full-time start-ups, but among migrants it was 47%. Second, they devote more time to start-up projects than the average entrepreneur in the country—3.2 hours a week or 11% more. Third, migrants are less likely to set up their businesses on their own, with nearly half of them starting with employees and/or with team partners—48%, compared with 37% for all business start-ups.

The above does not necessarily imply that the new migrants/refugees can make a major contribution to economic growth. Experience in Germany shows that if the rate of entrepreneurial activity is higher among migrants, so also is the rate of failure. In the first two years of the period under KfW survey, 22% of entrepreneurs abandoned their projects in Germany overall, but among migrant entrepreneurs it was 30%. While, as noted above, some of the newly arrived Syrian migrants seem to have the necessary skills and aptitude to ensure business success, it is not the case with the majority of them, especially those who arrived more recently. In fact, as past experience in Germany shows, many migrants are likely to start their own businesses for lack of wage-paid employment opportunities only as a fall-back position. Given the labour market trends and characteristics in Europe as discussed above, it is even more likely to be the case now and in the near future. Finally, some of the financial and other constrains that have placed the migrant entrepreneurs at a disadvantaged position compared with other, non-migrant ones in the past are likely to set limits to the new migrants' contribution to growth (further discussed below).

European Commission's Three-Year Projection of the Economic Benefits

On the assumption of the arrival of three million migrants over the next three years—one million in 2015, an additional 1.5 million in 2016 and then a half-million more in 2017—the European Commission made a forecast of the economic effects of the new arrivals and updated its projections of the EU's economic growth.

In line with the projections made by the banks cited above, it foresaw a possible net gain of a quarter of 1% (or 0.25%) to the Eurozone economy by 2017 as a result of the initial expenditure for welcoming the newcomers. It then based its forecasts of total gains by adding these effects of the extra public spending for the settlement of the refugees in the short run, and the medium-term growth boosted by an increase in labour supply. Taking these additional gains into account, the Commission predicted that the Euro area would grow by 1.6% in 2015, rising to 1.8% in the next year and 1.9% in 2017. The projections echoed the statement made by the Commission's President Jean-Claude Juncker in September 2015 saying that migration should be a "well-managed resource". And Valdis Dombrovskis, the European Commission's Vice-President, called the effects of the flows "temporary tail winds" and urged the EU governments to take advantage of them to manage the refugee crisis and stabilise national finances.

These projections like those made by the banks have, however, come under criticism as being a little too optimistic. Carsten Brzeski, the chief economist at ING-DiBa Bank in Frankfurt, was dubious of the reliability even of the near-term growth forecast about the Eurozone area. As he put it, "There is a big portion of wishful thinking underlying the forecasts, and the downside risk should not be underestimated". Several other analysts wondered if many of the newcomers had the right skills or were young enough to make long-term contributions or if the majority of the countries were equipped or willing to integrate the migrants effectively in their labour markets.

It needs to be mentioned that in a statement the European Commission added some qualifications to its upbeat forecasts. It clarified that the positive long-term impact of the admission of the new workers on growth would occur "providing the right policies are in place to facilitate access to the labour market". As Pierre Moscovici, EU commissioner for economic and financial affairs put it, "This is a public policy issue, it is not going to be spontaneous economic impact".

Further, the report itself tacitly recognised that all the successful asylum-seekers may not have the same level of skills or productivity as the local workers in a country like Germany. It thus presented two simulations of the growth impact of the employment of the new workers. One scenario assumed that the new workers would have the same skills as the German workers, which, the report estimated, would add about 0.2% to the country's economy in 2015, 0.4% in 2016 cent and 0.7% in 2017. In the other simulation, based on the assumption that the new arrivals will all be low-skilled, the Commission recognised the growth impact would be somewhat less—0.4–0.5 in the medium term. The report also acknowledged that in either scenario German employment would increase by about 1% by the end of the decade, but there would be stronger downward pressure on real wages.

These clarifications make the Commission's projections more insightful, although they do not necessarily reflect the full realities of the situation. For instance, as mentioned earlier, all the newcomers are not likely to have the same levels of skills as existing German workers; nor are all of them likely to be low-skilled. Also, as already noted, even if the newcomers have the same levels of skills, they are not likely to have the same level of productivity immediately and that the transition may take quite a bit of time. As for the trends in wages, it is reasonably certain that as the newcomers join the labour force, there will be some immediate downward pressure on wages, although the effects may vary between high-wage and low-wage sectors, depending on the skill profiles of the newcomers and their distribution between the two sectors.

Conclusions

So, what is the conclusion? Overall, the economic costs and benefits of the current refugee inflows, when juxtaposed to each other, seemed to suggest that in the short-run they would not make a big difference either way for the EU's economy as a whole, although over the long term there is likely to be a mildly positive effect. In fact, shortly after the European Commission's report was out, Pierre Moscovici, the commissioner for economic and monetary affairs, took a similar view of the situation by admitting that the migratory inflows would have only a "weak" effect on the EU's growth, but it would be a positive one. He also hedged the European Commission's forecasts by adding that these needed to be checked in the coming months. The point he tried to underline was that the Commission's initial estimates challenged the misconception that the inflows of migrants or asylum-seekers would necessarily be an economic burden. Also endorsed by the OECD, this remains valid. Significantly, the European Commission's projections of the EU's economic growth have turned out to be roughly in line with the more recent estimates/projections by IMF which are as follows: 2.2% in 2015; 1.7% in 2016 and 2.2% in 2017 (projected).

It cannot be overemphasised that when it comes to bona fide asylum-seekers, the overriding considerations must be the humanitarian ones, especially the legal and ethical imperatives enshrined in international law.

A Corollary: The Dark Side of the Inflows, if Mismanaged

What also remains valid is the risk that if mishandled, the huge human influx could lead to significant economic and non-economic costs, some direct, some others secondary or collateral. To illustrate, if these people, especially the youth, are not adequately trained and gainfully employed, instead of becoming net contributors, they would be a burden on Europe's social welfare funds. This in turn is likely to create resentment among the local population and heighten anti-immigrant feelings, alongside increased populism, foster xenophobia and create social tension. The direct economic cost will then be compounded by social and indirect economic costs.

Perils of Reception Without Integration

In the absence of effective labour market integration and positive outcome in terms of employment, many of the jobless will swell the (mostly urban) informal sector. The rapid growth of Europe's informal sector, marked by low productivity and low income, alongside tax evasion and labour exploitation (including via subcontracting to the informal sector by well established firms, as in Italy) is already causing concerns as being a serious drag on European national economies and social progress.[11] If the newcomers are driven to swell this sector further, it will only worsen the situation.

The secondary and longer-term effect could be more worrisome as the expansion of the informal sector is most likely to create ghettos and slums (as in the edges of Paris or Brussels), with a large underclass living in the dark corners of the wider society. Once established, it is difficult to abolish them, and these could easily be breeding grounds of crimes, violence and conflicts. The wider community, too, suffers as the situation leads to a gradual ethical decline, including erosion of respect for law and order, while the levels of poverty and squalor, especially in cities, keep on rising. Lack of social inclusion, including that related to basic human and cultural values, is also apt to make the young migrants rowdy, misogynist and disrespectful of the cultural values of the host society, as seen recently in Cologne and other cities in Germany.

Even more disquietingly, the marginalised, disgruntled and socially alienated youth in these ghettos could turn radical, embrace revengeful fundamentalism and become active and virulent agents of social violence and disruption across Europe and beyond. While the quality of long-term integration is of crucial importance, the aversion of this potential danger needs careful attention right from the time of reception of these people. The seeds of resentment and hatred may be sown if these suffering people after their long and perilous journey are harshly

---

[11]For a discussion of the growth of the informal economy see: Bimal Ghosh, *Huddled Masses and Uncertain Shores: Insight into Irregular Migration*, Martinus Nijoff Publishers/Kluwer Law International, The Hague, 1998, Chapter 2. Also *Managing Migration: Inter-state Cooperation at the Global Level*, Berne Initiative Studies, The Berne Initiative/IOM, 2005, pp. 120–121.

treated at the reception or detention centres. The scars could remain embedded. In such a situation, at least some of them could be lured into fundamentalism and become easy preys to recruiters of terrorist organisations. As already noted, deplorable and degrading conditions in refugee camps and detention centres have been found to be easy hunting grounds for recruiters of fundamentalists.

Marginalisation of Migrants and Its Likely Wider Negative Effects

And if this happens, and European leaders become preoccupied with them, their attention could well be diverted away from urgent structural and economic reforms that Europe badly needs and is desperately trying to address. Meanwhile, conditions in the detention centres, notably gross violation of human rights, are already casting a dark shadow on private investment, as pension funds are coming under increasing pressure to divest from companies that run detention centres accused of human rights abuses. Recent cases of such disinvestment in Australia have drawn attention in Europe to the business model of the private companies such as G4s, the London-based security company, which runs detention centres for asylum-seekers. The situation could carry investment risks due to large-scale litigation or the removal of the service contracts under human rights activist pressure and thus damage the financial stability of the pension funds.

If these potential negative trends take hold as a result of bad management of the new arrivals, it could have a serious impact on European and even global economies. As noted, in April 2016, Jim Yong Kim, the World Bank President, hinted (without going into detail) at the possible destabilising effect of such a situation if it extended to the Sahel and the Horn of Africa and if, as a consequence, refugees started leaving those areas and moving to Europe or elsewhere. The danger cannot be ignored, even if its economic and geopolitical ramifications cannot be assessed at this stage.

In brief, if these mixed inflows are badly managed, not only will Europe forego the potential gains that can be reaped from them, but will also inflict on itself direct and indirect economic losses and make the way for the rise of fundamentalism and future social unrest and upheavals. It should not be forgotten that, so far, most of the violent terrorist activities have been home grown.

It is bad if refugees and those who deserve humanitarian protection are denied access to safe countries, it is no less unethical, and perhaps worse for all concerned if, once accepted, they are left marginalised in the dark corners of the host society.

Initiatives for Integration: A Supportive Approach Works Better

It is good, and not too early, that a few countries notably Germany and Sweden have started giving some special attention to this pressing issue of refugee integration. In April 2016, Angela Merkel announced a proposal for an integration law after six hours of overnight talks with her coalition partners in the government at the time. The centre piece of the proposed legislation spells out asylum-seekers' rights as well as duties; it includes sanctions on those who refuse to attend language lessons and integration training or fail to stay in assigned locations. It seeks to toughen existing German laws under which asylum-seekers are not allowed to choose where they live until they have secured asylum in order to prevent over concentration in cities and ensure small communities share the burden. The proposal also envisages providing 100,000 job opportunities for asylum-seekers with reasonable prospects of success, paying them small extra sums for simple work and facilitating access to apprenticeships.

The proposal, even if not perfect, contained several positive elements. It is unfortunate, however, that it was presented in the context of assuaging public concern at the influx of refugees and could be perceived as a coercive, and not as a supportive or promotional, approach to refugee integration. This perhaps explains at least partly the condemnation of the initiative by some NGOs such as the Pro Asyl as a "disintegration law" on the grounds that it assumed refugees did not wish to integrate and asserted that the real problem lay with the government's failure to provide adequate training facilities, support and job opportunities. Field studies showed that many of the new asylum-seekers were themselves anxious to learn the language of the host country and at least some indicated that Germany was their preferred destination country because of the facilities it offers to learn the language. Reports in June 2016 showed that although state funding for courses had doubled to EUR 559 million, the demand for them was already outstripping supply. However, according to Aydan Ozoguz, commissioner for immigration, refugees and integration, Germany's priority, unlike in the past, was not to find immediate employment for refugees but to ensure they have access to opportunities to learn German language and improve skills needed for an industrial economy. The approach has a twofold, interconnected merit of facilitating refugees' occupational mobility in an advanced economy and their social inclusion, and they do not swell an underclass in German society, which could become a potential source of social tension and conflicts.

While all migrants must abide by the basic human rights and core values of the host society, experience also shows that when measures for integration are coercive or are perceived to be so, they are not necessarily more effective than when they are supportive and seen by migrants as being conducive to their own interest as well as to the wider interest of the host society.

In trying to speed up integration, Sweden, which, with a population of 9.6 million, received 163,000 asylum-seekers in 2015 and saw 80,000 new asylum-seekers in two months in 2016 (equivalent to 25 million entering the EU in one year) seemed to be taking a slightly more flexible approach. Prime Minister Stefan Löfven wanted asylum-seekers to start learning Swedish while they waited for their claims to be processed and to recognise overseas qualifications. Three centre-right parties were in favour of a lower minimum wage to help immigrants/refugees get a job, while the Moderates, the biggest right-wing party, preferred a new job contract that would allow immigrants to study Swedish during almost half their working hours.

There are, however, some serious gaps in refugee integration into the economy of the host countries.[12] Language and vocational training is no doubt critically important, but this needs to be closely linked to

---

[12]Alex Dziadosz, "Syrian exiles in Lebanon seek a refuge in work", *Financial Times*, 21 November 2016.

employment both in existing industries and through creation of new jobs, including by the refugees themselves. Unless this is done, many of the refugees, including those who may have received *only* community-based training in a humanitarian context, are likely to remain jobless. Unemployment rates among Syrian refugees are over 60% in Jordan and 36% in Lebanon, together with large-scale underemployment, according to the ILO. This does not bode well for the future. Heavy, sector-specific employment restrictions on refugees—such as those imposed by the Lebanese government on Syrian refugees, who are allowed to work only in agriculture, construction and cleaning—also limits the scope of their training and employment. These restrictions, also discernible in Jordan, are not likely to change any time soon because of political and sectarian considerations, despite the fact that many consider this a missed economic opportunity.

There are, however, some encouraging signs that the importance of economic integration of refugees has started receiving increasing attention. For instance, under Jordan Compact, signed in July 2016, the EU agreed to provide preferential access to EU markets for Jordan's manufactures produced in 18 specific industrial areas and development zones with at least 15% Syrian labour in the first year rising to 25% in the third year. Also, some NGOs like Basmeh wa Zeitooneh, which organises largely in Lebanon's Palestinian camps where many Syrian refugees have now settled, train refugees to run their own businesses with skills needed such as basic accounting and management, and then give them grants of US$10,000 to get started. However, such programmes are far too limited to meet the needs. It also remains critically important to make sure that the small-scale projects are economically viable and to provide advisory assistance as they become operational so that they may survive and prosper. This is an area where the private sector can play a most valuable role as discussed below.

Role of the Private Sector in Migrant Integration

As mentioned above, at a time when governments are painfully struggling with the problem of reception and placement of record numbers of migrants and refugees, there is a risk that the issue of integration might receive much less attention than it deserves. However, the discussion above has also highlighted the perils that lie ahead for host societies facing a situation of "reception without integration". Refugees and migrants are often forced into lives of despair, which, as noted, can lead to social alienation and revengeful fundamentalism, while the host countries are denied the benefits that effective integration can bring in.

There are at least three important reasons why the private sector needs to play a supportive, but pro-active role to help avert this deplorable situation. First, even with new international aid, which is mostly directed to governments, public funding will remain awfully inadequate to meet the needs of effective economic and social integration of so many foreigners from such diverse cultures and countries. A second reason which constrains the public sector's role in this area is, as the recent experience in Germany showed, the likely resentment and even resistance of the national population to a sudden, big increase in public expenditure for foreigner's integration. A third reason that argues for a complementary role for the private sector lies in its comparative advantage over the public sector in interacting with refugees and migrants and providing advice and assistance for promoting certain types of economic activities and services by refugees and migrants themselves, including their access to government legal, financial, employment and health services. It has been already noted that relatively large numbers of the newcomers are sufficiently enterprising and a high proportion of them are young, and many of them are likely to respond positively to initiatives for setting up or helping such economic and social, including self-employment, activities. In Turkey, where although even recognised Syrian refugees are reported to have difficulties in participating in the labour market, at least some of them have been quite successful in setting up and running small enterprises on their own, and, in some cases with the participation of local workers (discussed later in this chapter).

Even in countries, such as Germany, where employers have taken some initiatives in promoting integration, the activities have been mostly limited to providing apprenticeship and other forms of vocational training. However, these activities by the private sector can be widened to include promotion of viable business activities, including small enterprises, start-up projects and social-impact initiatives.

Experience in Germany shows the proportion of the needs for external funding (around 21%) is about the same for migrant enterprises as for all enterprises. However, there are important differences in the funding sources they tap. Migrants are obliged to raise funds from their personal networks such as families and friends, which is not easy and the amounts remain limited.

Also, they are more likely to rely on bank overdrafts than the general average in the sector (29% compared with 18%) and bank loans less often (31% rent vs. 38%).[13] This makes borrowing more costly and is indicative of the difficulties they face in accessing bank loans not just because of their discounted social standing and perceived low credit-worthiness but also because of other constraints such as language barriers that make it harder to obtain and use all the relevant information or negotiate loans. The private sector can play an important role in removing these constrains and facilitate the supply of low-cost and safe credit to migrants' start-up businesses and help make them more viable and competitive.

At the September 2016 summit on refugees and migrants in New York, President Obama called for US companies to play a larger role in solving the refugee crisis. It is encouraging that in response to this call, George Soros, Chairman of Soros Fund Management and philanthropist, has announced the establishment of a US$500 million fund to promote precisely such activities.[14] It will invest in start-up and established companies, social-impact initiatives and businesses founded by migrants and refugees themselves. Its focus, according to Mr. Soros, is on products and services that truly benefit migrants and host communities. All investments will come from his own Open Society Foundation, and any profits will go to Foundation activities, including its programmes that benefit migrants and refugees.

Although at the time of writing full operational details of the new fund were yet to be formulated and known, it was announced that the new fund will work closely with the UNHCR, which has welcomed

---

[13]KfW, "Migrants start 170,000 businesses each year", op. cit.
[14]*World Street Journal*, 19 September 2016. http://on.wsj.com/2cEoJnK.

the initiative, and the International Rescue Committee for guidance related to its investment. The initiative is a step in the direction and should spur similar action by other actors in the private sector. This is also an area in which other international organisations too can play a useful role. As mentioned, the World Bank has already promised an interest-free loan of US$3–4 billion to the governments of Jordan and Lebanon to help them deal with the refugee and migration inflows. However, the situation also offers a wonderful opportunity for the Bank's private sector arm, International Finance Corporation (IFC), to stimulate and support private sector initiatives in support of refugees and migrants. Since private sector capital is shy for investment in this kind of refugee-related small enterprises for products and services, IFC can provide funds as seed money to create such private sector funds or to those already existing but are short of capital. This should go hand-in-hand with technical advice and operational support from IFC, including techno-economic viability assessment and marketing studies, whenever needed, for both start-ups and existing enterprises founded by or related to refugees and migrants. By stepping up action along these lines, the IFC could at the same time enhance its own social and economic relevance at a time when the world passes through the unprecedented migration and refugee crisis in decades.

Economic Impact of Terrorist Attacks and Human Resilience

Although most of the terrorist activities have been home grown so far, there have also been some notable exceptions. The November 2015 attacks in Paris, for example, were initiated by the ISIS group in Syria, planned in Brussels and then executed in France. Attacks in Belgium were also homespun, but with external links. The co-perpetrator of the San Bernardino attacks in the USA was a foreigner holding a K1 visa. And the risk of terrorists infiltrating into the migration-refugee flows is becoming increasingly real (see Chapter 7), as reflected in the acknowledgement by the US government sources that the ISIS group had tried to infiltrate into Syrian refugee flows to reach the country. At least 31 US states had expressed their reluctance to accept Syrian refugees mainly on grounds of security risks, although the US government had accepted 10,000 of them. It is no surprise that in the context of the growing concern over terrorist activities, both home grown and from outside, the question of economic impact of terrorist attacks has started receiving closer attention.

In the past, a few studies have been made on the cost associated with terrorism. In 2003, after the terrorist action by the ETA in Spain, two economists, Alberto Abadie and Javier Gardeazabal, made an estimate of the loss that the Basque county may have suffered as a result of the attacks.[15] They came to the conclusion that over time, they reduced the gross domestic product of the region by 10%. Another study, made in 2004 by Zvi Eckstein and Daniel Tsiddon of the economic effects of the terrorist attacks on Israel, came to the same estimate of the cost—a decline of 10% in the country's GDP.

However, as Tim Harford, an independent economist and a columnist at the London-based *Financial Times*, recently noted, the aftermath of the recent terrorist activities in the USA or Europe tells us a somewhat different story.[16] The 9/11 attack on Manhattan destroyed over $13 billion worth of office space, damaged $17 billion more and possibly led to the loss of 75,000–100,000 jobs mostly in the travel and tourism sector. Yet the city of New York bounced back rapidly, recovering losses, although rebuilding infrastructure, of necessity, took longer time.

A look back at three more recent attacks reveals similar human resilience. It is known that normally, stock markets show more volatility than the real economy. However, pull backs in the equity markets that occurred immediately after the Madrid train bombings in 2004 and the London bombings in the following year recovered soon after the attacks and the markets posted solid gains later on. What happened after the Boston Marathon bombings on 15 April 2013, the more recent ghastly

---

[15] Alberto Abadie and Javier Gardeazabal, "The economic cost of conflict: A case study of the Basque county", The *American Economic Review*, vol. 93, no. 1 (March 2003), pp. 113–132.

[16] Tim Harford, "Nothing to fear but fear itself?" 17 November 2015. http://timharford.com/2015/11.

attacks in Paris on 13 November 2015 and the suicide bombing in Beirut the day after reveal a similar effect. After an immediate fall as a panicky reaction to these attacks, the stock markets regained their composure. On Monday, 16 November, the first trading day following the attacks in Paris and Beirut, the US stock markets posted their strongest sessions in three weeks. The German stock market, DAX, climbed 2.3% in five days.

It would be misleading, however, to make too many generalisations or draw sweeping conclusions on the basis of these experiences, including the performance of stock markets. A violent geopolitical event can alter consumption and destabilise credit markets as well as investment. And the impact may vary depending on the type of economic activity, the intensity of violence, the actual or anticipated frequency of attacks and other surrounding circumstances, and the direct cost of the attack due to the extent of the loss or damage caused by it.

Even in the case of rapid recovery of the economy, including the stock market as a whole, from their knee-jerk reactions, the negative pressures are likely to continue for a much longer period in sectors such as travel and tourism, and as a consequence airlines, hotels and restaurants may suffer more and much longer than the rest of the market. In the short term, consumption may fall, although the demand for protective devices and selected non-perishable goods is likely to be boosted.

A study by Abel Brodeur at the University of Ottawa of the terrorist attacks over the period 1970–2013 in the USA reveals a more balanced picture of their effects on employment, while confirming human resilience to such attacks.[17] It shows that successful attacks, in comparison with failed attacks, reduce the number of jobs in the targeted counties by around 5% in the year of the attacks. The effects fade away after two years, and the neighbouring countries do not seem to suffer from the attacks. The decrease in the physical capital stock of a country partially explains the temporary reduction in jobs.

---

[17] Abel Brodeur, "Terrorism and employment: Evidence from successful and failed terrorist attacks". iza.org/dp9526.pdf.

Successful terrorist attacks and the fear of more such attacks may, however, have a big impact on public finances. Following the terrorist attacks on Paris on 13 November 2015, France, for example, announced public expenditure of 735 million Euros over a three-year period on anti-terrorist measures, including the creation of 2689 new jobs. In 2015, the government planned to meet the expenditure out of the reserve fund, without deviating from its commitment to save 50 billion Euros in an effort to bring the public budget deficit back to the Eurozone's limit of 3% of GDP. Since in the following two years the expenditure was to be accommodated in the budgetary allocations, it would imply a shift in its composition. In the USA, following the 9/11 attacks, the government may have spent $650 billion to enhance security in public places. This may have helped restore public confidence, but as vigilance has continued, it has also entailed recurrent public expenditure.

Frequency and intensity of attacks, too, play a critical role in shaping one way or another human attitudes and economic behaviour in the face of such events. When the attacks are sporadic but minor, people may get used to them and move on with their lives and economic activities with resilience, although the situation may not encourage new private investment, especially foreign direct investment and could lead to outflows of some skilled and professional people. There is some evidence that as attacks become frequent, investors tend to become inured to their effects and they rattle markets less than they once did. This probably explains at least in part why over the past five years or so the reactions of the market following attacks have been found to vary between an overall 0.5% fall and a medium gain of 2% in the ensuing five days.[18] However, if the attacks are flagrantly violent and multifaceted as well as frequent and unpredictable, as presently in several of the conflict-ridden Middle Eastern countries, the resultant insecurity and disruption invariably undermine all economic activities, especially long-term investment, both internal and from outside.

---

[18]Nicholas Wells/Mark Fahey, "Terror attacks don't rattle markets like they use to do", *CNBC*, 22 March 2016.

A special characteristic of terrorist acts as distinct from deadly accidents and natural disasters lies in its psychological impact. Tim Harford cites the example of a small plane that, a few months after the 9/11 terrorist attack in the USA, crashed into the Pirelli Tower in Milan killing three people. There was initially much panic as it was thought to be another terrorist attack, but when the news came that it was a not a terrorist attack it brought widespread relief. As Mr. Harford puts it, "this was strange. Knowing that the crash was an accident (and not a terrorist attack) does not make them any less dead. But it makes their death less unsettling". I am inclined to think that it was less unsettling because it was unlike a premeditated and targeted attack deliberately perpetrated by fellow human beings as all terrorist attacks are.

Part II

Challenges Across Regions

9

Conflicts in Eastern Europe: Exodus from Ukraine and Russia

Human Outflows Driven by the Vagaries of a Geopolitical Game

Migration in Ukraine has been seriously affected by the Russian annexation of Crimea in March 2014 and the subsequent violent fighting over two breakaway eastern provinces seeking independence with Russia's support. Even before the conflict, dissatisfaction with the quality of life, lack of economic opportunities, poor public services and endemic corruption had been encouraging people to emigrate from the country. A large-scale survey, predating the conflict, revealed that 49% of the respondents were interested in moving abroad.[1]

However, following the 2014 pro-reform EuroMaidan uprising, annexation of Crimea by Russia and, its proxy war in eastern Ukraine, a wave of patriotism surged through most parts of the country, raising hopes that with economic and political reforms emigration pressure would decline. There was a feeling of resurgence also within the already established global Ukrainian diaspora of 5–6 million and among the new migrants abroad. They took an active interest in the reform and reconstruction of their country of origin. In Britain, the Ukrainian community,

---

[1] Bilan, Yuriy et al., *Perceptions, Imaginations, Life satisfaction and socio-demography: The case of Ukraine*, EUMAGINE Project paper 11, 24 September 2012. Available online. As discussed in Chapter …, this, however, does not mean that they would necessarily move.

© The Author(s) 2018
B. Ghosh, *Refugee and Mixed Migration Flows*,
https://doi.org/10.1007/978-3-319-75274-7_9

London, EuroMaidan, for instance, launched a powerful fundraising campaign for the benefit of the Ukrainian army and the war victims.

Sadly, however, as the momentum soon shifted from reform to defence, and corruption remained unabated, the mood of the people changed again. War in eastern provinces was placing a heavy strain on the economy. With rising taxes and prices, a hike in energy cost, alongside cuts in wages and social benefits, many people were exposed to severe economic hardship, while corruption was still running rampant. According to a public survey, nearly half of the respondents thought corruption had not diminished while 52% thought it had increased.[2] As a Ukrainian businessman and philanthropist put it, "Billions still are being taken out of the state budget. Many politicians are in the pocket of oligarchs. Still, people 'practised' (sic) in the art of corruption hold senior positions in the ministries and in parliament".[3]

* * *

Two initially promising mass upheavals—the Orange Revolution in the late 2004 and the Maidan protests of 2013–2014—have failed to dislodge the entrenched and parasitic ruling class. With hopes for a better future thus receding, and war in the eastern part of the country turning increasingly violent, many were impelled to look for opportunities abroad.

Ukraine's Painful Reform

The situation, aggravated by the devastation in war-torn eastern Ukraine and Russian annexation of Crimea, led to large-scale displacements, both internal and external. In October 2014, the UNHCR estimated that since the beginning of the conflict a total of over 824,000 persons had

---

[2]Piechal, Tomasz, *Disappointment and Fear—the Public Mood in Ukraine*, 2015, Warsaw. OSW. Available online.
[3]Victor Pinchuck, "Only tough love can stop Ukraine squandering its last chance", *Financial Times*, 16 December 2014.

been affected—430,000 were internally displaced in Ukraine, 387,000 had moved to Russia, and 6600 were asylum-seekers in the EU and 581 in Belarus. Since then, with the worsening of the security situation in eastern part of the country, these numbers have increased. As of May 2015, over 6400 people had been killed, and an estimated two million were forcibly uprooted, of which 1.3 million (including those in Crimea) were internally displaced and 700,000 refugees (Fig. 9.1). Ukrainian asylum claims in Europe had jumped 13 times over the previous year to 14,000.[4] At the time of writing, despite several ceasefire agreements, including the one in Belarus in February 2015, sporadic,

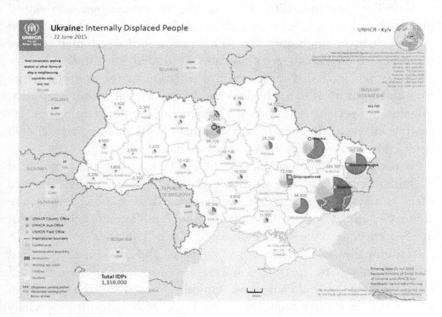

Fig. 9.1 Ukraine internally displaced people as a result of the conflict (*Source* UNHCR. http://www.migrationpolicy.org/sites/default/files/source_images/ukr_IDPs_A4L_22.06.2015.jpg)

---

[4]Franck Düvell and Irina Lapshyna, "The EuroMaidan protests, corruption, and war in Ukraine: Migration trends and ambitions", "*Migration Information Source*", 15 July 2015. MPI, Washington, DC. Part of the information concerning migration in Ukraine in this section is drawn, or adapted from this document.

but fierce, fighting was going on in eastern Ukraine along the border with Russia, uprooting many more people.

In addition to forced internal and external displacements by the Russian annexation of Crimea, and war in eastern provinces of Donetsk and Lugansk, the country has seen an increase in the outflows of people as a result of the flights to avoid military conscription and in search of better economic and educational opportunities or being driven by a combination of such motivations. A 2014 small-scale survey at Lviv Polytechnic/National University revealed that 82% of respondents wanted to work abroad, 80% wanted to study abroad, and 44 planned to live outside the country.

A similar trend was discernible among the professional and skilled people. For instance, according to a 2015 study by an employment agency, 80% of applicants for senior and middle-level management positions would like to work abroad; the underlying motivations for 41% of them included tense political situation in the country, desire for a stable future of their children and low salaries in Ukraine. Student migration, especially to Poland, for higher education or training has also sharply increased. In the first few months of 2015 alone, over 23,000 students had left to study at Polish universities.

At the time of independence in 1991, Ukraine had a population of 52 million and reached an all-time high at 52.8 million in 1993; since then, as a result of emigration and national demographic decline, the country's population had shrunk by nearly 10 million at 42.9 million in 2015, according to the State Statistics Service of Ukraine.[5]

Traditionally, Russian-speaking easterners and the lower educated in the country have in general migrated to Russia, while western and more educated Ukrainians have typically moved to the European Union and in smaller numbers to the USA. Male migrants, especially the low-skilled, would move east and west outside the country, working mostly in the construction industry. Female migrants, by contrast, would generally move south to Italy and work mostly as caregivers. If

---

[5]It should be noted, however, that during the period, 1960–2014, Ukraine's population averaged at 48.34 million, showing to date little change in the size of the country's population. State Statistics Service of Ukraine, *Population of Ukraine*. 2014, 2015. Available online.

the present conflict and accompanied violence continue, these trends in migration are likely to gather further momentum except that the non-Russian-speaking Ukrainians who might have otherwise headed to Russia would avoid doing so; many of them might be seeking asylum or move elsewhere in the EU. Meanwhile, the contraction of the Russian economy due to the decline in oil prices and western sanctions following its annexation of Crimea was also affecting the level and composition of Ukrainian migration to Russia, and related remittance inflows, which saw a decline of 9.9% in 2015, compared with 2014, according to the World Bank.

* * *

Driven largely by the continuing conflict and its ravages, as of early June 2015, some 900,300 Ukrainians are reported to have sought asylum or other forms of legal residence in neighbouring countries, with the majority in Russia (746,500) and Belarus (81,299). The authenticity of these figures has, however, been questioned. It is possible that many Ukrainian citizens who had been working as irregular migrants in Russia took the opportunity to declare themselves refugees to regularise their status. It has also been suggested that these figures are perhaps politically tainted and inflated, given the Russian overtures that continue to blame Ukraine and the EU for the conflict and thus for uprooting such high numbers of suffering people.

This apart, in 2014, 14,040 Ukrainians applied for asylum in the EU member states, the largest number in Germany (2705 applications), followed by Poland (2275), Italy (2080), France (1415) and Sweden (1320). However, of the 2985 Ukrainian applications processed in 2014, only 150 were accepted as refugees, and 500 granted other forms of protection, making a total of just over 22%. Poland, which as of March 2015, had rejected 645 applications and not granted refugee status to any of the applicants. In 2016, only 16 were accepted. It held the view that affected Ukrainians in eastern parts of the country could seek protection in other areas of the country as they are considered safe.

Even so, the EU portends to be a major player in Ukraine's migration. By 2014, Ukrainians already ranked fifth among the top non-EU resident groups in the European Union. They were also the top recipients of first-time residence permit holders, numbering 237,000 in 2013, compared with 150,000 granted in 2011. And, they were the second most common recipients, after Russians, of Schengen visas of all kinds, although the number of short-stay visas decreased from 1.54 million to 1.35 million in 2014. This was mainly due to a decrease in Ukrainians' spending power on tourism, combined with a decreased demand for short-term foreign labour owing to the economic downturn in the EU. The situation, however, has been changing fast, with a rapidly increasing number of Ukrainian temporary workers in Poland. This is being driven by labour shortages in Poland, caused by its economic recovery and falling birth rate and the previous emigration of 2 million Poles to other EU countries, on the one hand, and the economic recession, unemployment and a plunging currency in war-ravaged Ukraine, on the other. According to a recent report in *The Economist*, in 2013 there were only 527 temporary foreign workers in the central Polish town of Kalisz.[6] By July in 2017, there were nearly 10,700, most of them from Ukraine. Definitive figures are hard to come by, but it is estimated that at any given time around one million Ukrainians were working in Poland.

Equally important, as an EU Eastern Partnership member, Ukraine has been engaged in negotiations for a visa-free regime of movement to the EU for several years, and in May 2014, it initiated the second phase of its Visa Liberalization Action Plan, including implementation of the legal framework and institutional reform already developed in phase one.[7] In December 2015, it looked likely that Ukraine's efforts to secure a visa-free travel regime by July 2016 would be successful, but this was undermined by the postponement (until 1 January 2017) of a vital financial requirement—the filing of public declaration of assets—in

---

[6]"Plugging the gap", *The Economist*, London, 5–11 August 2017.
[7]European Commission, *Report from the Commission to the Council and European Parliament. Sixth Progress Report on the Implementation by Ukraine of the Action Plan on Visa Liberalisation* {SWD (2015)705} (final). Brussels, 18 December 2015.

the budget bill.[8] The government announced that this "shameful" error would be rectified soon through a new budget bill and had still hoped to secure visa-free travel facility by July 2016. It was also hoped that when this happens, and Ukraine makes significant progress in economic reforms, new possibilities might be opened up for Ukrainians to have more opportunities of legal entry through other migration channels.

In April 2016, there was, however, a setback in the process of Ukraine's integration with the EU when in a referendum the Netherlands voted against the EU–Ukraine free trade deal and gave a symbolic victory to Russia which had opposed the deal and sparked the Ukrainian conflict with Russia. The vote, however, was non-binding and the turnout at 32% was small, though it passed the threshold to be valid. Although the result did not necessarily derail the EU–Ukraine association deal, it was slowing down the overall integration process. It was nonetheless expected that visa-free travel for Ukraine might finally be approved by the EU in September 2016.[9] However, some uncertainty had remained. Finally, on 15 September 2016, the European Council agreed to grant Ukraine visa-free travel rights on condition that the scheme can be suspended in case of an emergency. The scheme went to the European Parliament, which duly approved it and confirmed that a visa-free travel regime for Ukraine would be effective as from 11 June 2017. However, at the time of writing, there was still some uncertainty regarding the fate of the proposed trade and security agreement because of the Dutch reservations, and negotiations were going on in Brussels to find a solution.

Integration of the internally displaced people has been placing a heavy strain on the economy of the country, especially on host communities, their infrastructure and budgetary resources. Field surveys carried out by the IOM showed that lack of employment and housing facilities were the biggest problems hindering the integration of the new arrivals in the local communities. Only a little more than half of those who had jobs before displacement managed to find new employment in their new places of residence, and nearly 40% of those surveyed were facing financial difficulties in

---

[8]Olena Goncharov, "Visa-free travel may be at risk after apparent tampering with budget bill", *KyivPost*, 4 January 2016.
[9]*Visa-Free Europe*, 10 June 2016.

meeting their needs. About 70% of them were living in rented accommodation, and the high rent was a concern for many of them.

In keeping with its policy of decentralisation, the government was laying emphasis on increasing the capacity of local communities as they grappled with problems of the displaced persons' social protection, accommodation, health care and education of their children. At a recent meeting, Vadym Chernysh, the minister for temporarily occupied territories and IDPs, recognised that the local communities needed state support as they faced these formidable challenges. With donor support, the IOM has initiated some activities to help the local communities and the displaced people. These included provision of training in business for IDPs and members of local communities, vocational training and grants for equipment. The organisation has also helped about 50 communities in seven regions of Ukraine by providing training in community development, as well as through social cohesion initiatives and refurbishment of social infrastructure and assets. However, the impact of these efforts remained to be seen, and in any case, these were still too little compared with the needs, especially for income-generating and quick-impact, but sustainable, projects.

After a difficult period, and despite continuing, but somewhat subdued, corruption, Ukraine was showing some signs of recovery. Growth was expected to reach 1.5% in 2016 and 2.5% in 2017. It received a long-delayed $1 billion tranche from a 17.5 billion IMF loan programme. However, as the IMF emphasised, more needed to be done to tackle corruption, attract investment, improve business environment and ensure fiscal consolidation in order to secure faster, sustainable and inclusive growth. As these lead to improvement of living standards of people, the prevailing undue pressure for emigration should also decline. Much, however, depends on the geopolitical situation, as noted below.

The situation in the conflict zone of Donetsk remained deplorable. Thousands of people were without electricity, gas and water, as the ongoing conflict continued to take heavy toll on civilian infrastructure criss-crossing the conflict line, according to OSCE chief monitor in Ukraine, Ertugrutal Apakan. Roadblocks installed by the Ukrainian army and the separatists were severely restricting freedom of movement. The long waiting time at the roadblocks with searches and interrogations was causing enormous hardships and provoking anger among the local population. As the UN monitoring mission observed, in the region of Donbas continuing conflicts and sporadic violent outbursts were unsettling the normal civilian life of people and depriving the most vulnerable of the basic necessities of life and threating their security.

Russia's Losses: Western Sanctions, Tensions Within the Middle Class

Just as the conflict was creating outflows of people and internal displacements in Ukraine, the economic consequences of the conflict, including, in particular, the western economic sanctions on Russia, were having an impact on emigration from Russia. Although the country's statistics are somewhat opaque to give a detailed breakdown of the situation, there is little doubt that there has been an exodus of foreigners from the country since the conflict began. According to the Russian government source itself, excluding those who fled to Russia to escape the conflict in Ukraine, there were 417,000 fewer foreigners in the country in January 2015 than a year ago—a drop of 4.7%. As of January 2015, the number of Germans, who have been among the largest foreign investors, had fallen to 240,113, representing a 31% decline since a year before. Likewise, the number of persons from the USA was down by 36%, from the UK 38% and from Spain 41% over the same period.

The data provided by the Federal Migration Service in Russia include tourists and visitors as well as those on short- or longer-term business assignments and settled expatriates. There are some clear indications that many of those leaving were on business assignments. Given the economic downturn and uncertain outlook, companies have been drastically cutting cost by reducing staff, and the trend has accelerated since the end of 2014. The number of German companies, for example, had fallen to 6000 from 6167 in late 2013, according to the German Chamber of Commerce.[10]

---

[10]Kathrin Hill, "Foreign exodus from Russia gathers space", *Financial Times*, 5 February 2015.

Russia's car market had seen a contraction of 10% by the end of 2014 and was expected to fall 35% in 2015. This was seriously affecting the scale of production of the western and Japanese car companies operating in Russia. Foreign companies in general were trying to ride out the storm by adopting what analysts dub "hibernation strategy" involving a mix of cost-cutting, production stoppages and job cuts to tackle low capacity utilisation.[11] Concerns have also been growing over emigration of Russians as the Federal Statistics Service announced that over 203,659 persons had left the country in the first eight months of 2014—a 70% increase on a year earlier. The sharp increase may at least partly be due to a change in the methodology used for the purpose, but there are indications that it may not be the only reason. For instance, a New York-based consultancy, run by Yuri Mosha, mentioned that while in 2014 they had dealt with just 60 clients, in 2015 they were signing up as many as 30 clients a month. Mikhail Denisenko, at the Moscow-based Higher School of Economics, estimated approximately 5000 Russians moved to Israel in 2014, compared with roughly 4000 in 2013.

The conflict has created a wedge through the Russian middle class and has also led to an opposite trend in emigration from Russia as those who are in favour of Mr. Putin's policy are now less likely to emigrate. The conflicting trends in emigration are also reflected in the number of Russian families who, due to the recent political and economic developments, want to send their children abroad for schooling and eventually emigrate themselves and the number of families who no longer wished to send their children abroad as it could be seen as unpatriotic or wanted to have their children back in Russia as a mark of patriotism. However, overall, the pressure for emigration is clearly increasing. What makes it more worrisome is that most of those who are leaving are the most educated and creative, the most financially secure and from Moscow where the sentiment is the strongest against the policy pursued by Mr. Putin.[12]

---

[11] "Western groups find Russia tough to harvest", *Financial Times*, 21 April 2015.
[12] "Putin drives a wedge through the middle class", *Financial Times*, 22 May 2015.

The Outlook

The future of migration in Ukraine is likely to be shaped mostly by the vagaries of the geopolitical game between the West (notably the EU) and Russia, and the attitude of the new US administration under President Trump. At the time of writing, the situation looked extremely uncertain. The Minsk agreement signed in 2014, and twice amended and reaffirmed, has been hanging in balance. The country is now gripped by a painful, frozen conflict, and bleeding from periodic outbursts of conflicts and violence. Durable peace has remained a distant dream. If the present stalemate persists, emigration from Ukraine and outflows from Russia (of both foreigners and some Russians) will continue. If, on the other hand, the political and/or military situation distinctly changes for the worse, these displacements could accelerate and turn disorderly and disruptive, though it is difficult to presage what might be their exact configuration. News coming at the beginning of 2017 revealed an escalation of what had become almost daily skirmishes. Unless arrested, this could add to the death toll of about 10,000 during the past three years and further threaten the Minsk agreement to end fighting and stabilise eastern Ukraine.

Adding to the tension, in July 2017, Alexander Zakharchenko, the pro-Russia leader of the self-proclaimed Donetsk People's Republic announced a plan to replace Ukraine (excluding Crimea) with a new state "Malorossiya" (Little Russia). The threat is not new. Already, in 2014, when Victor Yanukovich had lost the election, his supporters in Donetsk had used the slogan "Back Yanukovitch as President or we split the country". Although a Kremlin spokesman stated that it was a personal initiative and that Moscow remained committed to the Minsk agreement, the revival of the declaration (many analysts think it was Moscow-inspired) is a further blow to the agreement and the hope of a negotiated settlement of the three-year-old conflict any time soon.

10

Central America: The Unresolved Migration Conundrum

Children Trapped, Women Raped in the Midway to Escape

Migration from Central America towards Mexico and the USA is not new. In addition to the traditional migration in search of better economic opportunities, widespread violence and gross violation of migrants' human rights in recent years were generating huge flows of migrants seeking entries at the southern borders of the USA. The UNHCR has documented an increase of 1185% in the number of asylum applications from citizens—adults and children—of three countries, El Salvador, Honduras and Guatemala, dubbed "Northern Triangle", between 2008 and 2014.[1] During 1980 and 2015, Central American migration to USA had increased nearly 10 times—from 354,000 in 1980 to 3,385,000. According to the Council on Hemispheric Affairs, every year some 500,000 Central American migrants pass through Mexico, but it remains unknown how many reach their intended destination. Between October 2014 and April 2015, US immigration authorities detained over 70,400 non-Mexican migrants, mostly from Central America, along its southern border.

---

[1] UNHCR, Press Release, 9 July 2014, Washington, DC. http://www.unhcrwashington.org/children.

© The Author(s) 2018
B. Ghosh, *Refugee and Mixed Migration Flows*,
https://doi.org/10.1007/978-3-319-75274-7_10

This marked a sharp decline from 162,700 detained during the same period 12 months earlier. At the same time, however, Mexican officials detained 93,000 Central American migrants, far exceeding the 49,800 detained in the same period a year earlier.

The flow through Mexico has however continued unabated. According to a recent (2016) report of the Movimiento Migrante Mesoamericano (M3), driven by poverty, joblessness and violence, between 800 and 1000 people reach the southern shores of Mexico every day in an attempt to reach the USA to realise the "American dream".[2] As they do so illegally, they risk their lives and uproot their families. The first challenge is to avoid arrest on Mexico's southern border by the police who can deport them or drive them into sexual slavery or forced labour. The perils, they say, cannot be worse than "the threat of death, violence and hunger" that awaits them at home. During the journey, many fall victims to the violence of criminal gangs, resulting in assaults, sexual slavery, kidnapping or murder. Reports suggest that kidnapped migrants were often used to extort ransoms from their families while the migrants were physically abused. As the criminal gangs often act in collusion with migrant carrying transport agencies and reportedly at times also with the local authorities, migrants find themselves in an extremely vulnerable situation.

In an attempt to improve the situation, in 2014 the Mexican government, urged by the USA, launched its Southern Border Programme with the twin objective of protecting migrants' human rights and bringing the inflows under control by deploying more law enforcement agents. Five centres were set up at the Mexico–Guatemala border and 500 federal agents deployed to dismantle organised criminal groups that targeted the migrants and to discourage irregular migrants from boarding a cargo train—dubbed *The Beast* or *The Death Train*—that crosses the Mexican territory. Mexican official figures indicate that some 250,000 irregular migrants were deported in 2015—around 41% to Guatemala, 30% to Honduras and 19% to El Salvador. However, the unofficial sources put the number of deportations much higher—around 400,000.[3]

---

[2]World News Report, 3 January 2016, http://einnews.com.

[3]"Central America's unresolved migrant crisis", *The New York Times*, 20 June 2015. http://www.nytimes.com/2015/06/16/opinion/central-americas-unresolved-migrant-crisis.html?

The Mexican government claims that the programme has helped rescue large numbers of migrants. However, critics seem to think that the programme is unduly repressive. For instance, the Inter-American Commission on Human Rights thought the programme has not met its objectives. Following a visit to Mexico in June 2014, the UN High Commissioner for Human Rights said that the Mexican policies to prevent illegal immigration were excessively harsh. The harsh interception of migrants has also meant that fewer Central Americans who have genuine reasons to seek asylum were getting an opportunity to make their case. Mexico has a lengthy asylum application procedure and approved only 16% of claims filed by Central Americans during the first nine months of 2014.[4] Critics also argue that the crackdown on "the death train" as the route of choice for poor migrants is aggravating the risks that migrants will rely more heavily on human traffickers, making them even more vulnerable to extortion by corrupt officials and to abuse by criminal gangs who make promise of safe passage.

Another development was set to put additional pressure on Mexico's southern border. Rumours that Cuba's détente with the USA would soon remove Cuban's automatic entitlement to asylum once they reach the US shore, as provided in the 1996 Cuban Adjustment Act, led to a surge of arrivals of Cubans in Mexico on their way to the USA. Almost 6500 Cubans arrived in Mexico in the first nine months of 2015, more than five times as many as a year earlier. And the surge seemed to have continued as reflected in the fact that more than 8000 Cubans had been processed by November 2015, according to the Instituto Nacional de Migracion (INM), the national migration institute. The Centro Nacional de Derecho Humanos (CNDH), the national human rights commission, noted that more than a thousand Cubans had turned up at the Tapachula migration centre in the space of one week in October 2015, overwhelming migration officials.[5]

---

[4] *World News Report*, op. cit.
[5] "Cuba's détente with US drives Mexico migrant crisis", *Financial Times*, 10 November 2015.

At its south-western border, the USA has invested heavily over the past decade largely to stop illegal migration, with the budget of its Customs and Border Protection agency shot up from US$5.9 billion in 2004 to over 12 billion.[6] However, as in Europe and elsewhere, far less has been done to fight the root causes of the flight of desperate people seeking safety and a better life. The Obama administration did draw up a plan to help improve the region's economy and curb violence and crime, and had asked Congress for US$1 billion to implement the plan. However, in June 2015 the House of Representatives marking up the bill that allocates foreign aid set aside a paltry $300 million, and the lion's share of the financing was approved for border security. Subsequently, in an unexpected but encouraging move the lawmakers passed the new Appropriation bill of 2016 which included an allocation of $750 million to fund the Alliance for Prosperity plan for the three Northern Triangle countries (further discussed below).

Child Migrants: On the Run for Elusive Escape

> We have faith that we will make it. If we don't, it's God's will that we should remain in this hell of a country.[7]

A most worrisome feature of the Central American migration to the USA concerns the hapless child migrants. It is not that child migration is a problem unique to Central America. The number of refugees and asylum-seekers under the age of 18 has been on the rise reaching 50% of the world's refugee population at the end of 2013, and more separated and unaccompanied children are now claiming asylum than ever before, according to the UNHCR. In 2013 alone, more than 25,300 individual asylum applications for children were lodged in 77 countries,

---

[6]Ibid.
[7]Comment by Marisa Najar, a single mother from Honduras, travelling with her two children, ten and six, and 15-year-old niece, following her failed attempt to reach the USA through Mexico. "Under-age and on the move". *The Economist*, 28 June 2014, http://economist.com/node/21605886.

10 Central America: The Unresolved Migration Conundrum

excluding the USA. Minors represent an important share of migrants and asylum-seekers crossing the Mediterranean in appalling conditions, with as many as 14,000 children arriving in Italy alone in 2014. And their share is rising. For instance, the proportion of children among the new arrivals in Greece was one in three in January 2016, compared with one in 10 in September 2015. According to UNICEF, over 7000 unaccompanied minors arrived in Italy from North Africa during first six months of 2016—double the number of arrivals during the same period in 2015. The EU as a whole received as many as 88,000 minor asylum seekers in 2015, eight times the number received in 2013; between 2008 and 2013, the number varied between 11,000 and 13,000; by 2014, the number had already jumped to 23,000.

What has made the phenomenon especially disturbing for Central America was precisely the massive increase in the number of child migrants in 2014 (Fig. 10.1). The sudden spike of such flights created a serious problem also for the USA as some 68,541 children, both unaccompanied and accompanied by a parent, usually mother, sought entries at its southern borders. Apprehensions at the south-west border

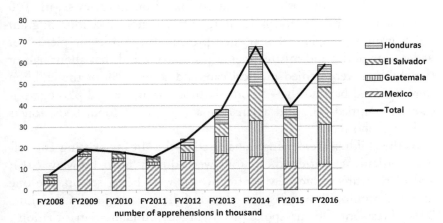

Fig. 10.1 Apprehensions of unaccompanied child migrants at the US southwest border by country of origin, FY 2008–FY 2016 (*Source* William A. Kandel, Congressional Research Service May 2016. US Department of Homeland Security, US Border Patrol; and Customs and Border Protection). *Note* The figure for 2017 is estimated on the basis of the numbers for the first quarter. https://www.cbp.gov/newsroom/stats/southwest-border-unaccompnied-children/fy-2015

were more than in any of the previous six years and four times as many as in FY 2011. After a decline in the number of arrivals of unaccompanied children from 68,541 in 2014 to 39,970 in 2015 due to increased enforcement efforts, it rose again to 59,692 in the FY 2016 (October 2015–September 2016), according to Customs and Border Protection.

The situation turned worse as a rising tempo of violence, increased frequency and intensity of assaults and extortion in these countries created a general climate of fear and insecurity, leading to massive outflows of unaccompanied children, who have been among the worst victims. In the face of attempts by criminal gangs to forcibly recruit them or subject them to kidnapping, murder and sexual abuse, especially of girls, Central American children flee or are led to flee in search of safety abroad.[8] The sudden and massive influx of children overwhelmed the US agencies that must deal with it. Under the Trafficking Victims Protection Reauthorisation Act of 2008, border agents cannot hold children for more than 72 hours at their facilities, after which they must either be placed with their relatives in the USA or sheltered at centres run by the Office of Refuge Settlement (ORS). Border Patrol facilities, where the children were being detained, were themselves cramped and ill equipped to cope with the situation. Based on interviews with 100 children in Texas, American Civil Liberties Union and four migrant rights groups complained that they presented a consistent picture of widespread abuse and mistreatment. They also found that about half of the children were denied medical care and some 70% of the children were detained beyond the 72 hour statutory limit. Leaked photographs showed cramped cells and an inadequate supply of food, beds, toilets and water showers.

As the children were being transferred to the already existing 100 refugee settlement centres, these, too, were already filled by May 2014; and of the three more new centres which were being set up, the one in San Antonio, Texas, was also already full by early June. On 2 June 2014, President Obama spoke of an "urgent humanitarian situation",

---

[8]For a detailed discussion, see Muzaffar Chisthi and Faye Hipsman, "The child and family migration surge of summer 2014: A short-lived crisis with a lasting impact", *Columbia Journal of International Affairs*, vol. 68, no. 2, 2015.

and in an environment of rising tension, there was a heated and wide controversy. Human rights organisations argued for the protection and fair treatment of the detained children, while the critics in US Congress blamed the Administration saying that the crisis was due to the leaky borders and its lax treatment of irregular migrants in the previous two years. Ted Cruz, a Texan Senator (and a Presidential candidate in 2016), fumingly remarked, "Children are pushed in the hands of criminals".[9]

True, in 2012 President Obama had ordered that illegal immigrants brought to the USA as children and had spent five consecutive years since 2007 should have their deportation deferred. However, as mentioned above, the law, already enacted in 2008, that intended to stop sex trafficking, basically allowed extra legal protection to unaccompanied Central American children pending a decision by court. President Obama blamed the instability in Central American countries for the sudden upsurge. However, the President of Honduras had a different view of the situation. On 13 June 2014, in a meeting at the US Chamber of Commerce he maintained that it was a security problem provoked by trafficking in drugs that were consumed in the USA.

The problem was aggravated by the delays in processing the claims in court. Since there were around 5000 immigration cases pending for every qualified judge, the delay was inevitable. Delays in detention centres and legal processing of claims created, in turn, yet another problem. Traffickers exploited the delays by circulating the wrong message and false rumours that the unaccompanied children would be automatically given permission to stay in the USA.

---

[9]"Central America's unresolved migrant crisis", *The New York Times*, 20 June 2015. http://www.nytimes.com/2015/06/16/opinion/central-americas-unresolved-migrant-crisis.html?

On 20 June 2014, President Obama dispatched Vice-President Joe Biden to Guatemala to meet the Central American leaders to quash the false rumours, explain the no "open-arms" US policy and discuss how the US government can help the Central American governments in addressing the child exodus. In the months that followed, the governments in the region stepped up their cooperation in managing the flows. The Mexican government initiated its new Southern Border Programme (discussed above), tightened its border control and deployed more resources to intercept and deport large numbers of migrants, including children. Also, the three Central American Presidents launched a set of coordinated measures to disrupt the human smuggling networks, increase public security to protect the children and facilitate reintegration of the children sent back by Mexican and US authorities. In fighting the false rumours, they also emphasised the perils and likely failure of efforts for the children to have access to the USA and gain residency status there.

However, these measures were clearly inadequate to deal with the root causes of child migration. After a relative lull in the earlier months of the year, the flows of migrant families and unaccompanied children increased in the fall of 2015, although they were smaller than the surge in the summer of 2014. In an environment of heightened security concern following the 13 November 2015 terrorist attacks in Paris, the US Border Patrol apprehensions, too, increased—a rise of 150% for migrant families over the same period in 2014, while the number of children apprehended more than doubled. Many of the women and children were fleeing violent gangs and endemic sexual violence, which led the UN High Commissioner for Refugees to issue an early warning of a "looming refugee crisis". A report released by the agency spoke of the women facing a startling degree of violence and assigned El Salvador to the top most position in the world for the rate of murders of women while Guatemala ranked the third, and Honduras had the highest murder rate over all. Given the high rates of murder in all three countries, not surprisingly, many of these women and children sought out Border Patrol agents, instead of avoiding them, for protection and eventual access to asylum-seeking procedure.

10 Central America: The Unresolved Migration Conundrum

In a recent book,[10] Oscar Martinez, a journalist, graphically describes the scary realities of organised crime in the Northern Triangle and reveals how politicians and police forces that are too corrupt, impoverished or incompetent fail to respond.

In El Salvador just two gangs, Barrio 18 and Mara Salvatrucha have around 70,000 members between them. Savage turf battles between gangs have made murder mundane, a daily event. A ceasefire truce between gangs had halved the number of murders from March 2001 until late 2013.

However, when the truce collapsed, and the rate of killings jumped, record numbers of unaccompanied children started fleeing to the USA in 2014. In 2015, the number of murders surged to 6700, representing a 70% increase compared with 2014 and making the tiny El Salvador the most murderous peacetime country in the world (Fig. 10.2).

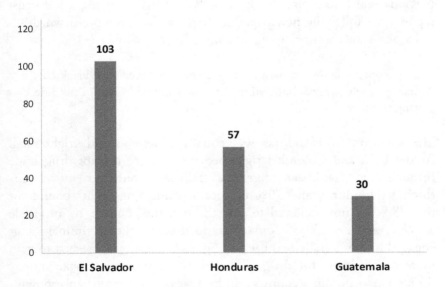

Fig. 10.2 Homicide rate in Northern Triangle countries (per 100,000 people) (*Source* Insight crime, David Gagne, January 2016)

---

[10]Oscar Martinez, *A History of Violence: Living and Dying in Central America*, Verso. March 2016.

Since then, the government has sought to respond to the situation by following an iron-fisted policy, but it has led to a twofold problem. The trigger-happy security forces have been empowered to shoot at gang members if they felt threatened by them, and they have since been using violence quite indiscriminately as part of the gang crackdown. According to El Salvador's human rights ombudsman, in 2015 they killed 13 people in two shoot-outs, including four teenagers, the youngest aged 15. At the same time, some were fearful that with the leaders of the gangs held in jail incommunicado, the gangs' younger members could become more radical leading to more violence again. The fragile, insecure situation has been encouraging the flight of Salvadorian children with or without their families.

Between October 2015 and March 2016, there were 11,000 apprehensions of Salvadorian children and their families trying to cross into the USA, more than three times the rate in the same period of the previous years, according to the Pew Research Center. As a journalist reports, the following newspaper coverage of the grisly pre-dawn death toll around the country on one day was a "matter-of-fact":

> One woman's body, her wrists and feet tied, dumped in a black bag; a man, possibly hanged, bundled in sheets and stuffed in a suit case; a dead gang member....

The situation in Honduras was equally gruesome and frightening. As the USA and Colombia tightened measures to disrupt drug trade through the Caribbean corridor, traffickers rerouted movements through Honduras, and 79% of cocaine-smuggling flights bound for the USA was now believed to pass through the country. In an article in *The New York Times*, Sonia Nazario describes how criminal gangs engaged in narco trade had been vying for control over the turf to gain more foot soldiers for drug sales and distribution and make money through extortion in a country run by a weak and corrupt government. The gangs have been putting pressure on children to work for them, using schools as a recruiting ground. The pressure to join the cartel is wide and relentless, and extortion under threat to life is common. As Ms. Nazario puts it, "Asking for help from the police or the government is not an option in what some consider a failed state. The drugs that pass through Honduras each year are worth more than the country's entire gross domestic product".[11]

In 2014, the US immigration authorities had expected more than 70,000 unaccompanied minors crossing into the country unlawfully, the majority of them from the three Central American countries. And the number of girls among them was increasing rapidly, according to a Pew Research Center study. Thus, not surprisingly, through May, the number of unaccompanied girls caught at the US–Mexico border increased by 77%. What was more disconcerting was that many of the girls who were fleeing their home country because of fears of being sexually assaulted were meeting the same fate on their journey, according to the UNHCR. Amnesty International reports that 80% of all women, including young girls, were raped on their way to the USA through Mexico—up from a previous estimate of 60%. Rape can be perpetrated by anyone along the route, including guides, fellow migrants, bandits or government officials, according to a recent investigation.[12] Many were critical of the US government policy in dealing with the situation. As Chan Greg Chan, director of advocacy group, American Immigration Lawyers Association, put it, the government response to the influx of the children has been "nothing short of a policy that undermines our basic humanitarian and asylum laws".[13]

Root Causes Inadequately Addressed

It is most likely that, unless the root causes of the problem are effectively addressed, protection of the vulnerable Central American children will remain a formidable challenge. Protection needs to go

---

[11]Sonia Nazario, "The children of the drug wars: A refugee crisis, not an immigration crisis", *The New York Times*, 11 July 2014.

[12]Eleanor Goldberg, "80% of Central American women, girls are raped crossing into the US", *Huffington Post*, 12 September 2014.

[13]Remarks to the Associated Press, cited in *International Business Times*, 23 April 2015.

hand-in-hand with prevention of the causes that generate relentless pressure for the children to flee. This calls for vigorous action to promote growth and employment, increased security and good governance. Sadly, these measures, involving structural reforms and good governance, have been receiving much less attention than they deserve. True, the US administration had taken some tentative steps towards this goal, but not in a systematic manner. For instance, on 8 July 2014 when at the cusp of the crisis President Obama had asked Congress for an allocation of funds to deal with the situation (mentioned above), none of the four proposed items of expenditure had anything to do with the root causes of the flight in the countries of origin.

However, subsequently, in January 2015 the US President proposed a Plan for Central America—a $1 billion aid programme for improving the economic and security situation in the three countries.[14] The funds were to be spent for increasing training and support for the police and armed forces, as well as measures to promote transparency and accountability, including strengthening tax collection and encouraging foreign direct investment through market liberalisation. The plan, modelled after the 1999 Plan Colombia, had drawbacks; nor was it free from criticism. But it was a step in the right direction for addressing the root causes of child exodus. In the event, as already mentioned, US Congress approved only $300 million and that mainly for border security. However, the spending bill passed in December 2015 mentioned above provides for an amount of $750 million to address the root causes of the human outflows, including child migration, by stimulating economic growth, reducing income inequality, promoting educational opportunities as well as for targeting human trafficking and improving governance. Insecurity, lack of economic opportunities and political instability, especially in Honduras, convulsed by a disputed election and claims of voter fraud could well have been a tremendous risk for the USA as well.

---

[14] Joe Biden, "A plan for Central America", *New York Times*, 29 January 2015. http://www.nytimes.com/2015/01/30/opinion/joe-biden-a-plan-for-central-america.html?

Clearly, the economic and political reforms needed to fight the root causes cannot be imported from outside. The USA can encourage and help the process, but the ultimate responsibility and prerogative lie with the people and leaders of the Central American countries themselves. They must have the ownership of the problem and its solution. Central America's problems did not start and will not end with Washington. As Professor Mike Allison at the University of Pennsylvania commented, "Whether the US is partly responsible, an equal or greater share of the blame lies with the [local] economic and political elites who have no interest in developing democratic political and economic systems".[15]

Child Migrants in Painful Limbo! Issues Involved

> I want to avoid drugs and death. The government cannot pull up its pants and help people. My country has lost its way.[16]

An important policy issue that has gained wide attention was whether or to what extent the children who were fleeing from their home country should be considered for protection as refugees. The answer calls for a clear understanding of the causes and conditions that have been driving them to flee. A number of studies, including field investigations, throw light on the situation.

A survey recently conducted by the UNHCR on the basis of interviews with 404 children who had arrived in the USA from Honduras, El Salvador, Guatemala and Mexico revealed that for 58% of those interviewed violence was the primary cause for leaving.[17] Another report by the same agency, based on interviews with 300 detainee children, put gang violence and domestic abuses high among the causes of the flights. The situation was quite different in the past, as reflected in a similar

---

[15]Cited in *Financial Times*, "Honduras crisis shines spotlight on Central America's problem", 1 December 2017.

[16]Comment in despair by Carlos Baquedano Sanchez, a 14-year old Honduran, explaining how hard it was to get away from the cartels. Cited in: "The children of the drug wars" op. cit.

[17]UNHCR, Children on the Run: Unaccompanied Children Leaving Central America and Mexico and the Need for International Protection, Washington, DC, July 2014.

survey made in 2006 of children arriving in Mexico which found that only 13% were fleeing violence.

These findings are in general confirmed by several academic studies. For instance, a field study[18] prepared during 2013–2014 by Elizabeth Kennedy at the American Immigration Council revealed that violence, extreme poverty and family reunification played important roles in pushing children to leave their country of origin. As many as 59% of Salvadorian boys and 61% of Salvadorian girls listed one of these factors as the main driver of their flight away from home. In some parts of El Salvador, however, poverty was the most common reason, especially for the adolescent males, to leave. One in three children cited family reunification as a primary reason for leaving, fear of crime and violence being the underlying motive to reunify with the family. Field surveys by several other organisations, including KIND (Kids In Need of Defence, a non-profit organisation), the US Conference of Catholic Bishops and the Women's Refugee Commission, confirmed that, while there were also other common considerations, the most common cause of the exodus had been and continued to be increasing gang and cartel violence that disproportionately affected young people, especially girls.

Significantly, studies also revealed that the children's urge to join their families abroad, too, was closely linked to pervasive violence and lack of security in their home country. Over 90% of the children interviewed had a family member in the USA, with just over 50% having one or both parents there. After three decades of migration from these Northern Triangle countries, about one in five of Salvadorians and one in 15 Guatemalans and Hondurans already live in the USA. Seemingly, the children and their families had decided they must leave due to violence and other coercive push factors and then chose to go where they had family connections, rather than chose to leave because they have family elsewhere.[19] Children were thus arriving not just in the USA

---

[18]Elizabeth Kennedy, "No childhood here: Why Central American children are fleeing their homes", American Immigration Council, Washington, DC, 2005. 1 July 2014. https://www.mricanimmigrationcouncil.org.

[19]Elizabeth Kennedy, "No childhood here: Why Central American children are fleeing their homes", op. cit.

but also in other neighbouring countries. The UNHCR documented an increase of 432% in asylum requests in other, relatively safe, nearby countries including Belize, Costa Rica, Nicaragua, Panama and Mexico (see Fig. 10.3).[20] It can be argued, as some analysts have done, that the urge or rather the coercive need for establishing connection with the family is dictated in most cases by rampant violence and lack of security in the home country.

Under the 1984 Cartagena Declaration on Refugees, those who have fled their country because of their lives, safety or freedom have been threatened by generalised violence, internal conflicts or massive violation of human rights should receive protection as refugees. Given the overwhelming evidence that rampant violence and lack of state security are a predominant cause of child exodus, most of them would seem eligible

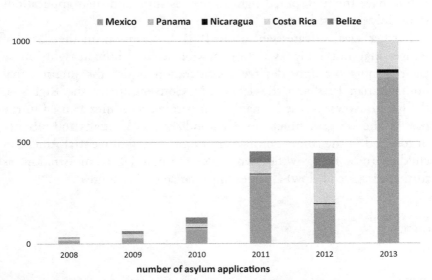

Fig. 10.3 Central Americans seeking asylum in neighbouring countries (*Source* UNHCR)

---

[20]UNHCR, "Children on the Run: Unaccompanied children leaving Central America and Mexico and the need for international protection", 2014. Available online. http:/unhcrwashington.org/children.

to international protection as refugees under the Cartagena Declaration. The situation may be a little less clear-cut under the narrower definition of a refugee posited under the 1951 UN Convention on the Status of Refugees, and its 1967 Protocol, although several UNHCR field surveys have confirmed that violence and in many cases individual persecution or threats thereof were the main causes of the flight. The organisation has also recognised the situation as a *refuge crisis*, and, as noted, in one survey it found that 56% of the unaccompanied children from these countries should qualify for protection as refugees. As for the public attitude in the USA, a survey by the Public Religion Research Institute shows that a majority (69%) of Americans think that children arriving from Central America should be treated as refugees and allowed to stay in the USA if the US authorities determine that it is not safe for them to return to their home.[21] In any case, all those fleeing violence and persecution have the undisputed right to seek asylum, and their applications to be duly processed.

Further, even in cases where the 1951 Convention on the status of refuges may not apply, as victims of violence and human rights abuse these minors certainly deserve consideration under the international humanitarian laws and the 1989 UN Convention on the Rights of the Child. Access to the humanitarian parole procedures as used in the past by the US government for Cambodians and Haitians and recently introduced in the context of in-country processing of Central American children (now being withdrawn under the new US administration, as further discussed below) assumes importance in this context.

---

[21]Religion and Politics Tracking Survey, 29 July 2014, Public Religion Research Institute. Washington, DC.

Determination of Eligibility to Protection: In Quest of a Child-Sensitive Approach

The determination of eligibility, however, poses many challenges for national asylum systems. It requires child-sensitive approaches and mechanisms to safeguard their best interests in keeping with the Convention on the Rights of the Child. Children need protection in terms of accommodation, basic health and social facilities and a caring environment. The EU's Humanitarian and Protection programme has been supporting some of the activities designed to meet the humanitarian needs of these children. However, safety and protection remain the paramount needs of these uprooted children.

The asylum officers and judges need to be trained and experienced in child-sensitive interviewing techniques to elicit full and frank information from fearful, often traumatised children. It is equally important that they are assisted by qualified and child-sensitive lawyers. The non-profit organisation, KIDS in Need of Defence (KIND), that provides *pro bono* lawyers to represent immigrant children, estimates that between 40 and 60% of these children potentially qualify to stay in the USA under current immigration laws—and they actually do so—if they have a lawyer by their side. Late in 2014, the US administration started a special US$2-million programme to provide 100 lawyers and paralegals to represent and help the children in court proceedings. In launching the programme, the then attorney-general Eric Holder remarked, "How we treat those in need, particularly young people who must appear in immigration proceedings, many of whom are fleeing violence, persecution abuse or trafficking—goes to the core of what we are". Although a step in the right direction, it has understandably come under criticism by some human rights groups as being long overdue and too little in relation to the urgency and magnitude of the need. Some others have expressed concern about the likely lack of training the lawyers needed to deal with this type of court cases.

In-Country Processing: Useful, but Inadequate

Another issue that has come under spotlight in the context of child exodus concerns in-country processing of protection claims (also discussed in Chapter 5, above). In December 2014, the US administration launched its in-country programme to provide the Central American children direct access to the US protection procedure and help avoid perilous journeys by unaccompanied minors. Three groups of Central American parents in the USA were eligible to sponsor in-country interviews for their children back home: lawful permanent residents, holders of temporary protection status and those recognised under Deferred Enforced Departure order. The eligibility of potential beneficiaries was also specifically defined: he/she must be under the age of 21, unmarried, resident of one of three Central American countries and the child of an eligible parent. It provides for admission of two categories of persons—refugees and those on parole on humanitarian grounds.

The in-country programme has the singular merits of providing unaccompanied minors direct access to the US protection procedure, without having to undertake labourious and perilous journeys. As discussed earlier in Chapter 5, in-country interviews as a screening arrangement are, however, not free from criticism; and the specific US programme for Central America suffers from some serious limitations which diminish some of its potential merits.[22]

First, its positive impact remains limited because of the narrow eligibility criteria for sponsoring parents in the USA as well as for the potential beneficiaries in home countries. Currently available statistics show the majority of the Central Americans living in the USA—1.4 million out of 2.7 million—have an unlawful or irregular status, and are therefore excluded.[23] The programme's real significance is also somewhat reduced by the fact that the lawfully resident Central Americans are already eligible to sponsor the admission of their children to the

---

[22] I wrote this comment when the programme was still in operation, pre-dating its termination in August 2017 by the new US administration, discussed later in this chapter.

[23] Faye Hipsman and Doris Meissner, "A piece of puzzle", MPI, Washington, DC, 2015. I wrote this comment when the programme was still in operation, pre-dating its termination in August 2017 by the new US administration, discussed later in this chapter.

USA. Making any such application effective may involve some delay (currently 2 years because of the backlog and quota limits), but many of them may have already gone through the process. Also, the recognition and admission of applicants as refugees under the in-country programme are subject to the overall regional ceilings for refugees which are already fixed, currently at 4000. However, these ceilings are considered to be somewhat flexible and they do not in any case apply to the beneficiaries of humanitarian parole.

Second, the screening process seems to be lengthy, complicated and time-consuming, with multiple interviews, laborious checking for security and medical clearances and DNA tests to validate parental relationship. The process is thus hardly congruous with the urgent need of those fleeing persecution. As a critic has put it, the programme is more suitable for orderly departure for immigration rather than for protection of persons fleeing persecution.[24] *Third*, as in other similar cases elsewhere, the arrangement may avoid the need for perilous and arduous journey to the destination abroad, but it is not totally bereft of dangers inside the country. In an environment of rampant violence, frequent extortion and pervasive insecurity, multiple trips to the screening centres are most likely to expose the unaccompanied minor children to retaliation and violence by gangs lurking in their neighbourhoods, as has also been the experience of many of the children sent back to the home country.

As of mid-August 2015, a total of 3344 applications were received (2859 in El Salvador, 426 in Honduras and 59 in Guatemala) under the programme. Given the short time that had elapsed since its inauguration, it was not possible at the time of writing to make a definitive assessment of the impact of the programme. At least some of the potential pitfalls of the programme can be mitigated by applying appropriate safeguards. These include: reducing the security risks for the applicant children by locating the processing centres in safe places and different areas of the country, and minimising the number of the applicant's personal visits to the centre; shortening the period of processing by using smart and streamlined application and interviewing procedures; timely

---

[24]Norman S. Zucker and Naomi Zucker, *Desperate Crossing: Seeking Refuge in America*, 1996, Routledge, New York.

security clearance and expeditious transfer of the eligible applicants to the USA. The arrangement allowing for the application to be initiated by a parent in the USA was already helpful in reducing the number of the applicant's personal visits to the processing centre and the related security risks; the plan to build in Honduras a shelter for the applicants during the screening process should also reduce such risks. Also useful were the provisions allowing humanitarian parole for those who deserve protection but not as refugees and those concerning expeditious processing for applicants reporting security concerns.

All in all, it is safe to say that while the programme, if thoughtfully implemented, would be useful for a limited number of vulnerable children, it cannot be expected to make a wide impact on the situation. In January 2016, the US government announced that working with the UNHCR would allow (adult) individuals in Northern Triangle countries who were facing persecution to apply for protection as refugees. The initial reception and screening would take place outside the USA and the origin countries, and the reception centres would be administered by the UNHCR. If the plan was properly executed, with adequate support, it could also indirectly help the child migrants' situation.

A Sad End of the Programme

In August 2017, when I had already finished writing the above, the whole saga of the Central American Minors (CAM) parole programme came to a sad end when the Trump administration formally terminated it, shutting the door on 27,214 children who had conditional approval to enter the USA. This also meant that 1465 minors already in the USA under the special parole programme will not be allowed to renew their status and find other pathways to extend their stays or return to their troubled home countries. The decision was based on an internal review of the programme as part of President Trump's executive orders seeking to tighten immigration control. The administration officials insisted that the decision to terminate the special parole did not end their chances of coming to the country, but they would need to apply through the standard parole programme that has long been in place. The snag in the argument is that it was precisely the inadequacies of the other avenues of entry that had prompted the Obama administration to introduce the CAM parole programme. Despite the difficulties involved, 99% of those who had applied won admission to the USA under the programme, according to the US citizenship and immigration service officials.

No surprise that the decision was sharply criticised by rights groups. "Our concern is that the administration is completely abandoning these children and leaving them in a real situation of immediate danger", remarked Lisa Frydman, Vice-President at KIND. Likewise, J. Kevin, a senior director at the Center for Migration Studies, was highly critical of the decision to terminate the programme and thought it was "mean spirited". "It is not a large number of kids, and they're really vulnerable" he added.

11

South-East Asia: The Sad Plight of the Rohingya

Persecuted on Land, Floating and Dying at Sea; Spiraling Violence, Hard to Escape

The sudden discovery in early May 2015 of seven human skeletons and subsequently mass graves containing 150 bodies at smugglers' camps on either side of the Thai–Malaysia border led to a process that brought under spotlight a human tragedy that had existed for quite some time but had attracted little attention of the outside world. At about the same time, a small vessel carrying journalists from the *BBC* and *The New York Times* spotted in the waters of the Bay of Bengal a small fishing boat packed with some 300 people, including 10 dead. For quite some time, traffickers have taken migrants—mostly Rohingya Muslims feeling persecution in Myanmar and some poverty-stricken Bangladeshis—to Thailand to extract ransom money and then to Malaysia and Indonesia (see Fig. 11.1). Those who could not pay were abused, raped or killed and left behind.

As Thailand, which was gaining notoriety as a hub of human trafficking, reportedly operating under the watch and not infrequently with the connivance of the local police and elite, decided in the face of the threat of US sanctions to close its borders to the traffickers' trade, the boats were not allowed to reach Malaysia or Indonesia. The traffickers then left the migrants in crowded boats with little food, water and other amenities.

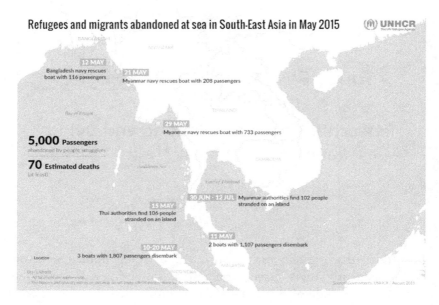

Fig. 11.1 Refugees and migrants abandoned at sea (*Source* UNHCR)

The boats were pushed back by each of the three countries as they tried to reach their territorial waters, and some 5000 migrants or more were thus stranded in high seas. Only the fishermen brought food and water to the boats. At least 300 died from starvation, dehydration and beatings.[1]

The source of the problem lies mostly in Myanmar where for years nearly one million Rohingyas, who are considered to be illegal Bengali immigrants, have remained badly persecuted. Many of them are in Rakhine state (formerly Arakan). They remain mostly stateless and are often considered the most persecuted minority in the world. They are asked to go back to Bangladesh, but those who do are typically denied Bangladeshi citizenship on the grounds that they are from Myanmar and remain isolated and exposed to persecution. In the mid-1990s, some 200,000 were brutally repatriated to Bangladesh (Fig. 11.2).

---

[1]The number (70) of deaths shown on the map refers to the month of May alone.

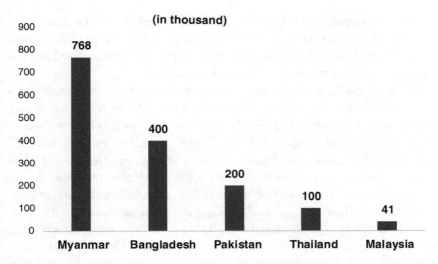

Fig. 11.2 The plight of the Rohingya: South and South-East Asia (prior to 2016) in thousand (*Source* IOM/FT)

More recently, in 2009 and 2010 there were anti-Rohingya campaigns and severe crackdowns in Bangladesh on the unregistered Rohingyas that led to large-scale forced displacement, distress and hunger. Some Rohingyas (until recently, numbering some 32,700) were accommodated in two official camps managed and recognised by the government as refugees. The others are labelled "undocumented Myanmar nationals".

According to the Arakan Project, a human rights advocacy group, on 10 January 2010 a crackdown was unleashed by law enforcement agencies was unleashed against these unregistered Rohingyas who had settled outside the two official refugee camps in Cox's Bazar district. More than 500 Rohingyas were subsequently arrested, and some of them were pushed back to Myanmar, and others were sent to jail under immigration law. Fearing arrest, harassment or facing expulsion, more than 5000 self-settled and unregistered Rohingyas fled their homes and most moved to a makeshift camp in Ukhia in search of safety, swelling its population to over 30,000. The Arakan Project suspects that the forced displacement may well have been a device to push the vulnerable unregistered Rohingyas into the makeshift camp. Until recently, the makeshift camp residents did not receive food assistance and were denied access to means of livelihood as they would face arrest if they left the camp to find work. Food insecurity and hunger were about to cause a humanitarian crisis.

In Bangladesh, until the more recent inflows, there were three categories of Rohingya refugees: there were some 30,000 refugees, as part of the inflows in the early 1990s living in two camps run by the government and serviced by the UNHCR. They have access to basic services, including food assistance, health care and education. The second category comprises an estimated 200,000–500,000 Rohingya who arrived before October 2016 and live in makeshift sites and local villages and, until recently, had no access to humanitarian aid, as mentioned above. The third category comprises over 70,000 Rohingya refugees who fled the conflicts and military operations in between October 2016 and February 2017 (discussed below); they lived a precarious life without any humanitarian assistance. Several thousand of them were, however, believed to be hosted in two official camps, straining the capacity of existing infrastructure and services. Overcrowding and poor sanitation carried the risks of outbreaks of diseases. Many more of these newly arrived Rohingyas were living in makeshift sites or new ones that had sprouted sporadically, with flimsy structures, and unhygienic latrines and miserable living conditions.

In Myanmar, the situation was tough for the Rohingyas due to the long-standing mistrust and animosity of the Rakhine community. The Rakhine, who have a proud history of independence, are themselves a persecuted minority. Following the British conquest of Arakan (now Rakhine), thousands of Bengalis were brought to Arakan from Chittagong and other parts of Bengal. Resentment grew among the Arakanese as they felt that jobs and land were being taken over by the irregular Bengali immigrants and that they had little control over it. Subsequently, the situation worsened during World War II when the retreating British forces armed some Muslim Arakanese to fight against the Buddhist Rakhine, who were mostly supportive of the Japanese. In post-war Burma, the Rakhine, like the other 135 officially recognised minorities, suffered from discrimination by the Burmese military governments.

Against this background of mistrust, in 2012 the murder and rape of a Rakhine woman by three Muslim Rohingyas sparked a violent attack on Rohingyas. The clashes between the state's Rakhine Buddhist community and Rohingya Muslims left at least 170 dead and 140,000 homeless. More than two years after the violence the government forcibly segregated Rohingyas from the rest of the population in the state. They live confined in enclaves—effectively rural ghettos—from which they are not allowed to leave. If they do, they are likely to be killed. The confinement has virtually destroyed their ability to rebuild their lives after the violence and arson of 2012. In 2015, as a backlash from the Rakhine Buddhist extremists, government scrapped the Rohingya's white identity card and the voting rights that go with it. As a spokesman for the UN office for the Coordination of Humanitarian Affairs in Myanmar put it, lack of citizenship rights and "of movement means people don't have access to their fields to go farming, don't have access to the sea to go fishing, and don't have access to markets to trade". Not surprisingly, trafficking networks sprang up to sneak Rohingyas away from such horrors and misery. The United Nations reckons some 100,000 may have surrendered to the traffickers following the violence of 2012.

Several South Asian countries have tolerated and indeed benefited from the people smuggling trade (Fig. 11.1). Thai officials gave the smugglers space to flourish not just by quietly allowing the boat people to proceed to Malaysia but tolerating the enrichment of a few corrupt locals through the human trade. Malaysians, for their part, have sometimes turned a blind eye to the influx which helped the country have access to cheap and docile unskilled labour.

A Human Ping-Pong Between Countries

On 19 May 2015, the news flashed that, with boats pushed back and forth between Thailand, Malaysia and Indonesia, thousands of migrants, trapped at sea for several weeks, were facing starvation and 100 people were killed in violent clashes between Rohingyas and Bangladeshis over food. On 20 May, with the international, including in particular the US, pressure mounting rapidly, both Indonesia and Malaysia changed their closed-door approach. Following a meeting in Kuala Lumpur, they issued a joint statement agreeing to rescue the stranded migrants at sea and provide them temporary shelter and assistance, to be followed by resettlement and repatriation within a year. They expected the international community to provide necessary support, particularly financial assistance, and also emphasised that they would take only those who were already in the high sea, and should not be expected to take in any additional ones. Thailand attended the meeting but declined to join in the offer of help, but specified that if the boats entered Thai waters and any migrants found hurt or ill, they would provide medical assistance.

Nine days later, on 29 May 2015, another big meeting with representatives from 18 Asian countries as well as Switzerland, the USA and several UN agencies was held in Bangkok. Among them were the representatives from Bangladesh and Myanmar, which had avoided the Bangkok meeting. At the Kuala Lumpur meeting, Malaysia and Indonesia had already agreed to stop pushing back boats with stranded migrants. Nearly 3000 were already registered as having landed, although many—estimated by some at 6000—were still adrift at sea. Expressing grave concern over the situation, the meeting also called for establishing task forces, and improving communications and data-sharing among various law enforcement agencies. The UN High Commissioner for Refugees and the IOM were promised access to migrants. The USA pledged aid to the IOM to ease the situation, and Australia did the same for humanitarian relief in Myanmar.

A Fragile Agreement, Uncertain Future

In a joint statement, the Kuala Lumpur meeting also called for addressing the root causes for the exodus. As always, this is where the future continues to look uncertain. At the meeting, the Myanmar representative rejected a suggestion from a UN official that his country's abusive treatment of the Rohingyas was the primary cause of the exodus. Given this attitude, when the attention of the international community drifts, how is the situation likely to evolve? An ominous sign for the future was that just one week before the Bangkok meeting, Myanmar's President had signed the Population Control Health Care bill. The measure empowers local authorities to ensure that mothers in areas deemed to have high rates of population growth have children no fewer than three years apart. Given the fears fomented by the Buddhist chauvinists of high birth rate among Muslims, it is likely to be used against Muslim Rohingyas. Under international pressure, the network of traffickers may have been dismantled for now, but as long as abused Rohingyas would remain desperate to flee, the traffickers' network would re-emerge.

The fear was real as recent events have revealed that trafficking still portends to be alive and kicking in both Thailand and Malaysia. In Thailand, as Manit Pleantong, a district chief supervising a people smuggling check point, said, "I believe the smugglers are going to stop for a while. But the government needs to continue to act to make sure everything is sustainable".[2] The key question remained: will the government do so? The extent of the influence traffickers and the elite supporting them can exercise may be gauged from the fact that although in November 2014 dozens of people, including a senior general, appeared before court to face charges of human trafficking, this happened only days after the officer in charge of the investigation resigned saying he feared for his life after implicating senior military figures in the grisly, multi-million-dollar trade. In an interview with *Agence France Presse*, the officer, Major-General Powen Pongsirin, said his investigation was closed too quickly, with too many suspects still at large and his unit disbanded.[3]

And yet some hopeful signs were fledgling. On 19 July 2017, a Thai court convicted in a landmark human trafficking trial, involving as many as 103 suspects, Manas Kongpan, a lieutenant army general, alongside dozens of Thai nationals, including a former mayor and a prominent businessman. The conviction was hailed by observers as a sign of the Thai government's resolve to aggressively deal with human trafficking. According to press reports, the army general was, however,

---

[2]Michael Peel, "Asia's Boat People", *Financial Times*, 3 June 2015.
[3]Agence France Presse (AFP), 10 November 2015.

planning to appeal the conviction, and many others were likely to follow suit, contributing to the uncertainty of the situation. As Puttenee Kangkur, a human rights expert, cautiously observed, "There is still a lot of work to do. Traffickers are still operating".[4]

As for Malaysia, the US State Department office, set up by Congress to independently grade global efforts to fight human trafficking, had recommended keeping Malaysia on the bottom grade (Tier 3) reserved for countries with the worst trafficking record. However, seemingly for geopolitical reasons, it was upgraded to Tier 2, and the country remains under watch list.

There was still another worrisome potential danger. At the height of the Rohingya crisis, as a mark of religion-based solidarity, a small group of Muslims in Indonesia staged a protest demonstration against the invasive stance of Buddhist monks and their abusive treatment of the Muslim Rohingyas. Luckily, it was a subdued protest and did not spread out across the region. However, the situation already foreshadowed that any worsening of the Rohingya crisis could spark off interfaith tension and conflicts between and within the countries with disastrous consequences. As discussed below, this is exactly what happened following the events of 25 August 2017.

Finally, the Bangkok meeting did not create an independent and credible mechanism to monitor the situation and ensure follow-up action. And the Association of South-East Asian Nations (ASEAN), which is notably conflict-averse and committed to the principle of non-interference in internal affairs of the member states, has not taken up the issue of human rights abuse of Rohingyas in Myanmar (which in fact chaired the ASEAN in 2014). Should the ASEAN decide to set up a mechanism to keep the situation under watch, it would lend credibility to its own declarations, including the adoption of a 2012 convention, in support of human rights.

---

[4]Puttenee Kangkur, a specialist at the human rights group Fortify Rights, *The Straits Times*, Singapore, 19 July 2017.

A Glimmer of Hope: Electoral Victory of Aung San Suu Kyi

The only glimmer of hope in an otherwise gloomy situation in the country was the victory of Aung Sang Suu Kyi in the recent parliamentary election. Ms. Suu Kyi had come under criticism overseas and by some in Myanmar for saying little about the abuse of Rohingyas. However, subsequently, she had made some gestures showing her concern in the issue. In June 2015, her National League for Democracy party had issued a statement calling for resolving the problem of "boat people" in keeping with the principle of human rights and addressing their citizenship question in a fair, transparent and expeditious manner. Pending the grant of full citizenship, the authorities can issue residency cards allowing them to move freely. If they could make a living and send their children to school, then Rohingyas might feel that they have a future in Myanmar. This will be a right step towards addressing some of the root causes of the problem. There was, however, no certainty that this was likely to happen.

Even so, since 24 August 2016 when the government announced the establishment of an independent commission, headed by Kofi Annan, former Secretary-General of the United Nations, to examine and report on human rights violations and abuses in the Rakhine state, there had been some fledgling hopes of improvement in the situation. The commission, which was composed of three international members and six from Myanmar, including the Muslim and Buddhist communities, was scheduled to submit its report in one year. While commending the initiative, the Amnesty International expressed disappointment that the commission did not include representatives of other minority and ethnic groups and the investigation was limited to Rakhine state. However, considering the constraints embedded in Myanmar's delicate ethno-political and religious situation, it was considered a small, but significant step in the right direction. Nor should it be forgotten that although Rohingya representatives welcomed the initiative, there was still considerable opposition to it—not just from members of the Rakhine community but also from several other groups. These included members of the former ruling party and a split group from Aung San Suu Kyi's own political party, who were protesting foreign meddling in what they perceived as essentially a domestic issue.

Given the situation, it was unrealistic to expect a total change in the situation immediately, but it would have been a worthwhile achievement if, as a first step, the restrictions on freedom of movement of Rohingya and other ethnic groups were lifted, and their access ensured to opportunities for education, employment and aid. International watch over the situation remained essential.

A Turn for the Worse

Sadly and disquietingly, the fragility of the situation came into focus when in October 2016 new reports came in suggesting a recrudescence of serious disturbances in Rakhine state. On 24 November 2016, a senior UNHCR official told the *BBC* that following coordinated attacks on border guards in October, for which some politicians blamed a Rohingya militant group, Myanmar armed forces were seeking the ethnic cleansing of the Muslim Rohingya minority. They were "killing men, slaughtering children, raping" in Rakhine state, forcing many women to flee neighbouring Bangladesh. The government denied the atrocities, expressed disappointment over these comments, and some officials claimed that Rohingyas were setting fire to their own houses.

However, Bangladesh foreign ministry confirmed that thousands of Rohingyas had already sought refuge in the country, while more were reportedly gathering on the border. It had summoned Myanmar's ambassador to express "deep concern" over the military operation in northern Rakhine state and asked Myanmar to "ensure the integrity of its border". Also, Human Rights Watch released satellite images which showed that more than 1200 houses had been razed in Rohingya villages. Likewise, according to the testimonies of several witnesses in refugee camps in Bangladesh, killings and burning of houses by the army were indiscriminate. In January 2017, the UN High Commission for Human Rights estimated that since October 2016 the operation had led to the death of several hundreds of Rohingyas, an outflow of over 66,000 of them to Bangladesh and internal displacement of 22,000 in other parts of Myanmar.

Bangladesh, which does not recognise Rohingya as refugees, has been detaining and repatriating hundreds of fleeing Rohingyas, which, as Amnesty International pointed out, is against international refugee law. The organisation also reported that some other Rohingyas who had gone into hiding had been suffering from a severe lack of essential supplies, including food and medical care. In 2011, Bangladesh had rejected UN aid of US$33 million to alleviate poverty in Cox's Bazar, one of the country's poorest areas, on the ground that this would have benefited the Rohingya refugees as well, encouraging their permanent settlement in the country and attracting new inflows.[5]

The tragic events renewed international criticism of the Myanmar civilian government led by Aung San Suu Kyi for not doing enough to protect the Rohingya minority. At the end of December 2016, nearly a dozen Nobel laureates sent an open letter to the UN Security Council criticising her and calling the military action against the Rohingya a human tragedy amounting to ethnic cleansing. Amnesty International has also been critical of Aung San Suu Kyi for failing to live up to both her political and moral responsibility to stop and condemn the atrocities. There was hardly any sign that the recommendation of the Kofi Annan commission for restoration of Rohingyas' citizenship would be implemented any time soon.

Her supporters pointed out that she did not have control over the army which still enjoyed full power. An additional complicating element in the volatile situation lay in a report by the International Crisis Group claiming that the Rohingya group that attacked frontier security forces in 2016 had international links to Pakistan and Saudi Arabia. The situation, already tense, took a still more disquieting turn when on 31 January 2017 Ko Ni, a prominent member of the Muslim community and legal adviser to Ms. Suu Kyi, was shot dead at Yangon International Airport. At the time of writing, the motive of the killing was unknown.

---

[5]In a paper published in 1979, soon after the 1978 influx of Rohingya refugees to Bangladesh, Alan Lindquist, then UNHCR representative in southern Bangladesh commented: "the objective of the Bangladesh government from the beginning was that the refugees should go back to Burma (Myanmar) as quickly as possible, whatever they may feel about it", cited in *The Economist*, 21 October 2017.

But it came at a time when the religious unrest and conflict were already running high in Rakhine state, and conditions for Muslims were also worsening elsewhere in the country. There were already 22 villages in Myanmar that had declared Muslim-free zones, according to U Kyaw Win, director of The Burma Human Rights Network, a watchdog NGO.

In February 2017, the UN High Commissioner for Human Rights stated that the systematic repression and attacks very likely amounted to crimes against humanity and possibly ethnic cleansing and made a renewed appeal for a full investigation by the United Nations. Ms. Suu Kyi thought that such an international investigation at the time would not help matters. In March 2017, the UN Security Council considered issuing a statement to express concern over renewed fighting and underscore the importance of humanitarian access to all affected areas, which could have served as a first step to possible further action. However, it was blocked by China and Russia, and in the absence of a consensus, no action was taken.

A Vicious Cycle of Violence

Most Rohingyas have long remained reasonably pacific in the face of extreme provocation. But the sufferings and lingering grievances have led to the rise of militant groups, including, notably, the Arakan Salvation Army (ARSA), which was formed in 2012 following the savage violence between the Buddhist community and the Rohingyas in Rakhine state. Although a home-grown organisation, it has gathered strength fast, with international links and support in Saudi Arabia and Pakistan, according to the International Crisis Group, a think tank.

The situation, already tense in Rakhine state, turned more ugly and worrisome on 25 August 2017 when some pro-Rohingya militants, led by ARSA, attacked some 30 police posts and a government military base and the army started a ghastly operation against the Rohingya minority in brutal reprisal, creating a vicious cycle of violence unleashed by both the militants and the troops. More than 100 people were killed in just a few days as troops started their assault, and the number rose to

414 in the Rakhine state in a few weeks. Satellite images showed burning villages across northern Rakhine, and there were horrifying reports of soldiers and Rakhine militias burning down houses, soldiers opening fire on villages and raping women, making the Rohingyas flee to Bangladesh across paddy fields, along narrow mountain paths and in boats.

On 11 September 2017, the then UN Human Rights Commissioner, Zeid Ra'ad al-Hussain, told the Human Rights Council in Geneva that his agency had received "multiple reports and satellite imagery of [government] security forces and local militia reports burning Rohingya villages" as well as "consistent accounts of extra judicial killings, including shooting fleeing civilians". He also called the military ravage against the Rohingya "a text book example of ethnic cleansing". In a softer tone, but provocative style, Antonio Guterres, UN Secretary-General, repeated the accusation: "When one-third of the Rohingya population had to flee the country, could you find a better word to describe it?" he asked. Mathew Smith, chief executive of Fortify Rights, human rights NGO, called the military atrocities "the most serious crime that could be perpetrated against a civilian population". "It has been described as genocide, ethnic cleansing, crimes against humanity: all of these terms apply to what we are seeing", he added. Despite a multitude of such denunciations, Myanmar authorities, however, maintained that ARSA posed a serious security threat and that they were just conducting an operation to destroy terrorism in the country.

With the Rohingya refugee flows rapidly rising, Bangladesh government, as in the past, lodged a strong protest at the "unprecedented level of influx of Myanmar nationals to Bangladesh". Also, with the situation turning increasingly gruesome, there were protests from around the world, including some Muslim majority countries. On 9 September 2017, there were reports of ARSA unilaterally declaring a ceasefire. And, at the urging of the United Nations, the Myanmar government which had earlier rejected any international intervention in the conflict, including the visit of a UN human rights investigation team, was reported to have finally agreed to set up three refugee camps in Maungdaw at Myanmar's border with Bangladesh. However, the government quickly rejected the ceasefire, saying "We do not negotiate with the terrorists".

By mid-September 2017, an estimated 370,000 refugees had streamed across the border into Bangladesh since 25 August and some were still on the move in the border area, creating concerns of food shortages and foreshadowing a humanitarian crisis. Many children and old people died on the mountain roads; several others, too weak to walk, were left behind. There have also been complaints about land mines being planted at the borders to prevent the movement across the borders.

Faced with the deepening humanitarian crisis, Bangladesh partly reversed its earlier policy stance against the new Rohingya inflows. Sheik Hasina, the prime minister, paid her first visit to Cox's Bazar, at the border of Bangladesh and Myanmar, and declared that her country would accept those coming across the border but adding that she had urged Myanmar "to take steps to take their nationals back".

Of the new arrivals in Bangladesh, an estimated 130,000 were living in the registered camps and the makeshift settlements; another 90,000 were sheltering in host communities, and nearly 50,000 had settled in new, spontaneous settlements. But as the flows were swelling fast—by the third week of September the number was hovering around 429,000—the country was struggling to cope with the situation.[6] As of 21 September, about half of them were living in makeshift camp sites with little access to basic amenities. While safety, especially of girls, has been a major concern for the new arrivals, humanitarian assistance in terms of shelter, drinking water, food and health care facilities and medical assistance were also urgently needed. One of the major problems was the lack of toilet facilities for the new arrivals. The government has promised to build 500 temporary latrines and the UNHCR 8000 more.

In order to avoid overcrowding in existing camp sites, Bangladesh government has allocated 2000 acres of land for a huge new camp where it

---

[6]As of September 2017, Bangladesh had a total of some 800,000 Rohingyas, according to IOM. It had already been hosting approximately 300,000 in official and informal centres, accepted 74,000 after the outbreak of violence in October 2016 and had been sheltering a further 429,000 Rohingyas following the incidents in 25 August 2017; at the time of writing, the inflow had not to totally stopped. By 18 September 2017, it may have swelled to 582,000, according to UNHCR, and by November to over 617,000, as estimated by IOM.

will also be easier for new arrivals to access some of the basic services and humanitarian aid, and has agreed to spend about US$4.88 million for construction of internal and access roads and drainage. External aid has been flowing in from countries like Saudi Arabia, Turkey, Malaysia and Indonesia; several other countries, including the USA and the UK as well as the European Union, pledged or were already providing aid to help Bangladesh cope with the situation. International organisations, some of which—like the IOM and the UNHCR—had already been helping the government in dealing with the previous Rohingya flows, moved in fast to cooperate with the government in avoiding a humanitarian crisis in Cox's Bazar which was swamped by the new arrivals. In order to meet the urgent needs of the suffering Rohingyas in a concerted and timely manner, aid agencies coordinated action in issuing an appeal for a total US$77.1 million to fund the emergency response through the end of 2017. Several agencies, including the United Nations and the IOM, have also committed funding from their emergency reserves. However, there was still a huge funding shortfall to meet the needs. This was likely to increase as people continued to arrive from Myanmar and especially if and when the return and resettlement process starts.

To avert an immediate humanitarian crisis in the overcrowded refugee camp and makeshift sites in Cox's Bazar area, principals of three international organisations—the United Nations (OCHA), UNHCR and IOM—made a joint appeal for an international aid of US$434 million which would help sustain and scale up the existing effort to meet the life-saving needs of all Rohingya refugees and the hot communities.

Meanwhile, Bangladesh government was feeling overwhelmed by the unprecedented level and speed of the new inflows, which by the end of September may have involved half a million persons. In late September, the authorities limited the movement of the newcomers inside Bangladesh, requiring them to remain in the designated centres until they returned to their country. They were not allowed to travel from one place to another by roads, railways or waterways. Other troubles were also brewing. Boat owners in south-east Bangladesh had made significant profits by picking up refugees and ferrying them to safety across the border. Bangladesh border guards started burning these boats—not just because of the unfair and unscrupulous practice, but also in an effort to stop more inflows from Myanmar, according to reports from human rights groups, cited by the *Daily Telegraph*.[7] Conditions in the congested camps were awful. There were also concerns that the helpless refugees could become easy victims of labour exploitation, sexual abuse and slave trade. According to a most recent IOM report,[8] desperate men, women and children were being recruited with false offers of paid work in various industries. Once on the job, they were usually paid less than what was promised, made to work more hours than was previously agreed, and not allowed to leave their work premises or contact their families. Girls were often physically or sexually abused. Some of them recruited as domestic aids in Cox's Bazar and Chittagong were forced to prostitution either locally or trafficked elsewhere. Such exploitations of Rohingyas and the related crimes had also existed before, but with the massive influx of refugees, they have become much more extensive.

There was also a concern that Bangladesh might revive a plan designed in 2016 to relocate the new refugees and another 232,000 already in the country to Thengar Char, an island in the Bay of Bengal, which first emerged in or around 2007, formed from the wash down of the Meghna River. It is low-lying, prone to flooding, and at present uninhabited. The nearest inhabited island is some 30 kilometres away, and the distance from the nearest camps is about 250 kilometres.

The government claims that the relocation would improve refugees' access to humanitarian assistance, but the rights groups are strongly opposed to the plan. The Asia Pacific Refugee Rights Networks has called the plan "dangerous, absurd and inhumane". The Bangladesh forest department has warned that the soil and environment of Thengar Char are not yet suitable for human habitation. And the responsible district administration in Noakhali has also informed the government that building a flood protection embankment, cyclone centres and basic

---

[7]"Local people told me boatmen caught dropping Rohingya people here are having their boats burned as a punishment and warning. It's deemed necessary as border control". Ashiqur Rahman at Odhikar, a Bangladesh human rights group. Kathleen Prior, *The Telegraph*, 22 September 2017.
[8]IOM Press release, 14 November 2017.

infrastructure and facilities for supply of drinking water would be essential before refugees can be relocated on the island.[9]

All in all, by the end of the year, as this script was in press, the Rohingya situation remained grim. More than 600,000 uprooted Rohingyas had arrived in Bangladesh in a desperate search of security, and most were living in sub-human conditions. While, according to the Myanmar government, 400 of them died as a result of the military assaults, Médcins Sans Frontièrs estimated that 6700 may have been killed in the first month of the crackdown, between 25 August and 24 September, including at least 730 children below the age of five years. Overall, 69% were killed by gunshots, 9% by being burnt to death and 5% beaten to death.

The Outlook

> I see only problems, I only see impossibilities. Possibilities I can't see for reasons of race, religion, ethnicity—and our culture.[10]

Given the ethno-political climate of the country, the Rohingya situation has become one of the toughest issues for the new government to handle. Although following the victory of her party in the elections, Ms. Suu Kyi has said that securing peace with ethnic minorities, including armed ethnic groups in the country's border lands, would be among her priorities, it should not be forgotten that the military still wields considerable political power. In particular, it will continue to control the defence, frontier and home affairs ministries. In addition, the constitution allows the army to veto any attempt at constitutional reform. As Gavin Jacobson put it in *The New Yorker*, "The irony is then if Aung San Suu Kyi once represented the power of the powerless, she is now powerless in power".[11]

---

[9]Ashraful Azad, "Banishing refugees to a flood-prone island will not solve Bangladesh's Rohingya refugee crisis". *The Conversation*, 27 March 2017.

[10]Reflections of a tearful Ziaur Rahman of the Rohingya ethnic group. Cited in *Financial Times*, 3 January 2015.

[11]Gavin Jacobson, "Aung San Suu Kyi, The ignoble laureate", *The New Yorker*, 15 September 2017.

The situation has put Aung San Suu Kyi, who kept silent in the weeks following the army incursion in November 2016, in a delicate situation, and more recently she had appealed for time. She had also come under criticism for appointing Myint Swe, Myanmar Vice-President and a former army general, to head the team charged to investigate the events in Rakhine state. Most Burmese have very little sympathy for Rohingya, and the army's action seemed to have considerable popular support. As *The Economist* crisply, and somewhat cynically, remarked "No Burmese politician has ever benefited by standing up for the Rohingyas".[12]

The spiral of violence unleashed since 25 August 2017 by Myanmar army's most brutal and indiscriminate assaults and the rapidly rising militancy among Rohingyas hold the potential of an imminent, multi-layered, and threefold, danger. *First*, there is a real risk that the unstable and tense situation in Rakhine state in Myanmar will drive ARSA, which already has international links, to attract foreign fighters, including jihadists, to join the conflict. And, many fundamentalists and terrorist groups outside Myanmar would doubtless be eager to fully exploit the situation. This would lead to further radicalisation, fuelling both Rohingya and Buddhist extremism, destabilise the country and retard much-needed economic development in Rakhine state, as the Kofi Annan commission forewarned. There was no dearth of provocation to incite such faith-based violence inside Myanmar and make this happen. Indonesia's militant Islamic Defenders Front (FPI), for example, has already called for volunteers to wage jihad against Buddhist-majority Myanmar in defence of the Rohingya. The call was in keeping with the religious opinions issued by Islamic scholars last year in Saudi Arabia, the United Arab Emirates, Bangladesh and India, who argued that resistance to forces opposing Islam was legitimate.

Second, fears of such links between Rohingya communities and internal and external terrorist groups are apt to harden the attitude of neighbouring countries towards the Rohingyas. This would make these countries more reticent to accepting new Rohingya refugees and may even make them anxious to expel the Rohingyas already

---

[12] *The Economist*, 4 June 2015.

settled in their territories, as reflected in India's recent announcement (but not yet implemented) to expel the Rohingya refugees already settled in that country.[13] Although not a signatory to the 1951 UN Refugee Convention, India has a long history of providing refuge to groups fleeing persecution. The new hard line seems to stem from New Delhi's belief that Rohingyas posed a potential security threat, especially due to the rising militancy among the Rohingyas and the emergence of ARSA. It also plays well with groups within the governing party which derives considerable support from its nationalist Hindu base. This has been causing anxiety among the Rohingya refugees in India. "If we have to go back, it is better that we are killed here. At least we will have proper funeral rites", says Fakir Ahmed, a Rohingya refugee in Hyderabad, echoing a sentiment expressed by several others.[14] Nepal has tightened up its control of its border with India because of its fear of the irregular entry of Rohingyas from India.

In September 2017, some neighbouring countries such as Indonesia, Malaysia and Thailand tentatively agreed to accept some Rohingyas, but the offers were already tempered with caution against possible terrorist infiltration into the new arrivals (even though they were most likely to be confined in detention centres). There is a clear risk that if such fears take hold or worsen due to even one or two terrorist incidents involving Rohingyas, the offers may very well remain unimplemented.

Third, given the faith-based ethno-political configuration of the region—majorities in Myanmar, Thailand and Sri Lanka are Buddhists while those in Bangladesh, Malaysia and Indonesia are Muslims—any worsening of the Rohingya crisis could spark off interfaith tension and conflicts between and within these countries with disastrous consequences. Worse still, if this happens, it could, directly or indirectly, suck into the conflict countries outside the region as well. Protests condemning violence against the Rohingya by the Myanmar army and Buddhist extremists have already stirred deep-seated emotions across the Muslim

---

[13]In subsequent official statements, India lowered the tone and the threat may remain unimplemented, unless there is new evidence of Rohingyas' links with terrorism.

[14]Amy Kazman, "Deportation hangs over India's Rohingya", *Financial Times*, 11 September 2017.

world. In September 2017, thousands of Muslims marched in cities across the globe demanding an end of what they called genocide (absent from the list were the Middle Eastern capitals (see footnote 16)).

Pressure or provocation for such involvement of governments of Muslim majority countries has been building up for quite some time. For instance, in a sermon given on 14 May 2015 by Abu Bakr al-Baghdadi, the leader of the ISS in Iraq was reported as saying, "Where is the support of al-Salul (a derogatory expression for Saudi royals) and their allies for a million of the weak Muslims who are all without exception being exterminated in Burma?"[15] According to SITE intelligence group, more recently, Al-Qaeda had sent messages urging governments of Muslim majority countries to provide financial and military assistance to Rohingya militants. If such incitements were to take hold, it could make South and South-East Asia a replica of the conflict-ridden MENA countries.

Governments in several of these countries could not avoid getting involved in the Rohingya crisis for a twofold reason. They felt the need to demonstrate their interfaith solidarity and were also fearful that the deep-seated emotions evoked by the violence against the Rohingya could strengthen the ultra-conservative and more militant Islamic forces in their own countries.[16] Thus, soon after the outbreak of violence, in the second week of September 2017, Indonesian Foreign Minister Retno Marsudi rushed to Dhaka with an offer of help to Bangladesh in sheltering 150,000 Rohingya refugees. Concurrently, Indonesian authorities forbade a rally in support of the Myanmar government at the Borobudur Buddhist temple in central Java. Likewise, Recep Tayyip Erdogan, President of Turkey, accused Myanmar of genocide, saying he would be raising the issue at the UN Security Council in consultation

---

[15]Cited in *The Economist*, 13 June 2015.

[16]The conflict-ridden Arab countries, which have already been fighting these radical Islamist groups, are in a different situation. They are more concerned that their involvement in the Rohingya crisis might give a new impetus to the radical Islamist groups which have lately become weakened inside their own countries and only open for them a new front to fight. "As an Arab diplomat observed, the last thing we need is an open confrontation between Muslims and Buddhists". James M. Dorsey, "Plight of Myanmar's Rohingya: Militant Islam's next rallying call?" http://www.scmp.com/author/James-m-dorsey.

with other Muslim majority countries. He also pledged to deliver 1000 tons of food, medicine and clothing to Rohingyas in the afflicted northwest region of Rakhine state. The then Turkish Foreign Minister Mevlut Cavusoglu, who was also due to visit the Myanmar–Bangladesh border, said the Rohingyas in Rakhine state lived in open prisons covered in mud and in conditions that were totally unacceptable and announced that Turkey would provide ambulances and other equipment to help the distressed refugees.

In her first comment since the latest crisis in August 2017, Ms. Suu Kyi said she was working to protect the rights of all the people in the country, including the Rohingyas. In her comment made during a telephone conversation with Turkey's President Recep Tayyip Erdogan, who had described the repression of Muslim Rohingyas as amounting to a "genocide", Ms. Suu Kyi also added that there was "an iceberg of misinformation", which was being spread with the aim of creating tensions between communities and promoting the aims of terrorists.

It is possible that ARSA deliberately pushed the army towards indiscriminate retaliation with the hope of attracting international attention. It was also understandable why Ms. Suu Kyi had to be cautious in handling the situation. But it was certainly unbecoming of her to attribute the whole problem to the rise of terrorism, as she did in her statement, and not to say a word against the excessive use of force by the military. Her equivocation of responsibility for violence was also wrong. After all, the rise of militancy among the Rohingyas cannot be separated from their long-standing persecution and sufferings.

Concerted international pressure remained critically important to attain a breakthrough. However, such pressure should be carefully calibrated to the fragile, complex and fast-evolving situation in the country. Just as international pressure on the government could give Ms. Suu Kyi's certain leverage in her negotiation with the army and those opposed to reform, including those in her own political party, it could also generate a nationalist backlash and induce the army to revert to the previous authoritarian and isolationist system of government. On the other hand, if she fails to play a more active role to protect the rights of the Rohingya and other minorities, she may lose her credibility among them and the world outside, as has been happening. In any case, international focus exclusively on Aung San Suu Kyi will not suffice; as discussed below, pressure must also be brought to bear upon the Myanmar army to achieve tangible results (further discussed below).

Aung San Suu Kyi's New Statement: A Mixed Message with Confusing Results

On 19 September, as this script was about to go to press, the situation seemed to be changing, with Ms. Suu Kyi making a new statement of the government policy on the Rohingya crisis. As mentioned, on 5 September she had called the reports about the army atrocities "a huge iceberg of misinformation" that was creating problems between communities and promoting terrorism. Two weeks later, in her new statement she softened the tone, though it was still defying, and vowed to address human rights violations and unlawful violence, expressed concerns that numbers of Muslims were fleeing across the border to Bangladesh and agreed to take back those found to be genuine refugees of all minorities after proper verification. She also affirmed her commitment to the restoration of peace and stability and rule of law throughout the Rakhine state and welcomed open investigations into the events in the troubled areas, which her government had previously refused to allow.

It was, however, a mixed and confusing message. It certainly did not herald a new dawn. It was not surprising therefore that the general reaction to her first public address since 25 August 2017 was underwhelming. Amnesty International said that she and her government were "burying their heads in the sand over the horrors unfolding in Rakhine state". The organisation's director for South-East Asia, James Gomez, later called it "a mix of untruths and victim-blaming", while the director of Burma Campaign UK, Mark Farmaner, thought the speech was "business as usual, denial, as usual". These criticisms were harsh, but not completely unwarranted. Ms. Suu Kyi avoided using the term "Rohingya" except in the context of the ARSA's involvement in the violence, nor did she address the allegations against the army and its indiscriminate abuse of civilians.

The validity of several of her statements has also been challenged. These include: the claims that there had been no clashes or clearance operations after 5 September, as earlier her own office had reported such operations since that date on its Facebook page that "more than 50% of the villages of Muslims are intact" and that "all people in Rakhine state have access to education, and health care without discrimination". Likewise, it was astonishing to hear her saying "we don't know why more than 400,000 people have fled" or her presentation as good news that half the Muslims in Rakhine state had not fled.

It seemed encouraging to note her assurance of "another round of humanitarian endeavour, which we hope will take care of all the peoples in the region". However, the Myanmar government had been blamed for a blockade on international humanitarian aid, including denying UN aid agencies' entry to the conflict zone, although recently limited access was given to the International Committee of the Red Cross. Significantly, following Ms. Suu Kyi's address, in a phone call the then US secretary of state Rex Tillerson urged her to facilitate humanitarian aid and address allegations of human rights abuses. Likewise, her statement that her government would welcome any investigations of the events in Rakhine state sounded encouraging. It seemed to bode well for the UN fact-finding mission, as the mission's chairman, Marzuki Darusman, put it. And the EU, too, called her invitation for international diplomats to visit the affected areas "a step forward". However, Myanmar's envoy at the UN, Htin Lynn, had said that Darusman's mission was "not a helpful course of action, that the country was taking proportionate measures against terrorists, and making efforts to restore peace". Significantly, within 24 hours of her speech, there was also a chorus of calls from rights groups to allow full access to the affected areas for independent investigations. Even by the end of September, this was not happening.

In brief, as noted, Ms. Suu Kyi's address did not usher a "new dawn" unfolding on the horizon nor was it the harbinger of a radical change in Myanmar's Rohingya policy. As Phil Robertson of Human Rights Watch put it, she was "trying to crawl back some degree of international credibility with the international community without saying too much that will get her into trouble with the military and Burmese people who do not like the Rohingya in the first place". In any case, as mentioned, international attention should not be focussed exclusively on Aung San Suu Kyi. To be effective, the pressure must also be brought to bear upon the Myanmar army to make it more amenable to stop the carnage and find a lasting settlement through negotiation. Broad economic sanctions should be too blunt a weapon; it will retard economic openness, push back the country to isolation and make the poor people suffer.

A preferred course would be to apply targeted sanctions on politicians who are stoking anti-Muslim sentiment and army generals who were known to be hawkish on the Rohingya issue. Not surprisingly, questions have been raised on the relationship of Western powers with General Min Aung Hlaing, commander chief of the Myanmar military, who was hosted by countries such as Germany, Austria and Japan. It is widely known that the Myanmar army has direct interests in a number of Myanmar important business enterprises. There have been suggestions to target economic sanctions on some of these companies and key persons associated with them, which would have a pinching effect on the army's interests and make it more amenable to a negotiated settlement. This deserves serious consideration.

An Action Plan: Short- and Medium-/Long-Term Measures

To redress the situation, a policy of harmonised short- and medium- to long-term measures will be needed. As part of the short-term measures, international pressure must be brought to bear upon the army through negotiation and targeted economic sanctions for (a) immediate cessation of all military and faith-based atrocities against the Rohingya and arrangements for ensuring full protection to restore their self-confidence; (b) return and resettlement of all displaced persons of minority communities, with bilateral and international assistance, as needed; (c) restoring citizenship to the Rohingya or at least granting them immediately a set of basic social and economic rights, such as freedom of movement, including for farming, fishing and search for jobs, access to medical and health services and opportunities for children's education; and (d) establishment in Rakhine state of an independent and trustworthy institution, backed by professionals, for mediation and conflict resolution at an early stage.

The medium- to long-term measures should focus on reconciliation and confidence-building between communities and promotion of interfaith understanding and peace on a durable basis. This must not be just political slogans or a bureaucratic artifice but be based on joint action on the ground involving common interests and stakes. Broad-based and inclusive development of Rakhine state which would ensure full and fair utilisation of its considerable natural resources and open up new economic and job opportunities for local populations should be an important component of this part of the programme. Hopefully, this would also help reducing the existing tension between communities in the state. Interestingly, a recent field investigation revealed that while there was a general antipathy towards the Rohingya, the feeling was much less so in the business sector. Finally, there must be an effective and credible mechanism to monitor progress in the planning and implementation of the whole programme.

Negotiations should also be initiated, preferably under the United Nations auspices and without much delay, on an agreed plan for orderly and safe return and peaceful resettlement of the eligible Rohingyas, including the rules governing the selection process. This will be difficult. In early October 2017, following Ms. Suu Kyi's assurances in September, governments of Myanmar and Bangladesh agreed to draw up a plan for repatriation, but the exact terms and conditions remained to be decided. Meanwhile, radical Buddhist monks staged a demonstration against the return of the Rohingyas. Clearly, the critical situation created by the latest outflows of Rohingyas to Bangladesh warrant urgent attention. However, in the din and hassle of this urgency the distressful Rohingya situation in Thailand and Malaysia, as discussed in the first part of this chapter, must not be forgotten.

The Delicate Role of Western Countries

As already mentioned, Western countries would do well in not pinning too much hope on Aung Sang Suu Kyi as the sole saviour of the Rohingya crisis. It will be a facile make-belief, even naïve to rely too much on her. Underlying the Rohingya crisis, there are powerful ethno-nationalist and faith-based political forces which Ms. Suu Kyi, even with her erstwhile much applauded democratic conviction and international clout, cannot match: they remain far beyond her control. In a recent book,[17] Francis Wade rightly mentions a toxic mixture of some of these factors: a weak state burdened by the past colonial rule, Burmanisation project of the military and the aggressiveness of the of radical Buddhist monks, all undeterred by the weak state and exploited by the elitist politicians. The mixture stifles the flowering of social cohesion and the emergence of a democracy. The tortured political landscape also largely explains the reawakening of the Rakhine Buddhists' deep-seated fears of losing their resources and power and their recent more aggressive stance. Instead of playing a pacific role promoting security and self-confidence of both communities, the army, driven by its authoritarian zeal for ethno-nationalist Bumanisation programme, has let loose unprecedented and partisan violence. The whole Rakhin state is now radicalised, alongside a growing anti-Western feeling and tensions between Buddhism and Islam in Asia and beyond.

Given the complexity of the whole situation, if Western powers wish to be helpful to Myanmar and its people, they need to move with patience, perseverance and extreme circumspection. Pressure on the army, as mentioned above, must be an integral part of a multi-pronged strategy. On 16 October 2017, the European Union severed ties with the army and banned senior officers from travelling to EU member countries. Wider and more effective measures, including selective economic sanctions, targeting at business enterprises in which the army has a direct interest as mentioned above, should receive serious consideration. At the same time, innovative ways of building social cohesion through civil society institutions and social promoters should be explored—without giving the remotest impression of direct political interference. Business community has been found to be potentially less partisan, less radicalised and potentially more open

---

[17] *Myanmar' Enemy Within: Buddhist Violence and the Making of a Muslim "Other"*, Zed Books, 2017.

to foreign participation. The private sector could therefore be a viable interlocutor for exploring these possibilities and for initiating some joint economic and social service projects involving common interests and stakes of all the communities. In planning and executing all these activities, representatives of Western counties should have close links with the proposed national mechanism to monitor the progress in implementing the whole reconciliation and rehabilitation programme.

Meanwhile, Western governments can show their human solidarity by joining others in contributing to the US$434 million aid fund set by the international organisations in order to sustain and scale up the ongoing effort to meet the life-saving needs of all Rohingya refugees and their host communities, involving 1.2 million people in Cox's Bazar area, mentioned above.

Part III

How to Manage the Crisis and Avoid Its Recrudescence

12

A Synoptic Overview of Policy Issues and Prescriptions

Discussions in the previous chapters have included references to policy issues specific to the four selected mixed migration and refugee flows in three different regions—western and eastern Europe, the Americas and Asia—along with possible remedial responses to them. Instead of repeating them all in detail, this chapter focuses on those policy concerns that are of major importance and are mostly common not only to these specific flows but also to those of an analogous nature elsewhere and are relevant for better management of global migration and refugee flows.

* * *

Institutional Weaknesses and Legal Deficiencies

Effective management of massive migration and refugee inflows, be it for an individual country or a group of countries, calls for an adequate institutional arrangement which is capable of meeting the complex challenges and exigencies they often present, especially when the flows are massive, sudden and mixed.

For the European Union, free internal movement of people is a proud achievement, but, as noted, it has been finding difficult to sustain it. This is because its existing institutional and legal set-up is not adequately equipped to uphold it. It suffers from a twofold inadequacy. First, as already noted, within the EU structure the competence to deal with migration and refugee flows is diffused. While the management of internal movement rests with the EU at the community level, individual member states retain the sovereign prerogative of dealing with inward movement of people to the EU from outside. The bifurcation of competence ignores the inexorable links between free movement within the EU and the protection of its external borders. Second, while under the EU system all member states are entitled to enjoy the benefits of free internal movement, it does not have a structural mechanism requiring all member states to share equitably the burden or responsibility it entails. In the face of this structural constraint, the EU Commission has been trying hard, recently with some slow success, to find new and innovative ways of introducing joint action with member states for better protection of the Community's external borders. These efforts should continue.

In South-East Asia, the experience of Rohingya refugee inflows also reveals the importance of adequate institutional arrangement and its effective use to deal with sudden waves of such refugee and migration flows collectively and in an orderly manner. Although the ASEAN provides an institutional framework for interstate cooperation, the organisation felt shy to get involved in the matter possibly because of its traditional consensual approach to decision-making, its policy of non-interference in member states' internal affairs and the high sensitivity of the issue in the region. Even so, a timely and effective use of the mechanism would have avoided much of the tension created by the "human ping-pong" between neighbouring countries and enhanced the credibility of the commitment already made collectively by the ASEAN member countries themselves to uphold the protection of basic human rights. This could have also helped in finding a negotiated settlement of the Rohingya crisis or at least in restraining the eruption of violence in Myanmar.

In the case of the Central American child refugee flows to the USA, institutional and political constraints in terms of a lack of bipartisan agreement and the consequent political stalemate delayed or denied necessary action by the USA. The institutional and operational deficiencies in the arrangement for in-country processing of asylum applications (partly remedied later) in the Central American countries are also an example of similar shortcomings. As for the origin countries, although Central America has various economic cooperation/integration groupings, the pressing problem of child migration in Northern Triangle countries has not received the focussed attention that it deserves. And the same applies to the Pueblo Process on migration, a regional consultative mechanism, which would normally be expected to be actively involved in the issue and come up with both some innovative ideas and practical suggestions, but this does not seem to have happened.

At the global level, the absence of a coordinated institutional arrangement has long been an important constraint to effective management of migration and refugee flows as a global process. The integration of the International Organization of Migration within the United Nations system in 2016 has been a step in the direct direction, showing tangible improvement in the coordination of operational activities such as rescue, relief and resettlement of refugees and migrants. However, the responsibility and mandate for normative activities still remain widely scattered. Given that different agencies have their constitutional mandate for normative work in their specific areas of competence, it is difficult to change the situation. Nor is it necessary, provided that a way can be found to address the interconnectedness of different types and aspects of migration. This, as mentioned in Chapter 4, remains critically important to ensure a cohesive policy approach to the global migration system as a whole.

This can be achieved through the direct involvement of the United Nations itself. It does not imply that the UN should duplicate any of the work already being done by its different agencies, each in its own area of competence. Its distinctive role should be confined to monitor and ensure the cohesiveness and coherence of the policy package and undertake any residual or complementary work needed to achieve this. And it is a hopeful sign that after long years of procrastination due to member states reticence, the UN General Assembly has now agreed precisely to play this role by sponsoring the development of two Global Compacts dealing with migration and refugees, respectively (further discussed below).

Early Warning System, Readiness Based on Circumspection, and Anticipatory Measures

Discussion in the previous chapters has also shown the critical importance of an early warning system and anticipatory measures in ensuring effective management of refugee and migration inflows. By the end of 2014, when the opportunities for entry in the neighbouring countries of Jordan, Lebanon and Turkey were nearly exhausted, there were already several ominous signs and warnings of the possibility that waves of displaced people from the strife-torn Syria and from sub-Saharan Africa would be seeking entry to Europe through Turkey and Libya. However, in the absence of a sound early warning system, the EU failed to initiate any action to cope with it until nearly the middle of 2015.

It also was late in installing a robust replacement of Italy's Mare Nostrum and in noticing several of the crucial turning points in the direction of the flows from both the conflict-ridden MENA countries and sub-Saharan Africa, and making necessary adjustments in its action with adequate speed and circumspection. In Germany, Chancellor Angela Merkel was both brave and ethical to welcome the deserving refugees, but, backed, as is now known, by the German mainstream media, she did so without adequate preparation and sensitising German citizens of the merits of her policy, despite the difficulties it entailed. All this is indicative of the critical need for a robust institutional system which is sufficiently alert not only about the likely incoming waves of refugees and migrants but also about the subsequent dynamics of the flows, including changing routes and human traffickers' agile, fast-moving machinations.

Likewise, in the case of Central American child migration, the USA found itself totally unprepared for the sudden spike in the inflows of unaccompanied child migrants in 2014, which overwhelmed the agencies responsible for their reception, accommodation and care, and led to widespread abuse and mistreatment of the children, alongside political bickering and finger pointing to lay the blame for the messy situation. The existence of an alert and well-organised early warning system could have avoided or at least attenuated some of these problems.

The existence of such early warning systems at the regional and global levels would be immensely useful. At present, there are several migration observatory posts scattered in different countries, but they are not well equipped to provide the kind of early warning needed to take anticipatory measures to deal with sudden inflows of migration. International organisations such as the IOM and the UNHCR which have a network of field offices in countries and regions could provide useful inputs which can be pulled together, processed and refined and at the regional and global levels and then expeditiously issued.

The 1951 UN Convention on Refugees and the Way to Meet Protection Gaps

A most serious constraint inhibiting effective management of refugee and mixed migration flows concerns the scope and thrust of the 1951 UN Convention on the Status of Refugees and its 1967 Protocol.[1] As discussed in Chapter 4, the Convention, designed at the end of World War II, played an historic role in protecting refugees from communist regimes. However, it is proving increasingly inadequate in the fast-changing world to meet the needs of many who are in a refugee-like situation and in genuine need of protection, but are not covered under the UN Convention (for an illustrative list of these groups, see Chapter 4, pp. 41–42). Other gaps relate, inter alia, to the exclusion of cases of persecution by non-state agents and situations of forced (collective) displacements, but without easily identifiable personal persecution (an essential criterion under the existing Convention). The efforts by the EU member countries and those in North America and Oceania to respond to some of these humanitarian emergencies on an ad hoc basis by accepting some of these victims as temporary refugees or creating special categories of refugees on humanitarian grounds are helpful, but not adequate as the extent of protection varies between countries and remains unpredictable, fragile and uncertain.

---

[1]For a more detailed analysis of deficiencies of the Convention, see: Bimal Ghosh, *Elusive Protection and Uncertain lands: Migrants' Access to Human Rights*, IOM. Geneva, 2003, p. 11 and pp. 21–25.

An ideal and long-term solution would be to include all or most of these refugee-like groups and humanitarian emergencies by amending the 1951 Convention or, preferably, by incorporating them in an additional Protocol. Pending this happening, efforts should be made at harmonising and codifying the wide variety of scattered arrangements existing in different countries for temporary protection of these vulnerable persons on humanitarian grounds.

Under the UN Convention, the restrictive requirement (albeit with some flexibility, as already noted) that for an asylum application to be valid it needs to be lodged from outside the country of origin also compounds the difficulties to cope with refugee flows as it induces many potential asylum-seekers to take perilous journeys to Europe, often with the help of unscrupulous traffickers. As discussed, in-country processing is not without potential perils and pitfalls. And yet, it is possible that at an earlier stage of the conflicts in MENA countries the establishment of in-country processing centres—under the UN/UNHCR auspices and with active backing of powerful nations—may have been, on balance, a less costly and painful approach to Europe's refugee the crisis. At least, it should have received more careful attention and scrutiny than it actually had.

Safeguard Against the Dilution of the UNHCR Mandate

At the height of the refugee and migration crisis in Europe and the overwhelming burden it imposed on the UNHCR and receiving countries, some analysts had argued that the protection of refugees should not be deemed to be the concern of the UNHCR alone, but should also be shared by other UN agencies and the private sector as well. This has become increasingly important, and, as discussed, it has already been happening, but needs to be encouraged and stepped up. It is, however, critically important that this does not in any way dilute the core mandate of the UNHCR to supervise the screening process and determine the admissibility of asylum-seekers under the Convention. This is so particularly because the existing Convention does not have a specific monitoring mechanism and a formal process of interstate scrutiny—let alone a system of individual petitions for verification. Clearly, once the admission process is completed, the cooperation of all the other agencies and entities, including the private sector and civil society, is clearly valuable in the following stages of resettlement and integration of the refugees, as argued in Chapter 8.

Inadequate Focus on the Root Causes in Origin Countries

In trying to avoid or tame massive refugee inflows, destination countries in Europe as elsewhere have taken a variety of measures. However, so far the focus has been not so much on the complex and often deep-seated root causes in origin countries as on subsidiary or secondary causes and conditions subsequent to the outflows. As already noted, many of them have thus erected walls and other physical barriers, some at high costs or have tried to stop the flows midway by signing bilateral agreements with transit or nearby third countries—to arrest the flows against compensations in the form of financial grants, trade concessions or other forms of reward. Additionally, some have made return and readmission agreements with origin countries for sending back the rejected asylum-seekers. And most of these receiving countries have stepped up their efforts to dismantle the networks of human traffickers who flourish by alluring, colluding and sometimes forcing the potential asylum-seekers to take perilous journeys and making unlawful gains through ruthless exploitation of vulnerable persons.

All these measures, which have had limited or doubtful success, share a common feature of attempting to push away the outflows, as distinct from tackling the sources or root causes themselves in origin countries. As noted, more recently, destination countries have started giving some attention to helping origin countries in promoting employment, training and development as a means of stemming emigration, especially poverty- driven movements—such as the EU's aid to Nigeria, Senegal, Niger and Mali and US aid to Central American countries. Somewhat exceptionally, however, the US-sponsored latest (2015) development plan for Central America includes, as noted, promotion of security and good governance as its objectives, although action has been mostly lagging so far.

The plans, however, suffer from several constraints and limitations. In the EU, the member states (as distinct from the European Commission) have been dragging their feet to allocate their contributions matching the funds committed by the Commission, just as until December 2015 the US Congress had been reticent to provide aid money for the Central American countries. Previous discussion has emphasised that aid money must be regarded as a critical input to forging a genuine partnership with origin countries aiming at promoting broad-based and sustainable development and good governance, and not as a dole. Nor should it serve as a carrot just to induce origin countries to take back some of their irregular migrants or tempt them to somehow stop the outflows.

Clearly, many of the other causes of disorderly emigration—such as the flagrant violation of human rights, ethnic and religious conflicts and civil wars, breakdown of law and order, insecurity and generalised violence and natural or man-made disasters—are generally not covered under these plans.[2]

It is not that the EU leaders are oblivious of the root causes of disorderly and forced migration. However, they have been reticent to focus on these issues, and the reasons are not far to seek. Not only do these root causes present *per se* formidable challenges but they also raise sensitive internal political issues and fall mostly outside the ambit of competence of government institutions responsible for refugee and migration flows. This is precisely why it is so important to ensure (a) a fully cohesive approach to multidimensional challenge of migration through close interministerial coordination in both origin and destination countries, and (b) aid-related reform programme is genuinely *owned* by the origin countries and not considered as externally imposed. A third consideration to address the difficulty is also relevant. It relates to the need for an increased awareness and

---

[2]As noted, somewhat exceptionally promotion of security and good governance are included as objectives of the US aid of $750 million to Central America, approved in December 2015, although action has been mostly lagging so far.

12 A Synoptic Overview of Policy Issues and Prescriptions

recognition of the close links between gross violation of human rights and disorderly, often unwanted, migration. In cooperation with civil society groups and other non-state actors, government migration services in both origin and destination countries can play an important advocacy and cautionary role by calling attention to the fact that, unless these challenges related to human and minority rights as well as other basic rights are effectively met in time, the consequent disruptions are most likely to be compounded by the unleashing of massive refugee and disorderly migration flows, which in turn can make the national situation worse and also a threat to regional peace and stability.

Significantly, it is this linkage that provided the main justification for the United Nations to authorise armed intervention in Iraq in 1999. The relevant Security Council resolution (No. 687) noted that the gross violation of human rights by the Iraqi regime was generating massive refugee flows, seriously threatening regional stability and that therefore the situation called for collective intervention under Chapter VII of the UN Charter.

Institutions responsible for refugee and migration issues should be enabled and encouraged to play an anticipatory role in connection with any internationally authorised and legitimate military intervention. This applies, even if somewhat belatedly, to the air strikes and other military operations by the "coalition governments" in countries such as Iraq and Yemen. As noted in Chapter 4, in the past the refugee and migration-related consequences of such interventions have hardly been taken into account as part of the strategic planning in advance of such operations even when they have been subjects of long political and strategic discussions. Governments have scrambled to cope with human displacements on a *post facto* basis under great urgency and extreme pressure, and people have suffered. This should be changed, and efforts made to ensure that in planning any such interventions the effects on internal and external human displacements are fully considered and, to the extent possible, remedial measures carefully thought through in advance.

Mixed Migration: A Conundrum Endemic in a Fragmented Migration System

The problem of mixed migration arises, as noted in Chapter 4, in two different ways, and both make the management of refugee and migration flows difficult, as revealed by the painful experiences with the current inflows from MENA and sub-Saharan countries to Europe and those of child migrants from Central America to Mexico and the USA. In the first of the two situations, the problem stems from mixed *motivation* underlying the cross-border movement—a potential migrant may be motivated by a mixture of reasons—political persecution in the home country may be combined with the person's desire to join the family or to improve job opportunities in the destination country. Such situations may make it difficult and time-absorbing for the immigration authorities to determine the person's eligibility to entry and the potential migrant could fail to find a specific slot for legal entry and fall through the gaps between the established legal channels of admission.

This calls for a flexible screening policy, sensitive to the reality of mixed motivation and not a valid ground for automatic rejection of an asylum application.

The second situation of mixed migration relates to *entanglement of channels of entry* or "*category jumping*" by a potential migrant. A potential migrant in a conflict-ridden country may be anxious to join family members in the destination country, but if the family reunion channel is already closed, the person may try to enter through the asylum-seeking channel. Or, as mentioned in Chapter 4, if a potential labour migrant finds that, despite unmet labour demand, the destination country has blocked the legal channel for labour immigration, the individual may try to reach the country through the asylum-seeking channel.

When this happens, the asylum-seeking channel becomes overcrowded and clogged, the screening process turns unduly onerous and slow, and the bona fide asylum-seekers suffer, as happened in Greece and Italy in 2015–2016. And if neither the asylum-seeking channel nor any other legal channel looks promising, the potential migrant may try entry through an irregular channel, with or without the help of a human trafficker or smuggler. Likewise, when persons deserving humanitarian protection find no other avenues to protection they are likely to overcrowd the existing asylum channel, even if they are not eligible, or try the irregular channel as a last resort.

As past experiences in Europe and elsewhere show, such diversion of the flows from one traditional channel to another, causing entanglement of channels, is not new. In 1973, at the height of the first oil crisis and rising unemployment western Europe put a total ban on labour immigration, but as the emigration pressure in the erstwhile sending countries continued (and the new openings in oil-producing Gulf countries could not absorb them all), the flow turned to irregular channels and the number of irregular migrants started rising. Again, in the early 1990s, the main industrial countries (excluding Japan) faced a dramatic rise in the number of asylum applicants. With stringent measures, including restrictive interpretation of asylum laws, the countries could bring down the number of asylum-seekers by 1997. Significantly enough, with the pressure for emigration to Europe continuing unabated, the drop in asylum-seeking coincided with a sharp rise in irregular migration.

Interlinkages Between Types of Flows and the Need for a Comprehensive Approach

Two important and interconnected conclusions should be drawn, and lessons learnt from the above. *First*, each main type and channel of migration has its specific characteristics and its management must be fully attuned to its distinctiveness. *Second*, at the same time, however, they are also interconnected, and the malfunctioning of one channel is likely to drive the flows to some other channel or channels, and as the latter channels become clogged by the intrusion, they, too, fail to function properly, and their management becomes more difficult. Hence, the imperative need to follow a comprehensive and cohesive approach encompassing the migration and refugee system as a whole.

The latter objective can be achieved by the United Nations itself playing a coordinating and complementary role to cement the cohesiveness of the entire policy package and ensure smooth working of the migration management system as a whole. This does not imply that the UN should duplicate any of the work already being done by different UN agencies, each in its own area of competence. Its coordinating role should be confined to monitoring the policies and practices operating in different types and areas of migration from the perspective of their coherence and undertake any residual or complementary work needed to ensure that the system of migration management works well. In the past, the UN General Assembly has occasionally performed this task, but only in a sporadic manner.

It is a hopeful sign that in September 2046, after long years of procrastination due to member states reticence the UN General Assembly summit agreed precisely to play this role by taking the initiative to develop two Global Compacts dealing with migration and refugees, respectively. This holds the potential, inter alia, of opening up the prospect of a continuing and active role for the United Nations in this area of migration/refugee flow management (further discussed below).

* * *

Mismatch Between Rising Emigration Pressure and Dwindling Opportunities for Legal Entry

Much of the present malaise in the global migration, including refugee, system stems from a growing imbalance between the rising emigration pressure, including refugee outflows, in origin countries, on the one hand, and dwindling opportunities for legal entry, especially for low-skilled, poverty-driven migrants and politically persecuted or otherwise discriminated persons, in the destination countries, on the other. Many of the big issues confronting the system, including migrant and refugee rights, irregular migration, human trafficking, anti-immigrant feelings and xenophobia, are closely interwoven with and embedded in the persistent mismatch between these two powerful trends. The big challenge today lies in bringing the two into a state of dynamic harmony. This cannot be achieved by the destination countries alone; origin countries, too, must play their part by taking complementary measures to tame the excessive pressure for disorderly and irregular migration and refugee outflows.

True, the imbalance is worsened by the present restrictive trends in immigration policies of most destination countries. But at least part of it is due to their perceived fear that they are losing control over immigration and their consequent anxiety to avoid being over-flooded by foreigners, whether as immigrants or as refugees. As discussed, the involvement of some miscreants of migrant origin, or who entered through asylum channels, in terrorist activities, has contributed to the rising anti-migrant and anti-refugee sentiments and made the situation worse. It is likely that origin countries' active engagement in taming excessive and disorderly migration and refugee outflows would help enhance the confidence of destination countries to allow more openness in immigration, including refugee inflows, in keeping with their humanitarian obligations, their labour market, demographic and other needs and facilitate their pursuit of scientific progress and cultural enrichment through diversity.

Origin countries should be encouraged and enabled to play their part by providing the necessary support not just because many of them are labour-surplus, capital-short ones but also, and even more importantly, because international migration and refugee flows have become a truly global process. The drivers shaping them are beyond the exclusive control of any individual county, be it a sending or receiving one. The fact that more and more countries, both developed and developing, are getting involved in both sending and receiving migrants and (to a lesser extent extent) asylum-seekers makes both important and practicable to follow a truly global approach.

A New Global Architecture for Cooperative Management of Migration and Refugee Flows

All this points to the need for nations to get together and develop a multilaterally agreed arrangement for interstate cooperation, based on mutual confidence and understanding as the basis for an orderly, safe as well as more predictable and manageable system of global migration and refugee flows. In my writings over several years, I have argued for such an arrangement and have also put forward, along with a few of my colleagues, some essential details of its configuration.[3] Based on the principle of regulated openness, the proposed new architecture will be sustained by three essential pillars: commonality of objectives, a set of harmonised normative guidelines and coordinated institutional arrangements. Thus, in effect, future interstate cooperation should take the form of an overall framework agreement as a soft instrument—or a solemn declaration—setting forth guiding principles applicable to all types of cross-border movements. This will be supported and supplemented by a set of autonomous but interrelated, sub-regimes as soft and hard instruments, depending on the type of flows and nature of the issues involved. It would thus constitute a mosaic of hard and soft instruments geared to the set of common objectives articulated in the solemn declaration mentioned above.

The Proposed UN Global Compacts on Migration and Refugees

It is encouraging that, propelled by the gathering migration and refugee crisis in Europe and elsewhere, the United Nations has finally stepped in and agreed to move in this direction by deciding to develop two Global Compacts dealing with migration and refugees, respectively. Much, however, depends on how the two compacts are conceptualised and designed. It is worth noting that for the reasons already discussed, it would be wrong to completely delink the two compacts and deal with each one in complete isolation. In the last analysis, the real impacts of them will also depend on whether nations—not just governments but

---

[3]See Bimal Ghosh, *Managing Migration: Time for a New International Regime?*, Oxford University Press, 2000; 'Inter-state cooperation and migration management at the global level', in: *Inter-state Cooperation and Migration*, The Bern Initiative/IOM. Bern/Geneva, 2005; 'Managing migration: Towards the missing regime' in Migration without Borders, A. Pécoud and P. Guchteneire (eds.), UNESCO/Berghahan Books, Oxford, 2007; 'Inter-state cooperation and global mobility', paper presented at the conference on global mobility regimes, New York, 2009; "The global financial and economic crisis and migration governance" in Global Governance: A Review of Multilateralism and International Organizations, 16(3), July, 2010; *The Global crisis and the Future of Migration: Issues and Prospects*, Chapter 9 (Towards a new global architecture for orderly and predictable migration, Palgrave/Macmillan, Houndmills, UK, 2013.

12 A Synoptic Overview of Policy Issues and Prescriptions

also other principal actors, notably civil society institutions and the private sector—are prepared to seriously take up the challenge of global migration and refugee flows. In the context of the proposed two compacts, and as a follow-up to my earlier writings, I intend to discuss the subject further in a forthcoming book tentatively foreseen for winter 2018. It is unfortunate that the Trump administration has decided to dissociate itself the initiative. Even so, the initiative offers a golden and long-awaited opportunity. It should not be lost to better manage global migration and refugee flows in future.

Glossary

The European Union is the political and economic grouping of 28 European countries including the UK, which, at the time of writing, was in the process of withdrawing from the Union.

The European Council is composed of the heads of state or government of the member countries. It has the responsibility of defining the European Union's over-all political and economic direction, setting its priorities and approving decisions, as appropriate.

The European Commission is the executive body of the European Union responsible for proposing legislation, implementing decisions, upholding the European Unions' treaties and agreements, and managing its day-to-day business.

The European Parliament is the directly elected legislative institution of the European Union. Together with the European Council and the European Commission, it discharges the legislative function of the European Union although it does not sponsor legislation. It acts on the basis of proposals presented by the European Commission.

The Schengen Agreement, signed at Schengen village in Luxembourg on 14 June 1985 (effective 26 March 1995), created arrangements for abolition of border control and visa-free movement within the territory covered by its signatory states, dubbed Schengen Zone or Schengen Area. Although it started as an independent intergovernmental agreement, with only seven original members, it later became incorporated into the body of the rules governing the European Union. However, not all European Union member states are members of the Schengen Agreement; conversely, some signatories to the Schengen Agreement are not members of the EU (e.g. Iceland, Norway, Switzerland and Liechtenstein).

Bibliography

Abadie, Alberto, and Javier Gardeazabal. "The economic cost of conflict: A case study of the Basque county." *The American Economic Review*, vol. 93, no.1 (March 2003), pp. 113–132.

Agence France Presse (AFP). "Thai military general, the alleged lynchpin in human trafficking, among 88 charged in junta-led crackdown …." *South China Morning Post*, 10 November 2015.

Amnesty International, London, UK. "Hotspot Italy: How EU's flagship approach leads to violation of refugee and migrant rights."

———. 2016. Annual Report, 2016/17. www.amnesty.org/en/latest/research/2017/02/amnesty-international-annual-report-2016/17.

Ardittis, Solon. "Matteo Renzi's 'Migration Compact' proposal: A step closer to a viable and comprehensive solution to the EU migrant crisis?" *New Europe*, 4 April 2016.

Azad, Ashraful. "Banishing refugees to a flood-prone island will not solve Bangladesh's Rohingya refugee crisis." *The Conversation*, 27 March 2017.

BBC News. "Migrant crisis; Italy a haven from killings and kidnappings." 4 September 2016.

Biden, Joe. "A plan for Central America." *The New York Times*, 29 January 2015. http://www.nytimes.com/2015/01/30/opinion/joe-biden-a-plan-for-central-america.html?

Bilan, Yuriy, et al., *Perceptions, imaginations, life satisfaction and socio-demography: The case of Ukraine*. EUMAGINE Project paper 11, 24 September 2012. Available online. www.eumagine.org>2016/03/03>gr.

Bonnin, H., et al., "Can immigration alleviate the demographic burden," *Franz Archiv*, vol. 57, no. 1 (2000).

Boubtane, Ekrame, et al., *Immigration and economic growth in the OECD countries, 1986–2006*. CESIFO Working paper no. 5392.

Brodeur, Abel. "Terrorism and employment: Evidence from successful and failed terrorist attacks." 2015. iza.org/dp9526.pdf.

Cali, M., and Samia Sekkarie. "Much ado about nothing: The economic impact of refugee "invasions"." Brookings Institute, Washington, DC, 16 September, 2015. www.brookings.edu/blog/future-dvelopment/2015/09.16/much-ado-about-nothing-the-economic-impact-of-refugee-invasions.

CNBC. "Greece's Varoufakis addresses EU migrant crisis." 3 March 2016. https://www.cnbc.com.

Dorsey, James. "Plight of Myanmar's Rohingya: Militant Islam's next rallying call?" *South China Morning Post*, 9 September 2017. http://www.scmp.com/author/James-m-dorsey.

Düvell, F., and Irina Lapshyna. *The EuroMaidan protests, corruption, and war in 15, 2015*. MPI, Washington, DC.

Dziadosz, Alex. "Syrian exiles in Lebanon seek a refuge in work." *Financial Times*, 21 November 2016.

The Economist, London, UK. "Under-age and on the move." 28 June 2014. http://economist.com/node/21605886.

———. "As the world's refugee problem grows, Japan pulls up the drawbridge." 14 March 2015. http://www.economist.com/news/asia/21646255-worlds-refugee-problem-grows-japan.

———. "Still in Peril." 4 June 2015.

———. "The Rohingyas: The most persecuted people on Earth." 13 June 2015.

———. "All down the line." 19 December 2015–01 January 2016.

———. "Burying drowned migrants is part of a broader Greek problem." 21 April 2016.

———. "Misplaced charity." 11–17 June 2016.

———. "Plugging the gap." 5–11 August 2017.

———. "Attitudes to immigration: Still yearning." London, 12–18 August 2017.

Euronews. Robert Hackwill "Norway under fire for deporting woman who was whipped in Iran." 22 September 2017. www.euronews.cm.

European Commission, Brussels. Press Release, 6 June 2016. "Partnership framework for a coordinated, systematic and structural approach matching the EU's interests with the interests of our partners."
———. Report from the Commission to the Council and European Parliament. Sixth Progress Report on the Implementation by Ukraine of the Action Plan on Visa Liberalisation {SWD (2015)705} (final). Brussels, 18.12.2015.
European Stability Initiative, Berlin. *ESI newsletter.* "Fire in the Aegean, scenario of failure, how to succeed." 11 October 2016. See also its enlarged PDF version.
Financial Times, London, UK. "Reflections of a tearful Ziaur Rahman of the Rohingya ethnic group." Cited in *Financial Times*, 3 January 2015.
———. "Western groups find Russia tough to harvest." 21 April 2015.
———. "Putin drives a wedge through the middle class." 22 May 2015.
———. "Failed asylum-seekers caught in no man's-land." 11 June 2015.
———. "Paris and Berlin urge EU unity on refugees." 25 August 2015.
———. "Mafia diverts funds from asylum seeker reception centres, say officials." 25 August 2015.
———. "Cuba's détente with US drives Mexico's migrant crisis." 10 November 2015.
———. "Brussels plans new force to police external borders." 11 December 2015
———. "Greece takes a fall for Schengen." 12 February 2016
———. "Berlin eases anger over migrants with welfare increase." 24 March 2016.
———. "Sweden faces new reality of heightened security and violence." 10 April 2017.
———. "Australia urged to close detention centre." 28 April 2016.
———. "Exodus from South Sudan creates world's biggest refugee settlement." 9 June 2017.
———. "Germany struggles to find employment for refugees." 23 June 2017.
———. "Lebanon's mood towards refugees darkens." 2 August 2017.
———. "Libya migrants' sufferings revive memories of 'dirty deal' anger." 9–10 September 2017.
———. "Austria's Sebastian Kurz leans towards tougher line on migration." 19 October 2017.
———. "Honduras crisis shines spotlight on Central America's problems." 1 December 2017.

Frelick, B. "Haitian boat interdiction and return: First asylum and first principles of refugee protection." *Cornell International Law Journal*, vol. 26 (Issue Symposium 1993).

Ghosh, Bimal. *Huddled masses and uncertain shores: Insights into irregular migration*. Martinus Nijhoff Publishers/Kluwer Law International, The Hague, 1988, pp. 42–43.

———. *Managing Migration: Time for a New International Regime?* Oxford University Press, 2000.

———. *Elusive protection and uncertain lands: Migrants' access to human rights*. IOM, Geneva, 2003, p. 11 and pp. 21–25.

———. "Managing migration: Interstate cooperation at the global level. Is the emergence of a new paradigm of partnership around the Corner?" in: *Interstate Cooperation and Migration*, Berne Initiative Studies, Federal Office of Migration, Switzerland/IOM, Bern/Geneva (2005).

———. "Managing migration: Whither the Missing Regime?" UNESCO, Paris (2005), in: *Migration without borders*, UNESCO, Paris (2007).

———. *Human Rights and Migration: The Missing Link*. University of Utrecht/THP, The Hague, 2008.

———. *The global economic crisis and the future of migration: Issues and prospects. What will migration look like in 2045?* Palgrave/Macmillan, Houndmills, England, 2015.

Goldberg, Eleanor. "80% of Central American women, girls are raped crossing into the US." *Huffington Post*, 12 September 2014.

Goncharov, Olena. "Visa-free travel may be at risk after apparent tampering with budget bill." *KyivPost*, 4 January 2016.

Harford, Tim. "Nothing to fear but fear itself." 17 November 2015. http://timharford.com/2015/11.

Hill, Kathrin. "Foreign exodus from Russia gathers space." *Financial Times*, 5 February 2015.

Hipsman, F., and Doris Meissner. *A piece of puzzle*. Migration Policy Institute (MPI), Washington, DC, 2015.

Howard Koplowitz. "Immigration Reform 2015: Unaccompanied minors from Central America…." *International Business Times*, 23 April 2015. www.lbtimes.com.

IFO Institute, Munich, Germany. *German companies mainly see refugees as unskilled workers*. November 2015.

The Independent, London, UK. *Refugee crisis: Orphan crisis locked up in medieval prisons…*, 14 October 2014.

———. "Attitudes to immigration: Still yearning." 12–18 August 2017.
International Business Times, Howard Koplowitz "Immigration Reform 2015: Unaccompanied minors from Central America…."
International Organization for Migration (IOM), Geneva, Switzerland. "IOM Calls for a Coordinated Response to "Unravelling" Libya, Danger to Thousands of Stranded Migrants." 16 February 2015.
———. *IOM News*. "Mediterranean migrants arrive in Italy, Greece—More deaths reported." 14 July 2015.
———. *IOM News*, 20 June 2017. "UN Migration Agency Launches Detention Centre Mapping in Libya."
———. *Fatal Journeys*, vols. 1–3. Various years. https://publications.iom.int>books>fata.
———. *Harrowing Journeys*, UNICEF/IOM, 9 September 2017.
———. IOM Press release. "Human trafficking and exploitation are rife among Rohingya refugees." 14 November 2017. https://www.iom.int/newsdesk/20171114.
Jacobson, Gavin. "Aung San Suu Kyi, The ignoble laureate." *The New Yorker*, 15 September 2017.
Kazman, Amy. "Deportation hangs over India's Rohingya." *Financial Times*, 11 September 2017.
Kennedy, Elizabeth. *No childhood here: Why Central American children are fleeing their homes.* American Immigration Council, Washington, DC. 2005. 1 July 2014. https://www.mricanimmigrationcouncil.org.
KFW. "Migrants start 170,000 new businesses each year." KFW Press Release 2017-04-04/Group. www.kfw.de/gruendungen-durch-migranten.
Lucht, Hans. "European anti-migration agenda could challenge stability in Niger." *DIIS Policy Brief*, 19 June 2017.
Martinez, Oscar. *A history of violence: Living and dying in Central America.* Verso Books, Brooklyn, USA March 2016.
The Migrant Files. "The human and financial cost of 15 years of fortress Europe." http://www.themigrantfiles.com (discontinued on 24 June 2016).
Muzaffar, C., and Faye Hipsman. "The child and family migration surge of summer 2014: A short-lived crisis with a lasting impact." *Columbia Journal of International Affairs*, vol. 68, no. 2 (2015).
Nasser, R., and Steven Symansky. "Calculating the fiscal cost to Jordan of the Syrian refugee crisis." IMF country report no. 17/232, July 2017; DAI 20 June 2014. www.Dai.com.
Nazario, Sonia. "The children of the drug wars: A refugee crisis, not an immigration crisis." *The New York Times*, 11 July 2014.

The New York Times. "Central America's unresolved migrant crisis." 20 June 2015. http://www.nytimes.com/2015/06/16/opinion/central-americas-unresolved-migrant-crisis.html?

Organization for Economic Cooperation and Development (OECD), Paris, France. *Migration policy debates.* No. 8 November 2015. www.OECD.org/migration.

Peel, Michael. "Asia's Boat People." *Financial Times*, 3 June 2015.

Pew Research Center. "European opinions of the refugee crisis in 5 charts." 16 September 2016. http://www.pewglobal.org/2016/06/07euroskepticism-beyond-brexit.

Piechal, Tomasz. *Disappointment and Fear—the Public Mood in Ukraine.* Warsaw. OSW, 2015. Available online.

Pinchuck, Victor. "Only tough love can stop Ukraine squandering its last chance." *Financial Times*, 16 December 2014.

Prior, Kathleen. "Bangladesh border guards 'burning boats'." *The Telegraph*, 22 September 2017. www.telegraph.co.uk/authors/kathleen-prior/.

Rabinovitch, Zara. "Pushing out the boundaries of humanitarian screening with in-country and offshore processing." *Migration information Source.* Migration Policy Institute, Washington, DC, 16 October 2014.

Religion and Politics Tracking Survey, 29 July 2014, Public Religion Research Institute. Washington, DC.

Reuters. "The idea to set up camps would be in total disregard of circumstances for the people." 2 May 2017.

Rich, Column. "The war over Syria's war dead." *Foreign Policy*, January 2016.

Soros, George. "Why I am investing $500 million in Migrants." 19/20 September 2016. *World Street Journal.* http://on.wsj.com/2cEoJnK.

State Statistics Service of Ukraine, Kiev. *Population of Ukraine.* 2014, 2015. Available online.

The Straits Times, Singapore, 19 July 2017.

United Nations Children Fund (UNICEF), New York. *Thousands of Yemeni children dying due to conflict*, 2016. https://www.voanews.com/a/children-in-yemen-bear-brunt-of…unicef/3259260.html.

———. *"Harrowing Journeys."* UNICEF/IOM, 9 September 2017

United Nations High Commissioner for Refugees, Geneva, 2014. "UNHCR urges focus on saving lives as 2014 boat people numbers near 350,000." 10 December 2014.

———. Press Release, 9 July 2014, Washington, DC. http://www.unhcrwashington.org/children.

———. "Children on the run: Unaccompanied children leaving Central America and Mexico and the need for international protection." July 2014. Washington, DC. Available online. http:/unhcrwashington.org/children.

———. UNHCR Global Trends, 2015. www.unhcr.org.

———. UNHCR Statistical Yearbooks. Various years. www.unhcr.org>en-us>statistical-yearb.

Visa-free Europe. "Georgia, Ukraine Ukraine's visas-free-access to EU delayed" Schengen Visa Information, 10 June 2016. www.Schengen visainfo.com.

Wade, Francis. "Myanmar's *Enemy within: Buddhist Violence and the Making of a Muslim "Other".*" Zed Books, 2017, London. www.zedbooks.net.

Wells, N., and Mark Fahey. "Terror attacks don't rattle markets like they use to do." *CNBC*, 22 March 2016.

World News Report, BBC. "Migrant crisis: People treated like animals in Hungary camp." 1 September 2015.

World News Report. einnews.com, 3 January 2016.

World Street Journal, George Soros, "Why I am investing $500 million in Migrants." 19 September 2016. http://on.wsj.com/2cEoJnK.

Zucker, N.S., and Naomi Zucker. *Desperate crossing: Seeking refuge in America.* Routeledge, New York, 1996.

Index

A

Abadie, Alberto 148
Abbott, Tony 82
abuse of children 85
abusive treatment 194, 196
acceptance rates of refugees 72
access to asylum-seeking 84, 174
accountability 178
action plan 32, 34, 160, 212
Administration 108, 109, 173, 186, 187, 204, 233
admissibility assessment 45
admission 38, 97, 107, 108, 119, 137, 184, 185, 187, 225, 228
advisory assistance 144
advocacy and cautionary 227
Aegean islands 29, 48, 51
    Sea 24, 27, 28, 51, 52; Sea route 28
Africa 17, 33, 57, 60, 64, 67, 80, 133
African 16, 17, 33, 56, 61–64, 76
    Middle Eastern countries 60; migration to Europe 31

Africa Trust Fund 33, 62
Agadez region 68
Agence France Presse 195
Ahmed, Fakir 207
aid fund 215
    money 55, 113, 226; related reform 226
air strikes 227
al-Baghdadi, Abu Bakr 208
Albania 30, 49, 50
Aleppo 12, 13, 28
Alfano, Angelino 34
Alliance for Prosperity 170
Al-Qaeda 10, 68, 208
al-Sarj, Faez 66
Alternative for Germany 58
ambit of competence 226
American child 220, 222
American Civil Liberties Union 172
    Immigration Council 180; Immigration Lawyers Association 177

Index

Amnesty International 3, 15, 46, 47, 61, 64, 84, 89, 96, 103, 177, 197, 199, 210
animosity 192
Ankara 28, 30, 45, 53
Annan, Kofi 197
anticipated frequency 149
anticipatory role 227
anti-immigrant feeling 20, 58, 230
  intervention 68; migration measures 68; Muslim sentiment 212; refugee sentiments 231; Rohingya campaigns 191; sentiments 231; terrorist laws 53; torture convention 84; Western feeling 214
appeal 23, 47, 72, 107, 112, 196, 200, 203
apprehension(s) 171, 174, 176
Appropriation bill 170
Arakan
  Project 191; Salvation Army (ARSA) 200, 201, 206, 207, 209, 210
arbitrary arrests 53
arduous journey 185
Aristide, Jean-Bertrand 82
armed conflicts 39
  ethnic groups 205
Army 13, 113, 195, 198, 200, 205, 206, 209, 210, 212, 214
ARSA. *See* Arakan Salvation Army (ARSA)
Asia 6, 133, 195, 210, 214, 219, 220
  Asia Pacific Refugee Networks 204
assaults 92, 98, 168, 172, 205, 206
association agreements 61
Association of South-East Asian Nations (ASEAN) 196, 220
asylum 1, 2, 10, 13, 16, 17, 20–24, 26, 29–31, 33, 35, 38, 40, 41, 43, 45–49, 51, 54, 55, 58, 64, 66, 69, 72–76, 79–87, 89–92, 95–107, 109, 110, 112–116, 118, 119, 121, 123–125, 128–130, 132–134, 138, 139, 141–143, 157, 159, 167, 169–171, 181, 224, 225, 228, 229, 231
asylum and refugee policy 53
  application 118, 167, 169, 224, 228; centre 23, 106; claims 20, 82, 98, 103, 114, 157; hearings 46; laws 95, 177, 229; officers 183; policies 72, 95, 97; procedure 79, 83, 134; processing of 29, 81, 221; registration 29, 50; service 46; systems 183
asylum-seeker(s) 20–24, 26, 29–31, 38, 43, 45–47, 49, 51, 54, 55, 66, 69, 72–75, 79–84, 86, 170, 171
  on arrival 73; registration of 21, 26
attempted coup 53
Aung San Suu Kyi 197–199, 205, 206, 210, 211
Australia 82, 84, 85, 109, 141, 194
Australian model of offshore processing 81
Australia's High Court 85
Austria 22, 23, 30, 34, 73, 93, 95, 124, 212
Austrian 30, 34, 81, 95
authoritarianism 53
authoritarian regime 86
  zeal 214
autocratic governments 41, 61
autonomous instrument, inter-related 232
avenues of entry 187

backlog of cases 52, 83
Balkans 43, 51, 100
  route 47, 50, 53, 102
Bangladesh 190–192, 194, 198, 199, 201–210, 213
Bangladesh foreign ministry 198
  government 201–203

Bangladeshis 189, 193
bank loan 146
bank overdrafts 146
Barrio 18 175
basic amenities 202
    infrastructure 204
Bay of Bengal 3, 189, 204
BBC 5, 61, 189, 198
beatings 66, 190
Beirut 12, 149
Belarus 157, 159
Belgium 147
Bengal 192
Bengali 190, 192
Berlin 23, 60, 92, 104, 105, 115, 125, 128
Berlusconi 61
Biden, Joe 174, 178
bifurcation of competence 220
bilateral agreement(s) 33, 41, 67, 225
    partnership 80
bi-partisan agreement 220
"black box of refugees" 29
Black Sea route 50
    Ukraine-Poland route 49
boat owners 203
Boko Haram 16, 68
border control(s) 11, 20, 26, 27, 29, 66–68, 70, 83, 95, 125, 174
    closures 28; guards 47, 103, 198, 203; Patrol agents 174; security 19, 170, 178; walls 29
Borobudur Buddhist temple 208
Bosnia in 1992 76
Boston Marathon 148
breeding grounds 140
Brenner Alpine pass 34
British conquest 192
broad-based development 32
Brodeur, Abel 149
Brussels 30, 45, 57, 65, 70, 72, 92, 99, 115, 128, 140, 147, 160, 161
brutal reprisal 200

Brzeski, Carsten 137
Buddhism 214
Buddhist 195, 197, 206, 207, 214
    community 193, 200; majority 206; monks 196, 213, 214; Rakhine 192. *See also* Rakhine
Bulgaria 30, 72, 73
Bulgarian 50
burden 21–23, 55, 58, 63, 72–74, 80, 113, 129, 139, 142, 220, 224
burden (or responsibility) sharing 20, 74, 80
Burmanisation 214
Burmese military governments 192
    people 211; politician 206
burning
    down 201; houses, of 198
business
    activities 145; assignments 163
    community 214; enterprises 212, 214; environment 162
business sector 213

C

Cambodia 82, 109
Cambodians 182
CAM parole 186, 187
camps 11, 14, 31, 34, 47, 48, 54–56, 61, 64, 65, 81, 103, 104, 111, 112, 115, 141, 189, 191, 192, 198, 201, 204
capacity-building 62
    absorb to 56; utilization 164
capital-short 231
Caribbean 82, 86
    corridor 176
Cartagena Declaration on Refugees 39, 59, 181
cartel violence 180
category jumping 38, 228
Cavusoglu, Mevlut 209
ceasefire agreements 157

ceilings 185
Center for Migration Studies 187
Central America 6, 87, 167, 168, 170, 171, 173, 175, 179, 181, 182, 184, 221, 226, 228
Central American children 172, 173, 177, 180, 182, 184
  Americans 169, 181, 184; Central American countries 87, 173, 177, 179, 184, 221, 225, 226; migrants 167, 168; migration 167, 170; Minors (CAM) 186, 187
central Mediterranean route 34, 35, 43, 49, 50, 52–54, 64, 66, 112
  Mediterranean 33, 43, 48, 49, 117
Centro Nacional de Derecho Humanos (CNDH) 169
cessation 212
Ceuta 43
challenge 67, 77, 78, 121, 168, 177, 226, 230, 233
Chapter VII of the UN Charter 227
Chernysh, Vadym 162
child exodus 174, 178, 181, 184
  migrants 104, 170, 171, 179, 186, 222, 228; migration 170, 174, 178, 221, 222
children 5, 6, 11–13, 15–17, 32, 37, 41, 47, 85, 95, 101–104, 106, 111, 112, 125, 126, 130, 158, 162, 164, 167, 170–174, 176–187, 195, 197, 198, 202, 204, 205, 212, 222
child-sensitive approach 183
China 200
Chios Island 47, 48, 50
Chittagong 192, 204
Christmas Island 82
circumspection 214, 222
citizenship 95, 187, 190, 193, 197, 212
citizenship question 197
civil society 225, 227
  society institutions 214, 233; war 39, 76
clamping down 60
clearance 210
clogged 228, 229
closed-door approach 194
close links 215, 227
coalition against human rights 66
  governments 227
coast guards 26, 28, 65
coastlines 21
cocaine-smuggling 176
code of conduct 35, 118
codify 224
coercive need 181
coherence 221, 230
coherent policy 62
cohesive approach 226, 229
  asylum system 23; cohesiveness 221, 229; policy 221
Cold War 10, 86
collective commitment 41, 70, 73
  responsibility 33
Colombia 176
Commission 16, 19, 20, 22, 27, 43, 48, 50, 69, 70, 72–74, 85, 118, 127, 137–139, 160, 169, 197, 220, 226
commissioner for home affairs 80
commitment 20, 30, 46, 53, 57, 60, 61, 71, 80, 150, 210, 220
commonality of objectives 232
common border force 26
  commitment 58, 76; EU Migration bonds 57; European Asylum Policy 80; external borders 27, 70, 71; interests 62, 69, 213, 215; objectives 232; responsibility 53; Security and Defence 21
communication 194
communist regimes 39, 223
community development 162
  level 20, 57, 220

Index

complementary measures 230
  work 221, 230
complete isolation 232
composite push factors 40
comprehensive approach 60, 229
compulsory quota system 22, 70
concentration camps 48, 65
conditional approval 186
Conference of Catholic Bishops 180
confidence-building 62, 213
configuration 165, 207, 232
conflict resolution 212
Congress 170, 178, 196
constitutional reform 205
consular standards 53
contravention of the right to asylum seeking 81
control over the army 199
Convention on the Rights of the Child 102, 182, 183
cooperative management 231
coordinated institutional arrangement 221, 232
coordinating and complementary role 229
core mandate 224
corruption 155–157, 162
Council on Hemispheric Affairs 167
country of origin 40, 79, 130, 155, 171, 180, 224
  settlement 74
Cox's Bazar 191, 199, 202–204, 215
crackdown on the media 53
cramped cells 172
credibility 53, 62, 75, 196, 209, 211, 220
credible mechanism 196, 213
Crimea 155–159, 165
crimes against humanity 200, 201
criminal gangs 111, 115, 116, 168, 169, 172, 176
  groups 168

crisis 1, 9, 20–22, 24, 27, 28, 30, 32, 34, 42–44, 48, 54, 57, 61, 69, 78, 122, 124, 168, 169, 172, 173, 177, 178, 209, 224, 229
Croatia 73
crowded boats 189
Cruz, Ted 173
Cuba 86, 169
Cuban Adjustment Act 169
Cubans 83, 169
cultural affinity 74
  enrichment 231; mores 135
Customs and Border Protection agency 170–172
Cyprus 28, 72
Czech Republic 71–73, 96, 100, 130

D

daily arrivals 48, 50, 51
  Daily Telegraph 204; skirmishes 165
Dark side of the inflows 139
Darusman, Marzuki 211
data-sharing 194
Davutoglu, Ahmet 28
DAX 149
death 3, 17, 68, 85, 98, 151, 165, 168, 169, 176, 179, 198, 205
death tolls 52
decentralization 162
declarations 196
Deferred Enforced Departure 184
delays 46, 115, 134, 173
democratic conviction 214
demographic
  expansion 56; groups 63; needs 60, 231; solution 135
Denisenko, Mikhail 164
dependency ratio 130, 135
deportation(s) 30, 46, 49, 90, 112, 168, 173
  deferred 173; migrants, of 49; process 118

250　Index

deprivation 38
designed 39, 53, 71, 118, 183, 204, 223, 232
destination country(ies) 38, 58, 60, 61, 65, 79, 81, 83, 84, 87, 88, 143, 225–228, 230, 231
detained/detaining migrants 64, 66, 67, 101, 167, 168, 172, 173
detention 47, 54, 66, 67, 75, 81, 83–85, 100, 102, 103, 105, 109–111, 113, 114, 141, 173, 207
  centre(s) 54, 66, 81, 84, 85, 100, 105, 110, 111, 114, 141, 173, 207
deteriorating mental conditions 85
development 21, 31, 32, 57, 63, 67, 127, 129, 144, 169, 221, 225
  aid 61
Dhaka 208
diaspora 155
Diffa region 68
Dijkhoff, Klaas 27
dirty deal 65, 66
discrimination 38, 192, 211
disintegration law 142
disorder migration 32, 56, 58, 61, 226, 227, 230, 231
  emigration 226; migration flows 227
displacements 1, 6, 9, 11, 14, 16, 156, 158, 163, 165, 223
distribution of asylum-seekers 80
DNA tests 185
dole 60, 226
domestic abuses 179
  aids 204
Donbas 163
Donetsk 158, 162, 165
downside risk 137
drug smugglers 49
Dublin Convention 73, 74, 105, 118
durable peace 165
Dutch reservations 161
dwindling opportunities 230
dynamic harmony 230

E

early warning system 42, 222
eastern Balkan route 52
  Europe 6, 125, 219; Mediterranean 33; Partnership 160; provinces 155, 156, 158; Ukraine 155, 156, 158, 165
East European member states 22
East Germany 53
Eckstein, Zvi 148
economic behaviour 150
  burden 139; co-operation 221; development 32, 206; growth 124, 135–137, 139, 178; hardship 156; integration 144; migrants 38, 89; reform 67; sanctions 163, 212, 214
The Economist 5, 60, 78, 105, 108, 113, 160, 170, 206, 208
educational opportunities 158, 178
Egypt 14, 41
Egyptians 49
Electoral victory 197
eligibility, determination of 183
  criteria 184
elitist politicians 214
El Salvador 87, 167, 168, 174–176, 179, 180, 185
elusive escape 170
emergency assistance 50
  clause 75; relocation 20; reserves 203; response 203; scheme 75
emigration 158, 160, 162–165, 225, 226, 229
  pressure 50, 60, 155, 229, 230
employers 122, 125, 126, 134, 145
employment 32, 56, 124, 130–134, 138, 140, 143–145, 149, 158, 161, 178, 198, 225
enclaves 12, 43, 193
enormous flow 135
entanglement of channels of entry 228

entrepreneurs 136
  entrepreneurship 135
equipment 35, 75, 118, 162, 209
Erdogan, Recep Tayyip 208, 209
erected walls 225
Eritrea 16, 20
essential pillars 232
essential supplies 199
ETA 148
ethical dimensions 64
  ground 46, 52; values 62
Ethiopia 11, 33
Ethiopians 49
ethnic cleansing 16, 198–201
  minorities 205; network 74
ethno-nationalist 214
ethno-political 16, 197, 205, 207
EU-Africa bonds 57
  aid 47, 125, 225; asylum rules 23, 35; asylum system 23, 75; economy 139; knee-jerk plan 44
EU Charter of Fundamental Rights 30, 81
EU Commission 19, 20, 22, 26, 48, 50, 69, 70, 72, 73, 118, 127, 130, 220
EU Council 22, 27, 57, 72, 73
EU countries 21–24, 27, 41, 63, 64, 68, 74, 80, 95, 97, 103, 105, 116, 125, 129, 130, 160, 223
EU directives on asylum and refugees 48
EU members 19, 22, 35, 41, 46, 55, 72, 78, 80, 91, 159, 214, 220, 223
  membership 53, 64
EU member states 2, 19, 22, 26, 27, 33, 35, 41, 42, 46, 69, 71–73, 75, 78–80, 91, 106, 119, 159, 220, 230
EU migration policy 22, 23
  Parliament resolution 20; partnership 61, 65
Eurobond(s) 57, 58

Maidan 155–157; stat 72, 97, 129; zone 19, 57, 58, 128, 137, 150
Europe 2, 5, 6, 10, 14, 15, 17, 18, 20–23, 26, 27, 30, 33, 37–39, 41–43, 45, 48, 49, 51, 52, 55, 57, 64, 66, 67, 69, 89–92, 95, 97, 99, 100, 102, 105, 107, 111, 112, 118, 121, 122, 126, 129, 131, 135, 136, 139–141, 148, 157, 161, 170, 222, 224, 225, 228, 229, 232
European Agenda on Migration 20
  Border and Coast Guard Agency 26, 75; border force 70; Coast Guard 28
European Commission 19, 20, 23, 26, 28, 30, 33, 35, 45, 51, 74, 78, 130, 137, 139, 160, 226
  Council 33, 72, 161; Council on Foreign Relations 27, 66; Council on Refugees and Exiles (ECRE) 64, 81; Court of Human Rights 81, 90; Court of Justice 72; migration policy 22; Parliament 20, 44, 46, 160, 161; Parliamentary Assembly 45; report 51, 118; Stability Initiative (ESI) 50, 51; values 46
European Union (EU) 2, 3, 18–24, 26–35, 40–81, 83, 90–92, 95, 97, 103, 105, 106, 116–119, 121, 122, 125, 127–131, 134, 137–139, 143, 144, 157–161, 165, 171, 183, 203, 211, 214, 220, 222, 223, 225, 226
EU states 19, 40, 73, 128
EU structure 220
EU summit 20–22, 28
EU Trust Fund for Africa 67
EU/Turkey agreement 44, 48, 54, 57, 63–65, 69, 125
EU/Turkey deal 31, 44, 51–53, 65
EU/Turkey plan 49
EU-Ukraine association 161

252 Index

evacuate 47
exclusive control 231
executive orders 186
existing infrastructure 192
exit visas 87
exodus of foreigners 163
expectant mothers 41
expeditious transfer 186
expulsion 47, 191
external aid 203
external border(s) 26, 27, 34, 41, 50, 70, 75, 220
    externalisation 79, 81, 83, 86; processing 79, 80, 82; processing centres 81
extortion 111, 169, 172, 176, 185
extort ransoms 168
extra judicial killings 201
extra public spending 137
extremism 206

F

failed asylum-seekers 31, 46, 105, 118, 119
    state 86, 177
fairer distribution of refugees 19
faith-based atrocities 212
    political forces 214; violence 206
false offers 204
family 41, 98, 99, 104, 108, 172, 180, 181, 228
    reunification 41, 90, 97, 98, 130, 180
Farmaner, Mark 210
fast-track basis 45
Federal Migration Service 163
    Statistics Service 164
fences 47, 56
field offices 223
    surveys 161, 180, 182
financial crisis 57
    grants 225
Financial Times 23, 30, 50, 66, 70, 85, 91, 95, 96, 113, 116, 119, 128, 132, 143, 148, 156, 163, 164, 169, 179, 195, 205, 207
finger-printing 24, 29
Finland 73
first country of arrival 35, 74, 118
fiscal consolidation 162
flagrantly violent 150
flee 55, 86, 87, 172, 178, 179, 195, 198, 201
flexible screening policy 228
flimsy structures 192
flood protection 204
food assistance 192
    education 192; healthcare 192; insecurity 192
foot soldiers 176
forced displacement 3, 16, 33, 191
    emigration 50; labour 168; migration 32, 39, 58, 61, 226; movements 39; transfer 81, 83
forcible/forcibly repatriation 84
    retuning 46; uprooted 2, 157
foreign-born 89, 92, 98, 133, 135
foreigner's integration 145
foreign fighters 206
    investors 163; labour 160; meddling 198
forest department 204
formidable challenges 162, 226
Fortify Rights 196, 201
fragile agreement 194
fragility 198
fragmented migration system 228
France 20, 22, 78, 92, 97, 104, 128, 147, 150, 159
free/freedom of movement 47, 74, 162, 198, 212
    internal movement 20, 26, 41, 70, 73, 220; movement of people 20; trade deal 161
French 35
frequency of attack/assault 150, 172
Frontex 26, 27, 42, 43, 49, 50, 70, 117, 118

Index

front-line member states 20
states 19
frozen conflict 165
Frydman, Lisa 187
fundamentalism 140–142, 145
funding sources 146

G

Gabriel, Sigmar 65
Gaddafi, Muammar 61, 65
gang 115, 176, 180
gang violence 179
Gardeazabal, Javier 148
generalised violence 39
genocide 53, 201, 208, 209
genuine claims 75
genuinely owned 226
genuine partnership 62, 226
geopolitical conflict 56
ramifications 141; reason 196; stance 28
German 23, 31, 35, 53, 56, 65, 91, 98, 101, 105, 115, 117, 125–128, 131–134, 138, 143, 149, 163, 222
Chamber of Commerce 163; Institute for Security Affairs 60; laws 142; Parliament 53; workers 138
Germany 19, 20, 22, 28, 51, 57, 58, 66, 78, 91, 92, 98–101, 104, 105, 115, 122, 124–130, 132–136, 138, 140, 142, 143, 145, 146, 159, 212, 222
ghettos 140
global basis 219
Compacts 232; crisis 23, 219; level 140, 221
Gomez, James 210
good governance 67, 68, 178, 226
governance 178
Greco-Turkish cooperation 28
Greece 5, 6, 10, 20, 22–31, 42–53, 70–74, 80, 92, 100, 130, 171, 228

Greece-Albania-Adriatic route 49
Greek Appeals Committee 45
Greeks 77; islands 28, 31, 48, 52; National Commission for Human Rights 45; Prime Minister 24, 29
gross domestic population 21
product 21, 148, 177; unemployment 21; violation of human rights 141, 227
growth impact 138
Guatemala 87, 167, 168, 174, 179, 185
Guatemalan 180
Guterres, Antonio 114, 201

H

Haiti 84, 86, 87
Haitian(s) 82, 182
Harford, Tim 148, 151
harmonise 40, 224, 232
harmonised normative guidelines 232
Hasina, Sheik 202
Havana 82
Heidenau 23
Higher School of Economics 164
high intensity business 136
high seas 40, 190
Holder, Eric 183
holding centres 65
hold-out countries 72
Hollande, François 23
Hondurans 180
Honduras 87, 167, 168, 170, 174, 176–179, 185, 186
Horn of Africa 141
host country 86, 133, 143
hotspots 24, 29, 103
House of Representatives 170
human and refugee rights 64, 83, 106, 107
human attitudes 150
casualties 13, 44; cemetery 19; displacements 1–3, 75, 76, 227; emergencies 223, 224; flows 21;

habitation 204; outflows 178; ping-pong 193, 220; resilience 147–149
humanitarian 11–13, 40, 59, 65, 82, 129, 131, 139, 144, 172, 177, 183, 193
  access 200; aid 192, 194, 203, 211; assistance 11, 12, 192, 202, 204; crisis 13, 16, 30, 47, 105, 192, 202, 203; disaster 24, 29; endeavour 211; grounds 114, 184, 223, 224; laws 121, 182; obligations 231; parole 182, 185, 186; protection 6, 17, 38, 39, 121, 123, 142, 229; Protection programme 183; values 61; visas 20
human rights 12, 34, 39, 46, 53, 81, 83–85, 90, 95, 97, 100, 103, 105, 110, 113, 121, 141, 143, 169, 173, 176, 183, 191, 196, 197, 200, 201, 204, 211, 220, 223
human rights abuse 21, 182, 196
  instruments 85; Rights Council 201; Rights Watch 100, 112, 113, 198, 211; violations 197, 210
human smugglers 50
  solidarity 215; tragedy 18, 189, 199
human traffickers 14, 15, 17, 19, 20, 31, 43, 49, 83, 111, 169, 222, 225
human trafficking 21, 28, 33, 44, 178, 189, 195, 196, 230
Hungary 22, 38, 42, 70–73, 92, 93, 96, 97, 103
Hyderabad 207

iceberg of misinformation 209, 210
identification documents 56, 87
  asylum-seekers, of 21
Idomeni 47
IDPs 1, 2, 12, 14, 162
IMF 55, 124, 127, 134, 139, 162
immediate danger 187

immigrant children 183
Immigration and Nationality Act 86
  authorities 228; control 58, 114, 186; law(s) 183, 191; proceedings 183
implementation of agreement 51
inadequacy 69, 99, 220
inclusive development 213
inclusive growth 162
income-generating impact 162
income inequality 178
incommunicado 176
in-country processing 41, 83, 86, 87, 182, 184–186, 221, 224
  programme 184, 185
independent commission 197
  investigations 211; mechanism 196
India 206, 207
indiscriminate retaliation 209
individual persecution 39–40, 182
Indonesia 189, 193, 194, 196, 203, 206, 207
Indonesian 82, 208
inflows 1, 11, 18, 20, 26, 29, 33–35, 37, 39–43, 51, 52, 59, 63, 64, 66, 67, 71, 74, 80–82, 91, 96, 116, 121–124, 126, 129, 130, 138, 139, 141, 147, 159, 168, 192, 199, 202–204, 219, 220, 222, 223, 225, 228, 231
informal consultations 69
  sector 140
ING-DiBa Bank 137
inhuman conditions 84
inhumane 82, 111, 204
INSA 58, 92
insecurity 6, 13, 76, 123, 150, 172, 178, 226
  pervasive 185
institutional arrangement 219, 220
  development 62; reform 160
Instituto Nacional de Migracion (INM) 169
integrated border control and management 26

integration 74, 96, 99, 100, 104, 115, 123–129, 133, 134, 140, 142–145, 161, 221, 225
  law 142; training 142
integrity of its border 42, 198, 207
intensity of attacks/assault 13, 150, 200
intensity of violence 11, 149
Inter-American Commission on Human Rights 169
interception 40, 79, 83, 84, 169
inter-connected conclusions 229
interconnectedness 221, 229
interdiction at sea 81, 83, 84
inter-faith tension 196, 207
  understanding 213
interior ministry 66
interlocutor 215
internal and external human displacements, effects on 227
  displacements 6, 9, 11, 14, 15, 157, 163, 198; movement of people 20, 220
internally displaced people 157, 161
international aid 145, 203
  (and) European human and refugee rights 45; attention 209, 211; Committee of the Red Cross 211; community 194, 211; Criminal Court 65; Crisis Group 199, 200; criticism 199; Finance Corporation 147; framework 232; intervention 201; law(s) 39, 45, 84, 139; links 199, 200, 206; workers 47
International Maritime Organisation (IMO) 42
  international organisations 66, 67, 147, 203, 215, 223; Rescue Committee 47, 147
International Organization of Migration (IOM) 3–5, 17, 18, 21, 65, 111, 140, 161, 162, 191, 194, 203, 204, 221, 223

international pressure 195, 209, 212
  protection 65, 179, 181, 182; refugee law 81, 83, 84, 199; response 55; standards 48, 85; watch 198
interpreters 47
inter-state cooperation 140, 220, 231, 232
  scrutiny 224
interviewing procedures 185
interviewing techniques 183
intra-EU solidarity 20, 75
investment 33, 62, 65, 75, 141, 147, 149, 150, 162, 178
investment forum 63
IOM. *See* International Organization ofMigration (IOM)
IOM Director-General 21
Iranian 85, 96
Iraq 10, 12–15, 20, 55, 76, 133, 134, 208, 227
Ireland 23
irregular Bengali immigrants 192
irregular channel(s) 32, 60, 98, 228, 229
irregular and disorder movements 63
  emigration 50; immigrants 41; immigration 19
irregular migrants 6, 31, 43, 65, 80, 159, 168, 173, 226, 229
irregular migration 31–34, 38, 60, 61, 63, 68, 140, 229, 230
ISIS 10, 13, 14, 43, 107, 147
Islam 206, 208, 214
Islamic Defenders Front (FPI) 206
ISS 208
Italian 15, 26, 34, 35, 42, 44, 49, 57, 58, 80, 103, 104, 116, 118
  government 34, 43, 57, 65, 104, 111; interior ministry 49
Italy 2, 6, 10, 17, 19, 20, 22–24, 26, 29, 34, 35, 42, 43, 48–50, 52, 56, 61, 65–67, 70–74, 80, 81, 92, 95, 103, 104, 116, 118, 128, 140, 158, 159, 171, 222, 228

J

Jacobson, Gavin 205
Japan 113, 114, 212, 229
Java 208
jihadist militants 68
   jihadists 43, 49, 115, 206
Jim Yong Kim 55, 141
job creation 32, 57
   opportunities 105, 142, 213, 228
Johnson, Sterling 84
Jordan 14, 55, 113, 123, 124, 144, 147, 222
   Compact 144
judges 183
judiciary, independence of 46, 72
Juncker, Jean-Claude 20, 78, 137
Justice and Home Affairs Council 80

K

K1 visa 147
Kangkur, Puttenee 196
Kennedy, Elizabeth 180
Kerry, John 55
Kevin, J. 187
KfW 127, 135, 136, 146
kidnapped migrants 168
KIDS in Need of Defence (KIND) 180, 183, 187
killings 15, 17, 61, 175, 198
Kipping, Katja 66
knee-jerk reactions 69, 149
Kofi Annan commission 199, 206
Ko Ni 199
Koplowitz, Howard 177
Kremlin spokesman 165
Kuala Lumpur 194
Kurdi, Alan 23

L

labour demand 38, 60, 228
   exploitation 140, 204; immigration 38, 228, 229; migration 62; productivity 135; surplus 231
labour market(s) 56, 60, 123–127, 129, 130, 132, 134, 136–138, 140, 145, 231
Lagos 63
land mines 202
land route 42
language lessons 142
Latvia 73
law enforcement agents 168
Lebanon 14, 55, 112, 113, 123, 124, 143, 144, 147, 222
Left Party 66
legal aid 47
   migration 33; processing of claims 173; protection 45, 173; representatives 47
legitimate military intervention 227
Lesbos 5, 29, 47, 50, 102
liaison officers 27
liberalisation of trade 64
Liberal-National coalition government 82
Libya 5, 10, 15, 17, 18, 34, 35, 42–44, 49, 54, 61, 64–67, 76, 80, 81, 106, 110, 111, 222
Libyan authorities 35, 117
   detention camps 66
life-saving missions 21
linkage 227
Lithuania 73
Liu, Dr. Joanne 66
livelihood 192
local authorities 168, 195
   communities 161, 162
Löfven, Stefan 96, 143
logistics 46
London 12, 42, 55, 78, 104, 108, 141, 148, 156, 160
losing control 231
low-skilled worker 124, 134, 138
Luxembourg 73
Lynn, Htin 211

Index

M

Macedonia 30, 47
    Macedonian 29, 47
Macron, Emmanuel 78
Madrid 148
Maidan protests 156
makeshift arrangements 24
    camp 191, 192, 202; settlements 104, 202
Malaysia 189, 193–196, 203, 207, 213
malfunctioning 38, 59, 229
Mali 33, 67, 225
Malorossiya 165
Malström, Cecilia 80
Malta 64, 72, 73, 81
Malta Declaration 33
Maltese 33, 34
management of refugee 223
managing the flows 38, 174
mandatory offshore detention 82
Manhattan 148
Manit Pleantong 195
man-made disasters 39, 226
Manus Island centre, Papua New Guinea 85
Manus Island, Papua New Guinea 82
Mara Salvatrucha 175
Mare Nostrum 19, 42, 222
marginalise 140, 142
market liberalisation 178
Marshall Plan for Africa 32
Marsudi, Retno 208
Martinez, Oscar 175
massive
    flows 6, 227; massive refugee 227
Médecins Sans Frontières (MSF) 5, 47, 61, 66
mediation resolution 212
medical assistance 194, 202
    care 172, 199
Mediterranean 3, 5, 6, 14, 15, 17–19, 21, 23, 35, 37, 42, 81, 109, 117, 171
    migration crisis 20

Meghna River 204
Melilla 43
member states 2, 19, 20, 22, 26, 27, 29, 33, 35, 41, 42, 46, 54, 57, 62, 69–75, 78–80, 91, 106, 119, 159, 196, 220, 221, 226, 230
MENA countries 10, 16, 17, 41, 208, 222, 224
Merkel, Angela 23, 30, 53, 56, 57, 65, 78, 91, 98, 105, 142, 222
Mexican government 168, 169, 174
Mexico 3, 167–170, 177, 179–181, 228
Mexico-Guatemala border 168
middle class 123, 164
Middle East/Eastern continent 76
    capitals 208; migrants 49
migrant arrivals 44
    -carrying boats 35; entrepreneurs 136; Operations Centre 82; reception centres 34; migrant smuggling 33, 61
migrant(s) 1, 3, 5, 9–11, 15, 17, 19–21, 26, 27, 29, 30, 32–35, 38–44, 46, 47, 49, 51, 52, 54–56, 59–62, 64–67, 69, 72, 74, 79–82, 89, 90, 95, 98–100, 102–107, 110, 111, 115–117, 121, 122, 124–126, 128, 129, 131, 134–137, 139, 140, 143–147, 155, 158, 167–169, 171, 172, 174, 177, 189, 190, 193, 194, 221, 222, 226, 228, 230, 231
migrants' human rights 65, 167, 168
migration 1, 3, 6, 9, 20, 23, 26, 27, 31–33, 35, 37–41, 52, 56–61, 63, 64, 66, 67, 71, 72, 75–77, 82, 95, 96, 99, 103, 106, 109, 115, 117, 121, 124, 129, 133, 137, 140, 147, 155, 157–161, 165, 167, 169, 170, 172, 180, 219–223, 226–233
Migration Compact 57

conundrum 40, 59, 167, 228; crisis 5, 6, 19, 20, 26, 27, 31, 43, 56, 57, 69, 96, 224, 232; history 39; flows 30, 43, 65, 79; specialists 46
migration management 39, 40, 63, 219, 221, 230, 231
  policy (cies) 22, 75, 76, 124
militancy 206, 207, 209
militant Islamic forces 208
military
  interventions 76; operations 76, 192, 227
militia reports 201
militias 10, 65, 66, 111, 201
Minniti, Marco 34
minor asylum seekers 171
minorities 192, 209, 210
  and ethnic groups 197; rights 39, 227
Minsk agreement 165
mismanaged inflows 139
mismatch, emigration pressure-dwindling opportunities 230
mistrust 192, 193
mixed flow(s) 6, 38, 39, 89, 123
  message 210; migration 6, 37–40, 43, 59, 110, 219, 223, 228; motivation(s) 38, 40, 228
mixture of reasons 228
Moderates 143
monitoring 27, 42, 68, 163, 230
  mechanism 224
monitor progress 213
moral responsibility 199
Moria 47
Morocco 43, 99
Moscovici, Pierre 138, 139
Moscow-inspired agreement 165
Mosha, Yuri 164
movement(s) 11, 20, 25, 28, 37–40, 53, 56, 62–64, 68, 73, 74, 93, 95, 122, 160, 176, 193, 202, 203, 220, 225, 228, 232

Movimiento Migrante Mesoamericano (M3) 168
Müller, Gerd 32
multifaceted attack 150
multilaterally agreed arrangement 231
multi-pronged strategy 214
murder rate 174
murders 53, 115, 174, 175
Muslim majority countries 201, 208, 209
  Muslim-free zones 200; Rohingya minority 198; Rohingyas 193, 195, 196, 209
Muslims 5, 107, 195, 196, 200, 207, 208, 210, 211
Myanmar 189–209, 211–214, 220
  ambassador 198; army 206, 207, 210, 212; influx 201

national income 75
  League for Democracy 197; mechanism 215; prerogative 20; sovereignty 26, 69, 70, 76
nationalist backlash 209
NATO 27, 28
natural disasters 39, 151
Nauru 82, 84, 85
Naval Station at Guantanamo Bay 82
Nazario, Sonia 176, 177
negotiated settlement 165, 212, 220
negotiation 86, 87, 209, 212
Neighbourhood cooperation 60
neighbouring countries 14, 16, 149, 159, 181, 206, 207, 220, 222
neo-Nazi 23
Nepal 207
net gain 137
Netherlands 126, 161
networks 28, 43, 54, 117, 193, 225
new architecture 232
  workers 137, 138

Index

new arrivals 22, 26, 34, 38, 44, 49, 51, 54, 69, 82, 90, 116, 122, 126, 127, 130, 131, 135, 137, 138, 141, 161, 171, 202, 203, 207
New Delhi 207
New York 146, 148, 164, 185
The New York Times 168, 173, 176–178, 189
NGO 65, 102, 117, 118, 144, 200, 201
Niamey 68
Niger 5, 15, 33, 43, 67, 68, 81, 225
Nigeria 15, 16, 33, 49, 56, 63, 225
Nigerian 68, 113
1967 Protocol 182
Nobel laureates 199
no-man's land 119
non-interference 196, 220
    perishable good 149; refoulement 64, 65, 83, 84; state agents 40, 223
normative activities, mandate for 221
North Africa 6, 43, 80, 81, 171
    North African 80, 99; North America 40, 223
Northern Triangle countries 167, 170, 175, 180, 186, 221

O

OAU convention on refugees 39, 59
Obama administration 83, 108, 109, 170, 187
Obama, Barrack 83, 108, 109, 146, 170, 172, 173, 178, 187
occupational mobility 143
Oceania 40, 223
Office of Refuge 172
official camps 191, 192
offshore centres 84
    policy of screening 82; processing 41, 79, 82–87; processing centres 80, 100; screening 41
ombudsman 176
ominous sign 194

one-shot operation 74
open borders 70, 74
    openness 31, 62, 96, 212, 231; Society Foundation 146
operational activities 221
    response 69
Operation Sovereign Borders 82
opportunity-seeking migration 32
oppressive regimes 81
Orange Revolution 156
orderly and safe return 213
Orderly Departure Programme 86
    orderly immigration 87; orderly migration 58, 60, 61
origin country(ies) 21, 31, 32, 56–58, 60–64, 66, 68, 77, 84, 87, 186, 221, 225, 226, 230, 231
OSCE 162
outflow 113, 198
outsourcing 46, 63, 66
overcrowding/overcrowded 29, 47, 100, 102, 192, 202, 203, 228
over-flooded 231
Oxfam Italia 65, 111
Ozoguz, Aydan 143

P

Pacific Solution 82
Pakistan 17, 113, 134, 199, 200
Palestinian camps 144
Papua New Guinea 82, 84, 85
parental relationship 185
Paris 23, 26, 99, 104, 107, 140, 147, 149, 150, 174
parole 184, 186, 187
parolees 86
partisan violence 214
partnership 21, 33, 61–65
    agreements 63, 68; between Europe and Africa 58; Framework for Africa 67; plan 60
passport-free travel 74

Past colonial rule 214
Patriotism 155, 164
pension funds 141
perilous journey(s) 14, 18, 41, 42, 67, 140, 184, 185, 224, 225
permanent residents 184
  settlement 199
permit holders 160
persecuted minority 190, 192
persecuted person 86
persecution 1, 6, 40, 87, 90, 112, 182, 183, 185, 186, 189, 190, 207, 209, 223, 228
personal networks 146
personal persecution 223
personal visits 185, 186
Pew Research Center 3, 77, 92–94, 131, 176, 177
physical barriers 225
Pirelli Tower 151
Plan Colombia 178
Plan for Central America 178, 225
Poland 50, 71–73, 92, 93, 96, 97, 158–160
police and armed forces 178
policy package 221, 230
  response 37
political interference 214
  issues 226; landscape 97, 214; stalemate 220
Pongsirin, Powen 195
poor sanitation 192
Pope Francis 19, 65, 90
Population Control Health Care bill 195
  growth, high rates of 195
potential asylum-seekers 80
  asylum-seekers, removal of 66, 79; pitfalls 185
poverty 1, 6, 12, 32, 33, 38, 63, 121, 140, 168, 180, 189, 199, 225, 230
poverty-driven migration 32
powerless in power 205
precarious life 192

predictable and manageable system 231
preferential access 144
President of Honduras 173
President Obama 146, 172–174, 178
Pressure 17–20, 24, 34, 45, 46, 48, 50, 56, 58, 60, 61, 63, 68, 71, 76, 96, 122, 138, 141, 162, 164, 169, 176, 178, 193, 208–211, 214, 227, 229, 230
primary cause 179, 194
private investment(s) 31–33, 62, 141, 150
  contractors, for-profit 85; militias 66; sector 144–147, 214, 224, 225, 233
Pro Asyl 142
processing centres 48, 81, 84, 87, 100, 185
projections 51, 62, 137–139
promotion of security 226
pro-Rohingya militants 200
protection 27, 30, 39, 40, 45, 47, 64, 66, 67, 70, 83, 85–87, 96, 98, 102, 103, 109, 121, 159, 173, 174, 177, 179, 181–186, 212, 220, 223, 229
protection of borders 26
  gaps 223; needs 39, 83, 103, 177; procedure 184; of refugees 33, 224
protective devices 149
protest demonstration 196
psychological impact 103, 151
public attitude 89, 91, 182
  concern 58, 99, 142; expenditure 124, 127, 145, 150; funding 135, 145; investments 31, 32; Religion Research Institute 182
Pueblo Process 221
push factors 56, 180
Putin policy 164

radicalisation 206
Rakhine 192, 193, 201, 214

Buddhist extremists 193; community 192, 197; state 190, 197, 198, 200, 201, 206, 209–213; woman 193
rampant violence 181, 185
rape 89, 126, 177, 193
Rapid Reaction Pool 75
raping women 201
rate of failure 136
readmission agreements 56, 61, 225
reception without integration 100, 140, 145
recognition 62, 73, 133, 185, 227
reconciliation building 213
  programme 215
recrudescence 198
Refugee Action Coalition 85
refugee camp(s) 29, 31, 56, 111, 114, 115, 141, 191, 198, 201, 203
refugee crisis 23, 71, 77, 91, 92, 95, 96, 109, 137, 146, 147, 174, 177, 182, 204, 232
refugee flows 61, 71, 75, 92, 93, 96, 99, 107, 108, 125, 132, 147, 201, 219, 220, 224, 231, 233
  integration 142, 143; laws 39, 40, 105; -like flows 76; -like situation 39, 223; protection 53, 84, 114; registration centres 23; -related expenditure 32, 58, 127, 128; status 45, 86, 99, 100, 159
refugee/migration crisis 5, 6, 19, 20, 26, 27, 31, 43, 56, 57, 69, 224
refugee(s) 1, 2, 6, 9, 12–14, 16, 19–21, 23, 29–31, 33, 34, 39, 40, 43, 45, 48, 51–53, 55, 56, 58, 61, 64, 65, 67, 69–72, 74–77, 79–83, 85, 86, 89–93, 95–100, 102–112, 114, 115, 117, 121, 124–138, 141–148, 157, 159, 170, 172, 174, 179–182, 184–186, 191, 192, 198, 199, 201–205, 207, 209, 210, 219–228, 230–233
refugee status 45, 86, 99, 100, 159
regional level 223

peace 227; processing centres 84; solidarity 69, 76; stability 227
registered camps 202
regular migration 69
regulated openness 58, 64, 232
rehabilitation programme 215
reintegration 33, 105, 174
religion-based solidarity 196
relocation(s) 19, 20, 22, 24, 26, 70–73, 80, 204
  scheme 22
rented accommodation 162
Renzi, Matteo 22, 44, 57, 80
repatriation policy 84
rescue programmes 55
resettlement 16, 30, 52, 64, 83, 85, 107, 109, 110, 133, 194, 203, 212, 213, 221, 225
  shelter 87
residency status 174
residual work 221, 230
responsibility restrictions on refugees 19, 90, 108, 144
restrictive immigration policies 79
  interpretation 114, 229; trends 231
retaliatory violence 87
re-training 135
return 16, 33, 44, 46, 61, 62, 75, 84, 90, 98, 103, 105, 113, 182, 186, 203, 212, 213, 225
  migration agreements 56
rights groups 34, 45, 54, 61, 64, 90, 98, 103, 105, 106, 126, 172, 183, 187, 203, 204, 211
  detainees of the 34
right to seek asylum 83, 84, 182
Rintoul, Ian 85
riot 85
Rohingya crisis 196, 207, 208, 210, 213, 214, 220
  militant group 198; minority 199, 200; Muslims 189, 193; refugees 192, 199, 203, 206–208, 215; situation 205, 213

Rohingya(s) 189–194, 196–213, 215, 220
Rohingyas' citizenship 199
Rome 35, 65, 95, 116
root causes 21, 31–34, 50, 53, 54, 56, 58, 61, 63, 170, 174, 177–179, 194, 197, 225, 226
rule of law 31, 61, 210
rural ghettos 193
Russia 13, 28, 155, 157–159, 161, 163–165, 200
Russian annexation 155, 156, 158
  bombing 28

safe countries of origin 23
  country 64, 99; migration 68; third country 30, 45
safeguards 41, 185
safeguards for refugee protection 45
safety zones 41
Sahel of Africa 141
Salvadorian boy 180
  girls 180; Salvadorians 180
Samos 48, 50, 102
Samson, Diederik 30
Saudi Arabia 11, 199, 200, 203, 206
Save the Children 118
scapegoat 29, 30
Schäuble, Wolfgang 53
Schengen agreement 27, 73
  area 74; system 26, 27, 29, 73, 74; visas 160
scientific progress 231
screening arrangement 184
screening process 38, 40, 81, 83, 185, 186, 224, 228
sea route 20, 28
secondary causes 225
sectarian conflicts 56
security clearance 186
  concern 174; Council resolution (no. 687) 227; forces 68, 176, 199,
201; promotion of 214, 225; risks 92, 148, 185, 186; situation 1, 15, 157, 178
selection process 213
self-confidence 212, 214
self-employment 135, 136, 145
self-settled Rohingyas 191
Senegal 33, 225
sensitive internal political issues 226
sensitivity 26, 220
Serbia 30, 50, 102, 103
service contracts 106, 141
  providers 85
settlement 20, 23, 80, 91, 108, 109, 122, 137, 172, 212
  centres 90, 172
sex trafficking 173
sexual abuse 172, 204
  assaults 58, 177; slavery 168; violence 174
shelter 16, 30, 104, 126, 127, 186, 202
sheltered centres 172
short-stay visas 160
SITE 5, 208
slave trade 111, 204
Slovakia 22, 71–73, 96, 97
Slovenia 28
small-scale projects 144
smugglers 21, 27, 43, 111, 117, 189, 193, 195
smuggling networks 174
  trade 193
social benefits 74, 156
  cohesion 162, 214; economic rights 212; inclusion 140, 143; infrastructure 162; promoters 214; protection 162; reform 62; violence 140; welfare 58, 128, 133, 135; welfare funds 129, 139
soft and hard instruments 232
solemn declaration 232
solidarity among member states 57
Somalis 49, 112
Soros, George 146

sources 17, 70, 101, 126, 147, 168, 171, 225
Southern Border Programme 168
　southern border(s) 20, 103, 167–169, 171
South and South-East Asia 191, 208
　South Asian Countries 193
sovereign prerogative(s) 41, 42, 220
Spain 22, 23, 43, 44, 50, 128, 148, 163
special categories of refugees 223
　programme 186
specific characteristics 229
speedy and fair processing 75
spiral of violence 206
Sri Lanka 84, 207
standard parole 186
start-up activity 136
　businesses 146
starvation 16, 190, 193
stateless 190
State Migration Service (SEM) 51, 106
Steudtner, Peter 53
stick and carrot approach 62
strategic planning 75, 76, 227
strategy paper 34
streamlined application 185
strife-torn Syria 222
structural approach 33
　dichotomy 72; and economic reform 141; mechanism 220
subcontracting 140
sub-regimes 232
sub-Saharan Africa 6, 15, 17, 43, 49, 56, 112, 222
　African 65
subsidiary causes 225
Sudanese 49
sudden influx 24, 74, 75
summit 20–22, 30, 34, 35, 69, 146, 230
supportive approach 142
Supreme Court 85, 108
sustainable development 68, 226
　solution 77
Sutherland, Peter 21

Sweden 20, 72, 73, 96, 99, 124, 130, 133, 142, 143, 159
Swedes 77, 133
Swe, Myint 206
Swing, William 21
Switzerland 51, 72, 98, 106, 122, 130, 194
Syria 10, 12–15, 20, 28, 76, 113, 124, 133, 134, 147
Syrian refugee(s) 14, 20, 31, 46, 107, 113, 123, 132, 144, 145, 147
　migrants 136
Syrian(s) 12, 13, 17, 20, 31, 45, 46, 49, 52, 107, 112–114, 123, 124, 132, 136, 144, 145, 147
systemic deficiencies 26

T

take-back programme 75
Tapachula 169
targeted economic sanctions 212
task forces 194
tempo of violence 172
temporarily settlement 80
temporary derogation 74
　detention 54; protection 45, 59, 99, 122, 184, 224; refugees 40, 223; shelter 194; workers 160
territorial waters 28, 35, 117, 190
　integrity 68
terrorist activities 99, 142, 147, 148, 231
　attack(s) 26, 43, 68, 97, 99, 109, 147–151, 174; groups 206; recruiters of 141
terrorists 89, 92, 99, 113, 121, 147, 202, 209, 211
　infiltration of 26
Thai court 195
Thailand 189, 193–195, 207, 213
Thai-Malaysia border 189
Thengar Char 204
third countries 65, 83, 225
Tillerson, Rex 211

Tirana 50
Toaldo, Mattia 66
toilet facilities 202
trade concessions 225
traffickers 15, 21, 28, 38, 43, 44, 48–50, 54, 55, 65, 68, 125, 173, 176, 189, 193, 195, 196
traffickers' network 195
trafficking 68, 173, 183, 193, 195, 196
  boats 44; Trafficking Victims Protection Reauthorisation Act 172
tragedies in the sea 42
transit countries 34, 55, 57, 67
  transit and processing centres 80
transition 77, 138
translators 46
transparency 81, 116, 178
travel documents 40, 118, 119
Tripoli 6, 15, 66
Triton 19, 28, 42
  operation 42
truly global process 231
Trump, Donald 107–109, 165, 186, 233
Tsiddon, Daniel 148
Tsipras, Alexis 24, 29
Tuareg rebels 67
Tull, Denis 60
Tunisia 41, 55, 99
turf battles 175
Turkey 6, 13–15, 17, 27–31, 34, 41, 44–46, 48–53, 55, 63, 64, 101, 102, 106, 123, 124, 130, 145, 203, 208, 209, 222
Turkey's accession to the EU 31
Turkish 23, 28, 30, 45, 53, 123, 208
Tusk, Donald 57
two Global Compacts 221, 230, 232

U

Ukhia 191
Ukraine 50, 155–163, 165
Ukrainian army 156, 162
  conflict 161; Ukrainians 158–161
U Kyaw Win 200
ultimatum 35
ultra conservative 208
unaccompanied children 87, 170, 172–175, 179, 181, 182
  minors 47, 171, 177, 184
UN agencies 194, 211, 224, 230
  aid 199, 211; Convention on refugees (1951) 30, 39, 40, 51, 59, 64, 83, 85, 86, 96, 114, 182, 223, 224; General Assembly 221, 230; monitoring mission 163; Office for the Coordination of Humanitarian Affair 193; on/relating to the Status of Refugees 39, 64, 83, 86, 182, 223; Refugee Convention 96, 114; Security Council 11, 17, 199, 200, 208; Special Rapporteur on torture 85
underclass 140, 143
underdevelopment 33
undocumented Myanmar nationals 191
unemployment 19, 21, 38, 122, 126, 128, 133, 134, 144, 160, 229
UNHCR 2, 3, 12, 15, 16, 18, 23–25, 34, 45, 47, 48, 54, 64, 65, 81, 83–85, 91, 98, 100, 102, 103, 106, 109, 112–114, 146, 156, 157, 167, 170, 177, 179, 181, 182, 186, 190, 192, 198, 202, 203, 223, 224
  mandate, dilution of 224
UN High Commissioner for Refugees 114, 174, 194
  Commission for Human Rights 198
UN Human Rights Commissioner 90, 95, 198, 200, 201
unhygienic latrines 192
UNICEF 11, 13, 16, 102, 104, 106, 111, 112, 171

unified migration and refugee policy 69
unilateral action 76
United Kingdom 2, 20, 23, 80, 130, 163, 203
United Nations (UN) 3, 10–17, 30, 34, 44, 45, 51, 59, 64, 66, 80, 83–85, 90, 95, 96, 98, 102, 114, 131, 135, 163, 169, 174, 182, 193, 194, 197, 199–201, 203, 207, 208, 211, 213, 221, 223, 224, 227, 229, 230, 232
United Nations reckons 193
United Nations Special Representative on Migration and Development 21
United Nations system 221
United States (USA/US) 3, 68, 82–84, 86, 87, 89, 106–110, 146–151, 158, 163, 167–180, 182–184, 186, 187, 194, 203, 220–222, 228
unlawful or irregular status 184
unregistered Rohingyas 191
unsafe migration 31, 32
unscrupulous traffickers 41, 224
unskilled labour 193
untruths 210
upheavals 10, 142, 156
uprooted children 183
    people 1, 2, 12, 37, 100
US administration 84, 106, 107, 165, 178, 183
    aid 225, 226; Chamber of Commerce 173; congress 109, 173, 178, 226; government 13, 82, 147, 148, 174, 177, 182, 186; immigration authorities 167, 177; $2-million programme 183; president 86, 178; sanctions 189; State Department 196
USSR 86

V

Valletta Action Plan 32, 34, 58
    programme 60; declaration 76; summit 32
Varoufakis, Yanis 48
verification 83, 100, 210, 225
verification of asylum applications 83
vessels 17, 21, 28, 35, 65, 117, 118
victim-blaming 210
victims of violence 182
Vietnam 86, 109
    War 86, 108
violation of human rights 89, 181, 226
violence 3, 11, 14, 15, 23, 47, 87, 96, 109, 115, 123, 126, 140, 159, 165, 167, 168, 170, 174–176, 179–183, 185, 193, 200, 202, 207–210, 214, 220, 226
violent attack 193
    clashes 126, 193
visa-free travel 31, 43, 46, 53, 55, 160, 161
    access 64; Liberalization Action Plan 160; regulations 64
"Vision Paper" 80
vocational training 143, 145, 162
voting rights 193
vulnerable 50, 83, 87, 115, 163, 168, 169, 177, 187, 191, 224, 225
    asylum-seekers 47; children 186

W

Wade, Francis 214
wage-paid employment 136
war-torn 156
watch list 196
weak state 214
welfare shopping 74
West Africa 43, 56
West African 43, 67
West Balkan route/Western Balkan routes 24, 29, 30, 51

western Europe 51, 92, 102, 122, 125, 229
    countries 15, 213; Mediterranean route 50; powers 212, 214
white identity card 193
wider community 140
Women's Refugee Commission 180
work permits 46
World Bank 55, 123, 124, 129, 141, 147, 159
World War II (WWII) 1, 37, 39, 93, 192, 223

X

xenophobia 95, 126, 139, 230

Y

Yangon international airport 199
Yemen 10, 11, 16, 76, 227

Z

Zakharchenko, Alexander 165
Zoido, Juan Ignacio 44

CPSIA information can be obtained
at www.ICGtesting.com
Printed in the USA
LVHW08*2032220918
591057LV00006B/57/P